Russian Radicals Look to America 1825-1894

RUSSIAN RADICALS
LOOK to
AMERICA 1825-1894
BY DAVID HECHT

＊ TO ＊
MY MOTHER and FATHER

Preface

I HAVE ATTEMPTED in these pages to trace the almost completely neglected impact of American institutional experience and example upon a numerically small, but especially significant, group of two generations of pre-Marxian Russian revolutionaries. The leading figures of the uprooted, and often tragically alienated, nineteenth-century Russian radical intelligentsia paved the way by their teaching and example for the generation that actually made the Russian revolution.

A fresh quickening of Russian and American understanding is now more than ever necessary because of the emergence of the two countries to positions of predominant power in the contemporary world. Hence a study of how the revolutionary doctrines espoused by the significant Russian leaders of the past century were modified by the actualities of American life in their time—actualities often regarded as the very embodiment of democratic freedom—ought, I am convinced, to be of particular interest to present-day Americans. It is my hope that this book will also help to dispel the mists surrounding the Russian soul, a supposedly discarded concept, whose foggy imponderables have once again begun to invade the sober analysis of Russian affairs.

I have not attempted to be definitive in the bibliography appended to this book; the subject was much too extensive for that. For practical purposes, I have confined myself to a selected list of the sources and studies chiefly used. All translations from the Russian and other foreign languages are my own except where otherwise indicated.

The kindness of the staffs of the Widener Library of Harvard University, of the Library of Columbia University, and of the Slavonic Division of the New York Public Library in placing their facilities at my disposal has been much appreciated. I should like also to take this opportunity to express my gratitude to the late Professor Samuel H. Cross, whose recent and sudden death is a tragic loss to Slavicists everywhere, to Professor Sidney B. Fay, and to Dr. Oscar Handlin of Harvard University, as well as to Mrs. Mary Handlin of Cambridge, to Mr. Boris Nicolaevsky of New York City, and to Professor Clinton F. Oliver of Virginia Union University for their sympathetic aid at various stages in the writing of this book. To Professor Michael Karpovich of Harvard University I am especially indebted for his wise counsel and profound knowledge of Russia, freely and generously proffered to me from the outset of this project. The Reverend F. Hastings Smyth, S.C.C., of Cambridge, has rendered me invaluable assistance in the preparation of the manuscript and in the tedious task of reading the proofs. For his constant encouragement and scrupulous care, I am deeply grateful.

Sections of Chapters II, VI, IX, and X first appeared in abridged and altered form in *The American Slavic and East European Review*. Part of Chapter V first appeared in somewhat altered form in *Science and Society*, New York, volume IX, number 4 (Fall, 1945), pp. 318–34. A section of Chapter IX first appeared in *The Russian Review* for Spring, 1946, under the title, "Lavrov and Longfellow."

Since this book went to press, a volume of memorial essays commemorating the fiftieth anniversary of the death of Nicholas Chernyshevski has become available in this country: *N. G. Chernyshevski 1889–1939*, edited by V. E. Evgenev-Maksimov, A. A. Voznesenski, and S. I. Ganelin (Lenin-

grad, 1941). In this collection, an important, if somewhat
one-sided, essay is included, by M. M. Malkin, on "Chernyshevski i Zaatlanticheskaia Respublika (S.Sh.A.) [Cherny-
shevski and the Transatlantic Republic (U. S. A.)]."

D. H.

Bowdoin College
Brunswick, Maine
June, 1947

PREFACE

Contents

Note on Transliteration

THE SYSTEM of transliteration used in this book is based upon that employed by the Library of Congress. I have introduced a few modifications which seem to achieve a somewhat greater simplicity in English orthography without doing substantial violence to the phonetic values of the Russian letters. Some proper names that have an accepted spelling I have not rendered according to this system or transliteration.

а	a		с	s
б	b		т	t
в	v		у	u
г	g		ф	f
д	d		х	kh
е	e		ц	ts
ж	zh		ч	ch
з	z		ш	sh
и	i		щ	shch
і	i		ъ	(omitted)
й	i (omitted when combined with i or и)		ы	y
к	k		ь	(omitted)
л	l		ѣ	e
м	m		э	e
н	n		ю	iu
о	o		я	ia
п	p		ѳ	th
р	r			

Russian Radicals Look to America 1825-1894

Liberty

Oh, happy people
Whom fortune granted freedom,
Preserve in your heart the gift of generous nature
Which the Eternal has predestined for you.
The abyss, yawning beneath your feet
Bestrewn with flowers, still stands ready to engulf you.
Never forget for a moment
A fortress of strength can be transformed into utter weakness
And light into darkness.

> — Alexander Radishchev's reflections
> on America (1781-83).

CHAPTER I

The Russian Background

SOCIALIST ideas in Western Europe had already
achieved wide circulation by the fourth decade of the
nineteenth century. Spread principally by Robert Owen in
England, by Henri Saint-Simon and Charles Fourier in
France, these were "Utopian" visions of future golden eras.
The heyday of Utopian socialism coincided in certain logical
respects with the maturing of romanticism in Western Europe. But Utopianism, generally speaking, exhausted its po-
tentialities with the failures of the mid-century revolutions.
In its place, Marxian socialism with its ideology of "scientific" socialist revolution appeared.

Russia, too, was penetrated in those times by the general
currents of Western European Utopianism. And even though
a few Russian radicals were acquainted with Marxian doctrine in the 1840's, Utopian socialist ideas persisted in Russia
long after they had lost all important influence in Western
Europe. Indeed, elements of Utopian thought lingered on in
the doctrines of the Russian Marxists of the late nineteenth
century, even as the pristine Marxism in Western Europe
was infiltrated by the "realistic" and "reformist" ideas of
Ferdinand Lassalle and Edward Bernstein.

The mid-century Russian radical intelligentsia, therefore,
played the important role of bearer and assimilator of Western European Utopian socialist ideas for the revolutionaries
of a later generation. Building in large part upon the ideas of

the French pioneer socialists, these Russians evolved their peculiar theories for application to their own national scene. The historical significance of the pre-Marxian Russian radicals who acted as positive intermediaries to the generation which was actually to make the revolution in Russia cannot be over-stressed.

Hence the real birth of Russian socialism took place in the era of Nicholas I. For although one might read elements of revolutionary socialist doctrine into the Decembrist Pestel's assertion that "the most important movement of the present century lies in the struggle between the popular masses and the aristocracy . . .," [1] nevertheless any attempt to go behind the reign of Nicholas can achieve at best but mere inspirational solidarity with the past.

Russian socialism in the proper sense of the word originated and developed in the period of Nicholas I under the influence of imported doctrine. It was at first a purely intellectual movement with no mass following. Only much later did it acquire a national character and strong ties with the people. Herzen, Bakunin, Chernyshevski and Lavrov, the men we shall deal with chiefly in this study of attitudes towards America, were all profoundly influenced by Western European ideas. And while the impact of America upon these men was a significant one, it must always be viewed within the larger picture of Western European and Russian conditioning influences. Accordingly, a sketch of the mid-nineteenth century Russian radical movement will help supply a framework for the proper perspective of these pioneer radicals' attitudes towards America.

Alexander Herzen was probably the first full-fledged Russian socialist. He was very much influenced by French and

[1] V. I. Semevski, *Politicheskiia i Obshchestvennyia Idei Dekabristov* (St. Petersburg, 1909), p. 504.

German sources, coming under the sway of Fourier and of St. Simon especially, in the 1830's. His was a pre-Marxian and Western European Utopian socialism. In a relatively short time, however, Herzen's views underwent an interesting and significant transformation. He migrated to Western Europe, was in Paris in 1848, and lent his sympathies to Louis Blanc and the workers in the revolution of that year. With the failure of the revolution, Herzen was terribly shocked and disappointed. He then reached the conclusion (which had been maturing for some time) that Western Europe by and large was unable to achieve a radical revolution because she was too "cultured." She had a plethora of inherited traditions and conventions such as private property, Roman law, and the Roman Catholic Church, which in his estimation had corrupted and made bourgeois even the workers.

The only country that could now accomplish the really radical revolution which Herzen felt was so necessary was Russia; and this could take place precisely because of the latter's "backwardness" in relation to Western Europe. The revolution in Russia would influence and inspire the rest of Western Europe to socialism. This was Russia's mission— a prophetic if somewhat impractical vision at the time. But if the revolution should fail in Russia, then the fate of the masses and of socialism would lie with the United States. America was the one significant country whose destiny could be linked with Russia's in opposition to the "normal path" of development in Western Europe. Bakunin shared many of these views.

From that time on, Herzen joined his hopes for socialism with his hopes for Russia, particularly with the Russian peasantry—for it must be remembered that neither he nor Bakunin was familiar with the industrial proletariat until comparatively late in life. By the *narod* (the people) they meant the peasants. Furthermore, both men sprang from the land-owning class, a fact which also tends to explain their emphasis upon the peasantry. Herzen and Bakunin idealized the Russian peasant and considered the village commune as the nucleus of socialist development. The peasant, in their estimation, was "a socialist by instinct and a revolutionary by tradition" (recalling the uprisings of Razin and Pugachev). Bakunin especially believed, therefore, that all that was necessary in the Russian situation was determined leadership, someone to explain to the peasants that they already *were* socialist revolutionaries. Herzen was somewhat more vacillating and thought on occasion that the tsar himself (Alexander II) might be the leader of this movement. And it was Herzen above all who looked to the United States for consolation in one or another way when the going in Europe seemed too difficult and who even believed in an American "exceptionalism."

The historical significance of these ideas lies in the fact that in the subsequent period many of them influenced people who actually worked in Russia. In the 1860's and 1870's, when Russian youth began to organize revolutionary groups (such as the *Velikoruss,* or Great Russian Group), it was for some time these ideas, together with those of Chernyshevski and Lavrov, rather than those of Marx, which were prominent. Herzen and Bakunin themselves did little of a practical character in Russia. They were *émigrés*, working abroad.

The first socialist circle organized specifically for the study of the foregoing basic ideas was that of Petrashevski in the 1840's. Petrashevski was a landowner of no great importance, and the circle involved no activity beyond the organization of meetings in his St. Petersburg home. The revolution of

1848 frightened Nicholas I beyond measure; hence when the existence of the Petrashevski circle was uncovered the government exaggerated its importance and decided to treat it most drastically as an example to others. The members were condemned to death but at the very last moment their sentences were suddenly commuted in a very cruel way. Dostoevski who was a socialist in his early days and a member of this circle has left reflections of this event in *The Idiot* and elsewhere in his writings.

While Herzen (later to be joined by Bakunin) was working for revolutionary ends abroad, a new group of radicals was rising to prominence in Russia during the 1850's. This group, whose advent had been heralded by Belinski, was known as the *raznochinets*—intelligentsia. Its outstanding leaders were Chernyshevski and Dobroliubov, and the magazine *Sovremennik* (Contemporary), the foremost progressive review of that period, was their primary organ. The *raznochintsy*, or men of different social classes, broadened the ranks of the Russian intelligentsia, hitherto dominated by individuals of gentry origin. This alteration in social composition was contemporary with the Russian defeat in the Crimean War. And this defeat was followed by a relaxation of censorship under a new imperial regime, which enabled the *raznochintsy* to express themselves with greater freedom than before. These specific factors within the general change of European thought from romanticism to realism were responsible for some of the new ideas and wider activity among the Russian intelligentsia. Accordingly, in Russia the humanist and idealist "fathers," with their dilettante interest in philosophy and art, who possessed "beautiful souls" yet lived unconcernedly upon the exploitation of their peasants, were attacked for these traits with extreme and sometimes unpleasant vigor by the "children." The latter were positivists whose main interest lay in the natural and social sciences. The "children" thus denounced aestheticism, particularly the doctrine of art for art's sake, and condemned the lyrical and individual strain in poetry, art, and music, their canons being rather the civic, the social, and the utilitarian. The famous dispute of Herzen with Chernyshevski and the *Contemporary* group in the late 1850's was symptomatic of this fundamental cleavage widening between the two disparate generations.

Chernyshevski's great work as the leading radical publicist in Russia of the 1850's and his later imprisonment and martyrdom exercised a great influence not only upon his own contemporaries but upon succeeding generations of Populists (and Marxists) as well. In this connection, his lavish praise of the institutions of the "free North" helped mold Russian radical attitudes towards the United States for at least a score of years—until the seventies when the adverse opinions of Lavrov became articulate in his journal, *Vpered!* (Forward!).

In the late sixties, there was a short-lived extension (and almost exaggeration) of this "Nihilist" movement of the "children." What had previously been denounced by the radicals as caricature, in Turgenev's portrait of Bazarov in *Fathers and Children* (usually translated freely as "Fathers and Sons"), was eagerly accepted as verity by Pisarev, the brilliant leader of the extreme rebels against convention. The whole "Nihilist" movement for egotistical and individual development of personality, even in its extreme stages, however, was limited to an *intellectual* rebellion only, and although it did achieve the emancipation of women among the *educated* Russians much earlier than anywhere else in Europe or in England, it must not be confused with the political terrorism of a later period.

A more far-reaching social movement, and the first perhaps that can be properly described as *socialist* in Russia, started afterwards, in the mid-1870's, partly as a revulsion against the extreme intellectual Nihilism just described. This movement of the *Narodnichestvo* (Going to the Peasants) has been called Populism. For many, Nihilism and Populism were two stages in their own psychological development. Populism was a kind of religion of civic duty.

A strong ethical strain in the radical movement of this time was stimulated in great part by Peter Lavrov's *Historical Letters*. In these widely read essays, Pisarev's doctrine of egotistical development was subsumed in the idea that "critically thinking individuals," that is, the educated classes, had a debt to pay to the peasants who by centuries of toil had made possible a leisured class. This debt could be repaid by *going back to the people,* by becoming "simplified" as Turgenev put it.

The Populists concluded understandably, if somewhat illogically, that one had to live with the people and finally to live like the people. Hence, in the mid-1870's several thousands of ardent men and women, mostly indigent middle-class students (but including a fairly numerous group of "repentant noblemen") did go back to the people, and became teachers in village schools, clerks in the village assemblies, innkeepers or storekeepers, and even craftsmen, such as tailors or blacksmiths. Some features of this pilgrimage were related to the developing revolutionary movement, but many more of them were sincere attempts at a peaceful education that would raise the economic and cultural standards of the peasantry.

Politically, Populism was a dismal failure. The Populist sense of almost religious dedication to civic responsibility did not succeed in offsetting the partial lack of a sense of reality and the total lack of preparation. But the failure of the

Populist movement was not absolute, for it drove the radicals into newer and more dangerous paths, those of political terrorism and assassination.

In charting these various phases of the Russian radical and revolutionary movement, it is of course plain that there were outside forces at work as well, which brought about these frequently almost cataclysmic shifts in tactics. Important in this connection was the governmental reaction during the reign of Alexander, the "Tsar Liberator." This reaction was fanned by the apostate radical Katkov, whose violent denunciations held Chernyshevski and the *Contemporary* group ultimately responsible for the great fire of 1862 in St. Petersburg. Beyond this the reactionary trend was heightened by the outbreak of the Polish Insurrection of 1863 and a few years later by Karakozov's attempt to assassinate the tsar.

Equally important in stimulating the revolutionary movement was the governmental program, which the radicals considered a temporizing policy of semi-reform. For an initial program of bold advance, aiming principally to abolish serfdom, to create an independent judiciary, and to erect functioning county and municipal councils, was hamstrung from the very beginning by dilution of the original principles of the reforms, and weakened in practice by opposition from powerful groups of reactionary landlords and their toadying adherents. Herzen has summarized the feeling of the revolutionaries in his bitter statement that it would have been best had Alexander II died on the morrow of the promulgation of serf reform. Too many extreme hopes had been raised among the advanced reformers which the autocracy could not or would not satisfy. And then as the vicious circle of reaction, revolutionary upsurge, and renewed reaction got under way, the government again and again lost its head. It never learned the English lesson of combating revolution by timely reforms. It never knew how to separate the moderates from the radicals in the opposition camp as it might well have done by granting the demand for a moderate constitution "to crown the edifice" of reform. These were the external factors which led to the upsurge of the radical and revolutionary movement in the 1870's.

But even in the 1870's Russian socialism was non-Marxian in source and character. Marxism, at least in rudimentary form, had, however, been known to the Russians as early as the 1840's.[2] The first volume of *Das Kapital* was translated into Russian, printed on the press of the Ministry of Communications in St. Petersburg, and passed by the tsarist censor in 1872. Only after several years was it confiscated, when the authorities began to realize that this book was not just another dull tome on political economy written by a pedantic German. Although this was but one of the channels which introduced Marx to the Russian radicals of those times, they received him simply as "another anti-capitalist." It was native tradition, Herzen and Bakunin, Chernyshevski and Lavrov, which influenced them chiefly.

The various trends in this pre-Marxian Russian socialism were distinguished for the most part by tactical differences. Yet certain fundamental traits do stand out in bold relief especially when contrasted with the Western European Social Democracy of the second half of the nineteenth century. There was firstly the *maximalist* trend; the tendency always to play for the highest stakes, a tendency coupled, naturally enough, with an abhorrence for gradualism. The hardy men and women who supported it had no doubt whatever as to the possibility and practicability of an immediate transition

[2] Pavel Sakulin, *Russkaia Literatura i Sotsialism* (Moscow, 1924), pp. 245–49.

to socialism. Lavrov, one of the most conservative of the
Russian radicals in this respect, believed in a great deal of
preliminary education and propaganda among the masses.
But even he considered that such a program would not take
more than two or three decades. Great contempt was manifested for any idea of intermediate stages on the road to
socialism.

A second trait of the pre-Marxian Russian revolutionaries
was their generally negative opinion of the Western European bourgeoisie, as they knew it, a feeling that this
meshchanstvo had already outlived its social and historical
function. Such attitudes were not founded primarily in Russian experience; for the bourgeoisie was not very strong in
Russia, even in the 1870's, ten years after the decade of the
"bourgeois" reforms. In this respect Louis Blanc's *Histoire
de Dix Ans* (written early in the 1840's) played an important
role; for it presented not only a sharp critique of the policies
of the Orleanist regime in France, but also described with
master strokes the economic and social relations of the July
Monarchy between 1830 and 1840—a period when French
society was dominated by the bourgeoisie whose rule of life
faithfully fulfilled Guizot's slogan *Enrichissez-vous!* Louis
Blanc's book had a long and significant career in the history
of Russian socialist thought and helped in great measure to
crystallize this anti- (or pre-) capitalist attitude. As a result,
the Russian radicals believed overwhelmingly that it was
highly undesirable for Russia to pass through a "Western
European" bourgeois and parliamentary stage. Common to
both Herzen and Bakunin, this attitude persists in the
thought of the Populists of the sixties and seventies. Chernyshevski himself exemplifies this trend except as American
governmental institutions influenced him otherwise.

Closely related to this view was the idea, held in com-

mon by these three figures, of the peculiarity of Russia's
historical development. Thus there was a kind of "back-
door" connection with the Slavophiles. Herzen's post-1848
"revolutionary Slavophilism" typifies this.

Not all of these revolutionaries were convinced, however,
that Russia would escape a capitalist phase. Lavrov, for one,
did see the seeds of capitalism in Russian life even while he
inveighed against Western European and American capitalism. Tkachev, a more extreme figure, developed in the
1870's the theory of the "preventive revolution." He observed
a capitalist development in Russia, and his theory, therefore, was to seize power in Russia *before* capitalism and
the hated bourgeoisie could become strong and obtain a
constitution and a parliamentary regime. In this same period,
by contrast, the German Social Democracy was becoming
more gradualist.

Another trait of early Russian socialism was its agrarian
character. The "people" were identified with the peasants
and no emphasis was placed upon the proletariat; hence
the idealization of the village commune, remarked above,
as the nucleus of a future socialist order. (In reality, of
course, the commune was a primitive form of agrarian organization not peculiar to Russia.) The revolution, it was
believed, would transform these communes into socialist
centers which would be joined with each other in a federalist
union. Tactically this was connected with expectations of
peasant uprisings and Jacqueries. Here the tactical diver-
gence between the Bakuninists and the Lavrists became
clear. Followers of Bakunin optimistically believed that the
Russian peasant was ready to flare into "elemental" revolution
if only the spark were supplied from above. The Bakuninists
were the agitators (*buntari*) who scoffed at the necessity of
preliminary propaganda, and were primarily active in the

South. Lavrov's disciples, who concentrated more in the North, believed, on the other hand, that twenty or thirty years were necessary to prepare the peasantry by careful and systematic propaganda. These two groups made up the revolutionary wing of the Populist movement.

All of these doctrines had to face practical obstacles. The peasants unfortunately were not very sensitive to these efforts exercised on their behalf. The "agitators" raised only one peasant revolt and that an unsuccessful one organized in the name of the tsar, in the Kiev *guberniia* (province). The government was also relentless in its counter-measures with mass arrests, protracted imprisonments before trial, severe sentences of exile and even execution. For these reasons the determined revolutionaries, finding agitation unrealistic, propaganda tediously slow, and driven to desperation by the severity of governmental repression, began more and more to believe that they must form themselves into a secret organization of combat, into a conspiracy, attack the government directly, destroy it at the center, and thus seize power. After the Revolution there would be time enough to educate the people. This "Jacobin" tendency was especially advocated by Tkachev in his organ *Nabat* (The Tocsin) published abroad from 1875 and on. The doctrine of the hero—the "critically thinking" individual—as the motive force in history must also be counted as an influence. This extremist trend met with opposition among revolutionaries still laboring under the earlier *Narodnik* illusions. Even so, the People's Will (*Narodnaia Volia*) was formed in 1879 following the dissension and split in the earlier Bakuninist Land and Freedom (*Zemlia i Volia*) organization. Vera Figner and Andrei Zheliabov were prominent in the formation of *Narodnaia Volia*. Theirs was the first tactically unified Russian revolutionary party and the weapon of the *Narodo-*

voltsy (as adherents of the People's Will were called) was political terrorism.

The theory of the use of terror (assassination) as a tactic was based primarily upon the idea that it would disorganize the government and thus render it more vulnerable to frontal attack. The government would also be intimidated into concessions, would become more liberal out of fear. Finally the *Narodovoltsy* believed that such spectacles would educate the people.

Although the People's Will advocated constitutional and political reforms, it was *not* a gradualist organization. Its members still believed in the earlier socialist doctrines. As the famous letter of the Executive Committee to Alexander III upon his accession clearly indicated, they hoped for a constituent assembly which, with an overwhelmingly peasant representation, would inaugurate socialism upon the morrow. But they did realize in practice what Tkachev had preached. A very small group (never more than thirty people at one time) made up the Executive Committee of the People's Will, in whose name its acts of terror were committed. Its total membership even including affiliated groups was never more than five hundred.

The terrorists succeeded in assassinating a number of important political officials, among them Kropotkin's cousin who was governor-general of Kharkov. Their chief aim, however, was to kill Alexander II. And from the fall of 1879 to the spring of 1881, a remarkable duel continued between the terrorists and the government. Finally, after a series of narrow escapes, Alexander was assassinated by a bomb in March, 1881.

Politically Alexander's assassination was fruitless except for the wild but short-lived panic which it occasioned in court circles. It was a Pyrrhic victory for the party. The

Executive Committee, in sadly reduced form, continued its work, and addressed a consoling letter to Alexander III. It offered a truce if he would convoke a freely elected constituent assembly and abide by its vote as to whether or not monarchy should continue in Russia. The new tsar paid no attention to this letter. The government was not disorganized. And during his thirteen years' reign, Alexander III pursued highly reactionary policies. Educationally, the assassination made a rather unfavorable impression generally. The peasants in particular probably thought, in traditional manner, that Alexander II was personally a good tsar, that it was the officials who interfered between him and the people, and that the assassins were perhaps dissatisfied nobles who killed him for his liberalism.

The *Narodnaia Volia*, as the culmination of pre-Marxian Russian socialism, arose because of the peculiar conditions of Russian life. These were different in many respects from those which conditioned the growth of Western European Social Democracy. Involved in the Russian development was the long separation of the educated classes from the masses, as well as the weakness of the working classes, the industrial proletariat. There was also an absence of representative assemblies, of political parties, and of trade unions throughout this period in Russia. Conditions were simply not ripe for a socialist revolution of the masses in a country which had not yet been deeply affected by the Industrial Revolution. Adding their weight to this economic immaturity were the factors of psychological alienation of the intelligentsia from the people; the former's conspiratorial conditioning through several generations of underground movements; and the prevalent and strongly persistent idea of Russia as a peculiar or "exceptional" country.

The repressions felt by the revolutionaries after 1881

compelled a thorough-going reorganization of the movement. The gloomy and depressed spirit of the intelligentsia
in this decade is reflected in great part in the works of the
writer Garshin and the poet Nadson. This was a transitional
decade, however, one in which the seeds of Marxism at last
found fertile soil in Russia. But the earlier revolutionary
movements were not completely ended; some of their features were to affect subsequent developments even of Marxism in Russia.

Clearly, Herzen, Chernyshevski, Bakunin, and Lavrov
represent four nodal points in the history of the mid-nineteenth century revolutionary movement. The following chapters will aim to establish what attitudes these men developed
towards America; to integrate these attitudes and their evaluations of American institutions and life into a pattern;
to see where this pattern falls within the larger whole of
Western European and Russian formative influences. Finally there will be opportunity to discover whether the
American example conflicted with, or corroborated, the experiences of Europe. To what extent did American society
change these stubborn minds?

CHAPTER II

The American "Exceptionalism"

ALEXANDER HERZEN

ALEXANDER HERZEN, one of the greatest Russian radical intellectuals, came to know America well in the course of a life devoted to the problems of Russia and Europe, and he formulated well-rounded attitudes and shrewd observations about the United States. He believed that there were significant common meeting points between Russia and America, despite their fundamental institutional differences. American democracy was an especially constructive influence on Herzen's ideas, and it often gave impetus to his activities during the difficult years after 1848, when the "springtime of nations" had subsided into frozen winter again. Nonetheless, even the most recent investigations ignore almost entirely the role of America in Herzen's world outlook.

To understand Herzen's thoughts on America, one finds it helpful to examine his career, which has been sharply summarized as "1848 in human form." [1]

Alexander Ivanovich Herzen, illegitimate son of a well-to-do nobleman of ancient lineage, was born in Moscow in 1812. That was the year of the Napoleonic invasion and debacle, a year of great nationalist feeling in Russia. The

[1] Georg Brandes, *Glimpses of Russia,* tr. (New York, 1889), p. 255. In more Russian terms, Herzen is also "1861" as well, as has been pointed out more recently; cf. I. Kamenev, *Gertsen i Chernyshevski* (Petrograd, 1916), p. 5.

young "Iskander," as he was later called, became aware of the atmosphere of 1812 through the tales of his nurse, Vera Artamonovna.[2] "Eighteen twelve" was further impressed upon Herzen's consciousness, for his father, trapped in Moscow by the French, had been the unwilling bearer of a peace message from Napoleon to Alexander I. The first volume of Herzen's *Memoirs* is replete with recollections of youthful, patriotic feeling for Russia,[3] which he retained even in the bitterest days of exile. Probably his early love for fatherland had much to do with the formation of his maturer views on the peculiar position of the Russian peasant as the bearer of socialism for his country.

But the pall of "restored" Europe soon succeeded the liberating and nationalist exhilaration of 1812, and the backward aspects of the last third of Alexander's reign offered fertile soil for the rise and growth of an organized opposition. It is impossible here to discuss in detail the origins and development of the "Decembrist" movement.[4] It is enough to indicate that many Decembrists stemmed from the highest Russian aristocracy and had served as officers in the Russian armies which had fought against Napoleon in 1812 and occupied Paris in 1815. Traveling across Europe to France as conquerors, they not only were exposed to liberal ideas which their fathers in many cases had imbibed in Catherine's time, but were also hailed as liberators from the Napoleonic yoke. After this experience, they found that returning to Russia with its stifling Arakcheev regime was like returning

[2] A. I. Herzen, *The Memoirs: My Past and Thoughts,* tr. (New York, 1924), I, 1–12.

[3] Herzen also read copiously while at home, especially in French, German, and Russian literature. *The Marriage of Figaro* and *Werther* impressed him strongly.

[4] Cf. Semevski, *op. cit.,* and Anatole G. Mazour, *The First Russian Revolution* (Berkeley, Calif., 1937).

to prison after freedom. Soon these liberal-noble gentlemen organized in secret societies united on two goals: the
abolition of serfdom and the desire for some form of constitutional regime. Significantly, both the "radical" Decembrists who, like Colonel Pestel, advocated a republic and the
"conservative" Decembrists who, like Nikita Muraviev, favored limited monarchy, were greatly influenced by American constitutionalism. Pestel, in company with many Decembrists, took interest in books that dealt with American
history and contemporary American life, and he praised the
American republican order highly. As for Nikita Muraviev,
"the North American constitution was the chief source of
his constitutional project," and his plan of a federal government for Russia was undoubtedly borrowed from the American example. A future Decembrist, Prince S. G. Volkonski,
dreamed of a voyage to America as early as 1814, while he
was still surrounded by the heady atmosphere of Paris. Volkonski contemplated such a journey because "the North
American States filled the minds of Russian youth at that
time," inspiring them with "their independent mode of life
and their democratic political order." The American Revolution also played a part in influencing the trend of Decembrist thought.[5]

The Decembrist conspiracy came to a head in the St.
Petersburg rising of December 14, 1825 upon the accession
of the new tsar. As Nicholas I sardonically remarked, "what
a beginning for a reign!", for after quelling the revolt by the
cannon of the loyal regiments, five of the Decembrist leaders were executed and over a hundred exiled to the depths
of Siberia. Then an even darker pall descended upon Russian
life, felt most keenly by the generation too young to par-

[5] Cf. Semevski, *op. cit.*, pp. 208, 223, 229, 234, 256, 456, 504, and
Mazour, *op. cit.*, pp. 78, 93.

ticipate in the secret societies of the Decembrist movement. Herzen's horror at Nicholas' victory over "The Five" was translated into grim resolution. He attended the Mass of Thanksgiving, celebrated by the metropolitan in the Kremlin. And within the citadel of autocracy, the "boy of fourteen, lost in the crowd," in front of "the altar defiled by bloody rites," determined to avenge "the murdered men" and dedicated himself "to the struggle with that throne, with that altar, with those cannons." [6] His *Memoirs* record that when he was some years older he and his life-long friend and collaborator Nicholas Ogarev ascended the Sparrow Hills overlooking Moscow and there, together, vowed to avenge those brave martyrs, to devote their lives to the struggle against autocracy and serfdom. Hence it was no accident that when Herzen began to publish his free Russian journals in London, the covers of the *Polar-Star* bore the pictures of the five executed Decembrist leaders.

Faced with the utter impossibility of acting upon their ideas within the repressive milieu of Nicholas I's reign, sensitive intellectuals began more and more to gather in private salons, there to talk and theorize. Herzen was one of them, and in his *Memoirs* has left an unforgettable picture of the circles of Slavophiles and Westerners, springing from Moscow University. In their midst he hotly discussed St. Simonian socialism, Hegelian philosophy, and the destiny of Russia with such friends as Ogarev, Granovski, and Bakunin. This stage of Herzen's intellectual development began chronologically at the university during the 1830's. It was interrupted by two periods of exile to the provinces for minor political indiscretions. Following this, in 1842, the ardent youth was allowed to return to Moscow, whereupon he renewed his intellectual contacts and, with Belinski,

[6] Herzen, *Memoirs*, I, 63n., 87–88.

became the mainstay of the circles of Muscovite intellectuals. Herzen wrote with deep feeling of this whole period of idealistic youth that even "the most grotesque period of German student life" was infinitely better than the "petty-bourgeois maturity" of young men in France and England. And, to his mind, "the elderly Americans of fifteen" were "simply disgusting." [7] Herzen's revulsion against petty-bourgeois attitudes, one of his main sources of complaint against American life, as we shall see, is here evident.

Herzen took a leading role in the circle of Westerners who looked to progressive Europe for example and guidance. And in this period, he learned to believe in Hegel's dialectics as the "algebra of revolution," and became a revolutionary, at least in thought. In 1843 he read Louis Blanc's *Histoire de Dix Ans* and professed as great an admiration for this work as Belinski had a few months before. In addition, Herzen always respected his Slavophile opponents, never linking them with the official representatives of Orthodoxy, Autocracy, and Nationalism. In fact, even a growing rapport developed as Herzen began to base his hopes for socialism in Russia on the peasant commune (concurrent with his increasing disillusionment with the "bourgeois character" of European life). [8] Thus the main outlines of Herzen's thought were formulated: the union of Western European science, techniques, and democratic political institutions with the peasant

[7] Herzen, *Memoirs*, I, 176.

[8] In this respect, interestingly enough, Herzen joined John Stuart Mill, the Westphalian baron Haxthausen, and "the American sociologist Carrey [*sic*]." All these men fully appreciated the Russian peasant's need for "land and liberty." They realized, in Herzen's estimation, that the preservation of the village commune, self-government, and individual liberty were quite compatible. *Polnoe Sobranie Sochineni i Pisem*, ed. M. K. Lemke (Petrograd, 1919–23), XX, 58–59 (hereinafter referred to as *Soch.*-Herzen). We shall note below Chernyshevski's great interest in Mill and Carey.

communal agricultural system. Together, these would provide the basis for a Russian socialist system that would learn from Western Europe and yet differ from it. Moreover, Herzen's socialism, like that of many Utopians, had a constant moral and individualist trend.[9]

Despite the intellectual excitement of the early forties in Russia, Herzen desired to live in Western Europe, to escape the repressive atmosphere of his homeland. After many difficulties with the Third Section of His Majesty's Chancery, the Secret Police headed by Count Benckendorf, he finally secured a passport. And in 1847, at the same time as he inherited a large fortune from his father, he left Russia never to return.

Thereafter, Herzen's career was that of a propagandist and a revolutionary. He was present during the Italian and French revolutions of 1848, and was on intimate terms with Garibaldi, Mazzini, Proudhon, Ledru-Rollin and many other revolutionaries of the 1848 period. His most important work, though, was to establish a Russian press in London, where he settled more or less permanently in the 1850's. Under the pseudonym "Iskander," Herzen edited *Polar-Star* and later the more famous *Kolokol* (Bell). *Kolokol* was a propaganda journal of the greatest significance during its years of publication (1857–65), and Lenin, among others, praised it as Herzen's highest achievement, "his great service." On one occasion Lenin wrote: *"Polar-Star* continued the tradition of the Decembrists. *Kolokol* erected a rampart for the liberation of the peasants. The slavery of silence was shattered." [10] This was the only Russian publication free of any censor-

[9] Cf. R. Labry, *Alexander Ivanovič Herzen: 1812–1870* (Paris, 1928), pp. 292–306.

[10] V. I. Lenin, "Pamiati Gertsena," *Sochineniia*, XV (Moscow, 1931), 465–69.

ship in those times, and its news coverage, though selective, was excellent. Herzen's circle of Russian friends kept him familiar with the details of official life in St. Petersburg, and thus supplied, *Kolokol* discussed the burning questions of Russian reform in the post-Crimean War period with great zeal and persuasion. Several thousand copies of *Kolokol* circulated surreptitiously within the Russian Empire; and even Alexander II was reputed to read it regularly.[11] However, the journal lost much of its influence when it supported the Polish cause during the Insurrection of 1863, and publication ceased presently. Herzen died in Paris soon afterwards, in 1870.

Herzen never visited America, but this fact does not discredit his abundant notes and observations on American life; rather it heightens the striking insight of many of his comments. A cosmopolitan Russian nobleman, Herzen spoke French, German, and probably Italian and Polish as well. His command of English was imperfect but sufficient to allow him to read and to get along in London. Thus he possessed the tools to "follow . . . every new scientific discovery and read everything new in the literary way that appeared in any European country or in America." [12] Familiar with *Democracy in America,* he characterized Alexis de Tocqueville as "the writer on America." [13] Indeed Herzen became acquainted with the Frenchman's classic study of American democracy as early as 1837. At that time he was in exile at Viatka, and the new governor, Kornilov, a schoolmate of Pushkin's, presented him with a copy upon his ar-

[11] Cf. K. Zilliacus, *The Russian Revolutionary Movement* (New York, 1905), p. 29.
[12] Herzen, *Memoirs,* VI, xvi.
[13] *Ibid.,* III, 23–24.

rival. This first reading impressed him strongly.[14] There are
frequent references, too, concerning James Fenimore Cooper,
Washington Irving, and Harriet Beecher Stowe in Herzen's
writings, indicating his considerable familiarity with American literature.[15] But equally important sources of Herzen's
knowledge of America were his friendships with such revolutionary figures of the epoch as Garibaldi, Kossuth, and
Bakunin, who had visited America. Lastly, his frequent travels and his practice of maintaining open house wherever he
resided gave him ample opportunity to meet and observe
American travelers. All of this is carefully recorded by
Herzen.[16]

It is interesting that all but one of Herzen's notes on
America occur after 1848—the great watershed of nineteenth-
century Europe. The exception was the sketch of the early
drama "William Penn," written in 1838. Herzen himself
criticized this work as "an unhappy dramatic experiment,
mercilessly slain by Belinski." The sketch contains several
references to America, and to Pennsylvania as the site of
what Herzen believed to be a Christian Socialist colony.
Although this was not intended to be an historical drama,
but a literary exposition of the transformation of a religious
outlook into a revolutionary or socialist one, Herzen's trib-
utes to Washington, Franklin, Penn (despite the "failure"
of his colony), and to America the land, foreshadowed some
of his later thoughts on America. No doubt Herzen's reading

[14] *Ibid.*, I, 350. A few of Herzen's comments are derivative of de Tocqueville. However, Herzen never warns, for example, against the "tyranny of
the majority," an important concept of *Democracy in America,* tr. (Cambridge, Mass., 1862), vol. I, chap. XV.

[15] E.g., Herzen, *Memoirs*, II, 61; *Soch.*-Herzen, VII, 339.

[16] Herzen, *Memoirs,* V, 238–39. Herzen also apparently invested part of
his fortune in American holdings; *Soch.*-Herzen, XX, 8, 14.

of *Democracy in America* inspired his choice of William Penn as subject.[17]

From 1848 almost up to the moment of his death, America loomed on Herzen's horizon, now waxing, now waning, but always present. That America was a source of hope to Herzen in the years when he was depressed by the failures of the mid-century revolutions and increasingly disillusioned with the prospects of democracy and socialism in Western Europe is profoundly important; for it was in these years that "Iskander's" influence was greatest.

Herzen's over-all views on the States of North America were expressed in a sketch written on October 1, 1855, in the Isle of Wight. He prefaced these observations with remarks on his depression over the failure of 1848, caused, in his view, by dishonesty in the ideas of the revolutionary leaders and the consequent inability of the masses to follow them; and his brooding intensified his feelings about the deadly "bourgeois" life of Western Europe. The "tragic" and "passionate . . . anguish" would, however, pass with time. Moreover, in the "new world of the United States," it scarcely existed. That enterprising young nation, "more practical than intelligent," knew nothing, he insisted, of the agonies of the European revolutionary because she was too busy organizing her own new life. At the same time, America did not possess "two souls." For, Herzen believed that the individual's position in American society was fluid; a function of his bank account. The "sturdy race" of English colonists was increasing swiftly, and should it achieve an "ascendancy," men would not be the "happier" for it, but

---

[17] Cf. *Soch.*-Herzen, II, 208–11, and Labry, *op. cit.*, pp. 197–201. For a fuller critique, cf. I. Novich, *Dukhovnaia Drama Gertsena* (Moscow, 1937), pp. 156–59. Cf. also Herzen's amusing remarks on these "historical scenes in the religious socialist spirit"; *Memoirs,* I, 341–42.

they would be more "comfortable." And even though their comfort would be "duller, poorer, more arid than that which floated in the ideals of romantic Europe," with it, the Russian insisted, there would be "neither Tsar nor centralization" and perhaps "no hunger" either. Herzen then advised all who could slough off the "Old Adam of Europe" and be reborn "a new Jonathan" to take "the first steamer to America and then to migrate to some place in Wisconsin or Kansas." There the pilgrim would surely be better off than in "decaying Europe." Those who could not undertake this course of action, Herzen concluded sadly, remained "to live out their lives, representatives of the fair dream with which men lulled themselves to sleep." They had lived too long in "fantasies and ideals to fit into the age of American good sense." [18]

In this commentary, amidst passionate, lyrical prose, are sharp insights into the character of American life.[19] The concept of the "two cultures," which recurs again in his writings, also occupies a prominent place in Lenin's thought, and is often utilized by contemporary Soviet writers.[20] As an overall picture of the American scene, his statement is generally accurate. If Herzen erred at all in this estimate, it was in failing to foresee the later development of centripetal tendencies in our political life and the existence, even in 1855, of a certain amount of class striation.

A few years earlier, when outlining his reasons for becoming a Swiss citizen, Herzen had also expressed thoughts about America. He considered America and Switzerland as

[18] Herzen, *Memoirs*, III, 135–36.

[19] De Tocqueville had earlier noted the powerful role of money and prominent place of the middling standard in American life; *op. cit.*, I, 64, 66.

[20] Cf. Joseph Stalin, *Marxism and the National and Colonial Question*, tr. (New York, n.d.), p. 209.

being the only two countries where he wished to take up residence, since he "did not want to change a bad master for a good one, but to escape from serfdom into being a free tiller of the soil." [21] In Herzen's judgment, America was "destined to a great future." She was now "twice as near to Europe" as formerly. Yet American life was "distasteful" to this exiled revolutionary. And even though it was very likely that "her angular, coarse, dry elements" would be welded into "something different," America had not yet "settled down." She was "an unfinished edifice" in which laborers in their "workaday clothes" were "sawing, hewing, hammering." Why, therefore, should outsiders "settle" in America before she became "dry and warm"? Beyond this, Herzen concurred with Garibaldi's aphorism that America was the "land for forgetting home"—where those who had no faith in fatherland might go. For himself, however, there was no desire to leave Russia permanently. "The more I lost all hope of a Latin-German Europe the more my belief in Russia revived. . . ." But while Nicholas was tsar, to return would have been "madness." Hence there was no better alternative than to ally himself with the "free men of the Helvetian Confederation." [22]

In these extracts, Herzen obliquely acknowledged his debt to Garibaldi for information on America. He also expressed a keen desire to use his revolutionary energy not in exile even in the most "progressive" of countries but at home for the benefit of his native Russia. This element of Herzen's patriotic feeling reappears below in another context.

Expanding these views later on, in 1867, Herzen declared that European revolutionaries must not permit themselves to be distracted from their own problems by making a fuss

[21] Herzen, *Memoirs*, III, 185–86.
[22] *Ibid.*

over America. For America, he wrote, "sails at full speed into
the open sea." To strengthen his point, he quoted Goethe's
"excellent verses" about America: "Useless memories and
vain disputes do not alarm your present." No doubt Herzen
here meant that America was untrammeled by the dense
layers of tradition that bound Western Europe; accordingly,
a simple approach to the solution of pressing social problems, incapable of application to the Western European
scene, was there possible.[23]

In the same year, Herzen again surveyed American life in
similar terms. He compared Western Europe with America,
developing his concept of "two civilizations" (or "cultures").
"Iskander" pointed out the ever-growing incompatibility of
living in the "two worlds" of leisure, supported by exploitation, while constantly talking of "liberty and equality." The
States of North America, he declared, "with their unity of
civilization" would "easily outstrip Europe." Their "position
was simpler"; for while the "standard of their civilization"
was "lower than that of Western Europe," they had "one
standard and all reach it." Therein lay "their tremendous
strength." [24]

No doubt, Herzen blurred over distinctions too readily in
viewing post-Civil War America as not having "two civilizations," but he managed to capture the flavor of the American
"chromo-civilization" which existed in that era of relatively
fluid class lines and of emergent captains of business enterprise.

In a letter to Ivan Turgenev, written in 1862, Herzen

---

[23] *Soch.*-Herzen, XIX, 114. And in *ibid.*, XX, 135, appears a similar
thought by Herzen: "America: strong, rude, powerful, energetic, without
the ruins of a past which would encumber the route of the present; America
can take care of herself—Let us leave her to the Americans."

[24] Herzen, *Memoirs*, V, 236.

sweepingly denounced what he considered the greatest short-coming in American life: "the United States present the spectacle of one class—the middle class—with nothing below it and nothing above it, and the petty bourgeois manners and morals are retained." [25]

Yet Herzen was no Henry James; he always retained a positive sense of American values, and in the same letter acknowledged that although, "in the whole of America, there is no such Campo Santo as in Pisa, . . . still Campo Santo is a graveyard." [26] In 1857, in a letter that was already a "variation on an old theme," "Iskander" asked his reader, "has not the European ideal [the best of everything in Western civilization] in one form, to wit, the Anglo-Saxon, found complete expression on the other side of the Atlantic Ocean?" [27]

Even in a moment of scathing anger, Herzen was on firm ground, although he carried his contempt for certain aspects of American life to extremes. His strictures may in this case be attributed to disgust with a certain charlatan-revolutionary, Golovin, who had abused his kindness and aid in London. When Golovin departed for America in 1856, Herzen exclaimed with relief that at last he was rid of this unpleasant man. For now Golovin had disappeared within that "ocean of swindlers, fortune-hunters and adventurers. . . ." Whether he would become "a pioneer, . . . a card-sharper or a slave-holder" in America, or perhaps be "hung by lynch law" did not matter, so long as he did not return. [28]

[25] *Ibid.*, VI, 11.

[26] *Ibid.*, p. 8. For an amplification of this view, also cf. pp. 4–5, and *ibid.*, V, 238–39 (March, 1867).

[27] *Ibid.*, VI, 86.

[28] *Ibid.*, IV, 320. As it happened, Golovin did return to plague Herzen.

The ephemeral quality of such a negative outburst is at once evident. This extract must not only be set within the framework of the many foregoing positive citations, but must also be counter-balanced by the excessively favorable view of America that appeared in *From the Other Shore* in 1849. This favorable reaction had a lasting character, for Herzen repeated it in 1851: "a free man who refuses to restrain himself before force will have no other refuge in Europe than the deck of a vessel making sail for America." [29]

This, one may argue, may be ignored, for it was written in the midst of the Revolutionary epoch and bears its imprint. On the other hand, only several months after the "Golovin" quotation, Herzen wrote, "if I were not a Russian, I should long ago have gone away to America." [30] And when the first Atlantic cable was laid between England and America in 1858, Herzen expressed unbounded admiration for the vigor of America. What could a country not do, he asked his readers, that felt "the beat of an uninterrupted pulse with America . . . ?" "Truly," he declared, "here are not two states, but two different shores belonging to the Anglo-Saxons." [31]

These rapid shifts in Herzen's view of America may in some measure be explained by the uprooted character of Herzen's life. Gathering together these various strands of opinion expressed throughout a score of Herzen's mature years, we may assert that this Russian socialist-aristocrat regarded the United States in realistic terms; was able to appraise both virtues and shortcomings. Moreover, his opinions revolved around a central concept: America as a vigorous,

[29] *Soch.*-Herzen, VI, 206.

[30] Herzen, *Memoirs*, VI, 95. Cf. *Soch.*-Herzen, IX, 190, for similar views expressed in 1858.

[31] *Soch.*-Herzen, IX, 200.

growing, unfinished, and unstructured nation, a land of pioneers and of material civilization, a land where the influence of the frontier was still visibly apparent; America as possessor of a militant, democratic order, with fluid class lines, nonetheless a place where the power of money had the highest significance. Practical values outweighed spiritual ones in this New World, to the detriment of art and culture; and they led to more comfort but less happiness. In the last analysis, however, America with her democratic vigor, would outstrip Western Europe. Her future was great and assured.

But Herzen did not, by any means, confine himself to generalized observations about the United States. He displayed a keen interest in many specialized aspects of American life, and was a close follower of the outstanding events in the nation's life. For one thing, Herzen was very interested in the character of the polity and the administrative organization of the United States.[32] In a letter written in 1857, he stated that "civic religion—the apotheosis of the state" was constitutionally a "Roman" idea, and in modern times, primarily "French." It was compatible with a "strong state" but not with a "free people." From it "splendid soldiers" might emerge, but never "independent citizens." "The United States, on the contrary," he declared, "have so far as it is possible abolished the religious character of the police and the administration." [33]

---

[32] This interest is surely traceable in part to the Decembrists and to the French Utopian socialists. De Tocqueville also deals with this subject, *op. cit.*, I, 73–79, 346–48. Labry categorically asserts, however, that Herzen was won to the idea of a federal republic while observing municipal life during his stay in Italy (October, 1847 to May, 1848). This belief in a federal republic "was born directly in contact with Italian life, outside of any and all direct influence of Proudhon"; cf. Raoul Labry, *Herzen et Proudhon* (Paris, 1928), p. 57.

[33] Herzen, *Memoirs*, II, 401–2.

Beyond reflecting prevalent nineteenth-century concepts of the limited function of the state, this was for its time an accurate observation of the American scene. Herzen frequently expressed his appreciation for American federalism, local self-government, and the absence of strong, centralized bureaucracy in America. He acknowledged the values of a centralized government for such practical purposes as "organization of the post and maintenance of roads and currency." But Herzen argued that while centralization was valuable for order and for various public enterprises, nevertheless, it, like "civic religion," was "incompatible with freedom." For this latter reason, "the Americans and the English" hated it "as much as the Swiss." And he added in a lighter vein that "a king is as great an absurdity in Switzerland as the grades of the Russian civil service in New York." [34]

Considering the early struggles of the American republic for the establishment even of a national bank, a uniform currency, and the national administration of internal improvements, we may say that Herzen was certainly correct when he declared that Americans of those times hated centralization. His view was stated most succinctly in a letter written in 1857, mentioned above. "The grand idea developed by the Northern States," Herzen insisted, was "purely Anglo-Saxon, the idea of self-government." Specifically this meant "a strong people with a weak government, the home rule of every tract of land without centralization, without bureaucracy, held together by an inner moral unity." [35]

And writing to the French historian, Michelet, in 1868, Herzen declared that the Russian Empire was "a monstrosity." His "wish and hope" was to see it "transformed into a federation on the American order." [36] This tribute to

[34] *Ibid.*, III, 105. [36] *Soch.*-Herzen, XX, 158–59.
[35] *Ibid.*, VI, 91.

the non-unitary American federal system certainly reflects its importance in the totality of Herzen's thought. In the same vein, Herzen applauded the separation of church and state in the "first Republic of our day." [37]

"Iskander," in his organic view of society, admired the qualities of the American mind, considering them amply suited to the political organization of the people. His powerful pen treated this issue in an interesting essay, where he maintained that American thought, in itself, was not original, but merely that of the eighteenth century Anglo-Saxon mind as typified in Washington, Franklin, and Jefferson. Two things, however, he found peculiar to American thought. In the first place, he was impressed by the fact that the federal democracy with its local self-government was the form of civil life that corresponded *completely* to the mode of life of the Anglo-Saxon colonists in the New World. Beyond this, he was struck with the "freshness and simplicity" that the Americans in their magazines and newspapers introduced to "the scholastic rubbish of political questions." This "simple, lively, healthy" approach of the American mind to political and economic questions corresponded entirely to the concept of a "democratic republic." [38]

There are some inaccuracies in this appreciation. Herzen's praise of the contemporary American magazines and newspapers seems fulsome when one recalls such a representative publication as the *North American Review*. Conversely, Herzen was narrowly European in estimating American thought as largely derivative.[39] For a moment he failed to see in

---

[37] *Ibid.*, V, 232.

[38] Herzen, "Amerika i Sibir," *Kolokol,* no. 29 (Dec. 1, 1858), p. 234.

[39] Herzen, however, was accurate in his noting of the non-American sources. Cf. V. L. Parrington, *Main Currents in American Thought* (New York, 1927), I, iii–vii.

entirety the transformation and development which occurred in the new frontier environment. This he corrected
in other statements, as when he wrote: "America is Europe
colonized, the same race . . . but living under different
conditions." [40]

Herzen violently opposed the institution of Negro slavery
in America—a view not unexpected in one who was a passionate partisan of the abolition of serfdom in Russia. At
one time in 1857, he compared the Russian landowner in
his worst aspects with the American slaveholder. "Iskander"
accused the Russian nobility of general "brutality, debauch-
ery and violence" in their relations with house-serfs and
peasants. And he insisted that while a minority of "cultured"
landowners did exist who were not constantly harrying and
"thrashing" their servants, "the rest" had "not yet advanced
beyond the stage of . . . the American planters." [41]

In a pamphlet on Russian serfdom, written in English for
the British public in December, 1852, five years before, this
parallel was drawn even more sharply, Herzen here pro-
testingly implied that the issue of American slave emancipation had received undue attention in relation to the burning
question of the liberation of the Russian serfs. "White

[40] Herzen, *Memoirs,* VI, 89.

[41] *Ibid.,* II, 198. Herzen also drew parallels between the temperament
of the Russian serf and the American Negro slave. In defense of both he
wrote that "of course, on the one hand, the lack of all education, on the
other, the simplicity of the peasant in slavery have brought out a great
deal that is monstrous and distorted in their manners, but for all that,
like the Negroes in America, they have remained half children; a trifle
amuses them, a trifle distresses them; their desires are limited and are
rather naive and human than vicious." *Ibid.,* I, 31. A recent writer on
Russian peasantry in the last decades of serfdom has suggested a close
similarity between the songs sung by certain Russian religious sectarians
and American Negro "spirituals"; G. T. Robinson, *Rural Russia under the
Old Regime* (New York, 1932), pp. 46–48.

slavery," Herzen suggested, had not been sufficiently attacked because it had not been defended with the same "fierce tenacity" of the American slaveholders. The "mask" had to be ripped from those "slaveholders of the North" who meandered over Europe "assuming the rank of civilized" and even "liberal minded men." These individuals read *Uncle Tom's Cabin*, "the great work of Mrs. Beecher Stowe." They shuddered "with horror" when they read of "sellers of *black* flesh." But these brilliant habitués of the salon were "the very men" who, upon returning to their domains, "rob, flay, sell the white slave, and are served at table by their living property." [42] Apart from the justified indignation here displayed against two systems of involuntary servitude, we can see that Herzen was also numbered among the many enlightened Europeans who were influenced by Harriet Beecher Stowe's novel.

Herzen waxed sarcastic about "the Washington Senators who proved the benefits of slavery on each other with sticks," [43] a plain reference to the state of the American Congress on the eve of the Civil War, when the caning of Senator Sumner of Massachusetts by a Southern pro-slavery Congressman was only the most notorious of several similar incidents.

It followed logically enough that Herzen was an avowed opponent of the Confederacy during the Civil War in America. With the cry "War for slavery! 'For our sacred cause,'" Herzen indignantly mimicked Jefferson Davis. He admitted the prevalence of "slavery and serfdom, unjust war and illicit money-grabbing" prior to the existence of the United States. But "this cynicism, this insolence, this criminal

[42] *Soch.*-Herzen, VII, 339–61.
[43] *Ibid.*, III, 216–17.

simplicity, this shameless nakedness—this" was "new" and belonged "to America." [44]

Indeed to Herzen, Jefferson Davis was "the greatest political criminal of our time," an opinion current among most of the radical Russian intelligentsia.[45] He went on to castigate the English government for aiding the Southern cause by deliberately allowing vessels such as the *Alabama* to be fitted out for the Confederacy. "The country of Wilberforce," he exclaimed, "equips vessels," notwithstanding their destined service for slavery. Rivers could "flow with blood into the Atlantic"; "the ships" could "sink to the bottom, but 'the sacred foundation of the Southern republic will be recognized by all of Europe.' " [46] Although the Polish Insurrection of 1863 crowded the American Civil War from the pages of *Kolokol*, this was by no means an isolated reference to the struggle in America.[47]

Herzen was also a firm defender of the rights of women— another group in society demanding emancipation along with Russian serfs and Negro slaves. In an open letter to Turgenev, he took the famous Russian novelist to task for misunderstanding his views on this subject. After designating this issue as "a question which stands in the forefront in Europe and North America," Herzen extolled the citizens of the United States for being first to rebel against the inferior status and subjection of women.[48]

An ardent supporter of socialism, Herzen was closely in-

[44] "Mortuos Plango," *Kolokol*, no. 118 (Jan. 1, 1862), pp. 981–82.
[45] *Soch.*-Herzen, XIX, 357.
[46] *Kolokol*, no. 118, *loc. cit.*
[47] *Ibid.*, no. 191 (Nov. 15, 1864), p. 1565. Also cf. Herzen, *Memoirs*, V, 47, 70, 175.
[48] *Kolokol*, no. 182 (March 20, 1864), pp. 1496–98. The Civil War was of course far more vital in the United States than this issue at the moment.

terested in what attitude America might take toward this issue. He found no definite indication. Herzen conceded that America possessed a "highly developed" sense of "association" and of comradely enterprise, but she lacked "common ownership," the Russian *artel* (artisans' guild), and the "village commune." In the United States the "individual" combined with others "only for a definite task"; apart from this, he "jealously" guarded "his complete independence." [49] On the basis of Herzen's analysis, one would have been foolhardy indeed to venture definite predictions about socialism in America. Certainly this meager analysis, while containing accurate insights, betrays the point of view of a Utopian socialist rather than that of an orthodox Marxist. From the standpoint of orthodox revolutionary Marxism, Herzen has lately been criticized—with some justification—for the vagueness of his "petty-bourgeois" reformist plans for achieving socialism as contrasted with the concreteness of his destructive critiques of European society.[50]

Herzen dealt at length with one of the most striking phenomena in contemporary American life: American energy and expansionism.[51] After describing the settlement of America as part of the "age-long movement to the west," motivated by such definite causes as hunger, persecution, and stifling European atmosphere, Herzen went on to describe the contemporary flow of population in America. Pressing their way through the settled population, the newcomers sometimes even drew this population with them. But in any case they crowded ceaselessly to the South—"today

[49] Herzen, *Memoirs*, VI, 91.

[50] Cf. the Soviet writers I. Novich, *supra,* and L. Piper, *Mirovozzrenie Gertsena* (Moscow, Leningrad, 1935).

[51] Already the rising trend of American industrial power may be discerned in Herzen's praise of the "American engineer"—a sentiment which Lenin echoed; Herzen, *Memoirs*, I, 333.

to the equator." And Herzen insisted that "a new meeting and a new combination of the Anglo-Saxon element with the Latin-Spanish" would ensue from this movement.[52] Here, in embryonic form, is an analysis which bears some resemblance to ideas advanced by Frederick Jackson Turner in his celebrated address on the significance of the frontier in American history.[53]

Herzen regarded this American (it would be inaccurate to repeat "Anglo-Saxon") energy as flowing into currents of "manifest destiny"—as a movement that relentlessly advanced upon the neighboring present and former possessions of the moribund Spanish Empire in the New World. He asserted that this ceaseless flow was but the "marking out of the arena." And "no power" could prevent the North Americans "with their overflowing strength, plasticity and untiring energy from reaching Central America and Cuba." Though Venice was "falling into ruins," though Rome was "reduced to beggary," and the Italian and Spanish provincial towns were "declining from lack of capital and labor . . . and lack of energy," the trend was otherwise in California, Honduras, and Nicaragua. There deserts "in a few years" were "transformed into cultivated fields and clearings into towns." The plains were "lined with railways," capital was "abundant," and "the restless vigor of the Republic [absorbed] more and more. What is growing is young." [54] These sentiments supplement Herzen's views that Western European institutions were "bourgeois" and "decadent," and reveal that he tended to believe that America

[52] *Ibid.*, VI, 89.
[53] This address, delivered in Chicago, 1893, appears in a selection of Turner's writings, *The Significance of the Frontier* (New York, 1920), pp. 1–39.
[54] Herzen, *Memoirs*, VI, 89–90.

and Russia had certain good features in common. Furthermore these points of contact would draw the two countries closer together in the future.

Herzen resented any suggestion that Russia must inevitably follow the evolution of the Romano-Germanic peoples. There were no fixed lines of cultural evolution for every nation. America was the supreme vindication of this view. He wrote in January, 1863, that the Americans had developed their own peculiar character, that a "fresh soil" alone had sufficed to mold a new nation out of "old peoples." Why, therefore, should Russia, a nation that had developed "in her own way under completely different conditions" from the Western European states, live through "the European past," especially when she knew what that past led to? [55]

Six years before, "Iskander" had boldly linked Russia and America as the "only two progressive countries" outside Europe.[56] He elaborated this thought in an article entitled *France or England?* [57] In this work, Herzen urged Russia to withdraw from the sordid arena of European politics and diplomacy and instead to seek solid friendship with the United States. The Russians, he asserted, had absorbed all that was useful from Western European countries—"their theoretical thought." Now, only a "barren" and "German"

---

[55] *Ibid.*, VI, 83. Herzen also tended to feel that the nationality problem, i.e. the absorption of "aliens and vagabonds from all over the world" who came to America, was greatly aided by the hardy republican form of government. Switzerland also served him as an example of how the nationality problem might be solved. *Soch.*-Herzen, XIX, 109 *n.* Also cf. note 40 *supra.*

[56] Herzen, *Memoirs*, VI, 89. Herzen could, however, slyly note the contrast of Russian absolutism and American republicanism in terms of the complications of diplomacy. "Acquaintance with the Yankee has its inconveniences!"; *Soch.*-Herzen, XIX, 56.

[57] *Soch.*-Herzen, IX, 182–222.

ambition impelled Russia to mix in the affairs of Western Europe. Blindly Russia had failed to perceive that "humanity is sailing away from the European continent." Thus Herzen asserted that if she would but free herself from "the Petersburg tradition," she would have "but one ally—*The Northern American States!*" [58] The appearance of these views in an article entitled "France or England?" gains them greater significance. It offered Russian revolutionaries two alternatives: "With England—freedom and peace!" "With France—slavery and war!" The American example, however, was transcendent. Almost word for word these thoughts were reiterated in *Kolokol,* showing the great importance that Herzen attributed to them.[59]

The same article listed the points of contact between Russia and America which would effect lasting friendship between them—friendship that could be realized were it not for the "Petersburg military dictatorship that submerges all persons in the person of the absolute ruler." Both countries, he observed, possessed "a super-abundance of strength, plasticity, the spirit of organization and pertinacity" which recognized no obstacles. Both were poor in a past. Both were spreading over unending valleys, searching for boundaries. From different directions and across fearful distances, both were approaching the shores of the Pacific. Herzen referred to the Pacific as the " 'Mediterranean Sea of the future?' "—and so beguiled was he by this phrase that he announced a feeling of joy when he saw that American magazines and newspapers repeated it many times.[60]

[58] *Ibid.,* p. 203.

[59] *Kolokol* (Dec. 1, 1858), p. 233.

[60] *Ibid.* Also cf. *Memoirs,* I, 299–300. For the genesis of these Russian and American parallels, cf. de Tocqueville, *Democracy in America,* I, 558–59.

The sale of Russian America to the United States in 1867, of course, made the two countries neighbors across the Behring Straits. Herzen noted this event by insisting that the future close proximity of the North American Union with Russia "now" stressed by "all Russian and non-Russian newspapers" was first pointed out in *Kolokol* eight years before— on December 1, 1858.[61] Herzen, however, did not ascribe the transfer of Alaska to the United States to pure altruism and friendship on the part of Russia. "Russia did not donate the Aleuts, the Choukchy, and their compatriots with such gentle names as a simple gratuity for the *beaux yeux* of America." [62]

Herzen perorated: "If reaction and absolutism finally vanquish the revolution in [Western] Europe," then even Russia would not be immune and "perhaps . . . will perish." In that gloomy eventuality, however, Europe, too, would perish "and progress will pass to America." [63] "The dying gladiator," as Merezhkovski called Herzen, despite doubts concerning the future success of socialism in America, felt that the United States had thus far advanced beyond any other nation. This was a precious judgment from a man who loved and understood his own country and people as much as Herzen did. And one may certainly conclude that it was the progressive democratic strain in America to which Herzen quickened. Thirty years after de Tocqueville's classic study, American democracy, plunging rapidly into the pit of the "Gilded Age," was still a beacon light and a source of optimism in the thought of this Russian radical.

[61] *Soch.*-Herzen, XIX, 62–63; also cf. *ibid.*, p. 279.
[62] *Ibid.*, XIX, 264.
[63] Herzen, *Memoirs*, VI, 242.

CHAPTER III

Poet of Freedom

NICHOLAS OGAREV

NICHOLAS OGAREV occupies a distinctly secondary position among the mid-nineteenth-century Russian radical intellectuals. His background and development were closely related to Herzen's. He was born in 1813 of a wealthy noble family in Penza *guberniia;* studied in Moscow University; and was exiled to Penza in the 1830's for participation in the same student "incidents" for which Herzen was banished to Viatka. In 1856, Ogarev left Russia forever, and attaching himself once more to Herzen, became one of the leaders of the emigration. He was actively associated with *Kolokol,* wrote several revolutionary proclamations in the first half of the 1860's, and was supposedly one of the organizers of the first *Zemlia i Volia* society. Ogarev died near London, in 1877.

Ogarev's importance lies not so much in his own independent contribution or even in his position as a kind of poet laureate to the radical movement, but in his life-long friendship and collaboration with Herzen. The relationship of Ogarev and Herzen was indeed so close that Herzen in 1853 dedicated *My Past and Thoughts,* "our memories," to the poet, "I present them to thee," he wrote, "for thee they have a double meaning, the value of tombstones on which we meet familiar names." [1]

Ogarev's career was less devoted to "political" writing

[1] Herzen, *Memoirs,* I, 91.

than was that of most of his contemporaries. Therefore, it is not surprising to find fewer comments on American life in his works than appear in those of men like Herzen and Bakunin. The references to America which do occur appeared in *Kolokol* in the years immediately following the serf emancipation of 1861. One may regard these observations almost as supplements to Herzen's own views.

Ogarev's few comments on America, written during the two- or three-year period when enthusiasm over the reforms in progress in Russia was very great, contain none of Herzen's ambivalence of view. Generally they show Ogarev as looking to America as teacher and guide for a Russia entering with unfirm tread upon the road of democracy and constitutionalism. In this connection Ogarev, in a letter to "One of Many," defended a broad program of civil liberties for Russia. He declared that "religious freedom and . . . the development of . . . science" comprised the "sole path for the liberation of the masses from intellectual stagnation." These were also the fundamental conditions for participation by the masses in social life. The "Northern States" of America vindicated Ogarev's belief. There, "the greater the development of sects, the more the masses take part in public life." The mind, once "educated in controversy over social convictions, participates in everything." Hence, Ogarev concluded that the "furthest intellectual development" could take place only under conditions of "freedom of belief, freedom of speech and absence of an established church." [2] This was a plea for what might be almost synonymous with our own "Four Freedoms"—a desire for "freedom from want" being axiomatic, surely, among the Russian radicals. Ogarev's belief that religious freedom and civil liberties had liberated the intellect of the average American was in large

[2] *Kolokol,* no. 189 (Sept. 15, 1864), p. 1551.

measure true; especially if one considers the period since independence. It should be added that Ogarev discussed these constitutional virtues of American life somewhat abstractly, for the Civil War was then raging in America, and civil liberties were somewhat curtailed. Lastly these passages tend to illustrate the conservative-constitutionalist streak in the Russian radical intelligentsia, which was transiently visible in these years.

In a series of articles on the pending Judicial Reform (consummated in the Law of 1864), Ogarev used the example of the American judicial system as an argument for direct election of the new Russian judges.[3] He emphasized the evil of infringing upon the independence of the judiciary, and the danger of subservience to the tsar, the supreme power. He asserted that in England, governmental appointment of justices arose under the stress of historical circumstances and not from "scientific considerations." In the United States, the revolutionary break from England involved a shattering of this tradition also, and consequent election of American judges by "society as a whole." The latter was a much better system, in Ogarev's estimation, for it reduced the possibility of governmental interference with the judicial power—interference which only "a strong guild" of lawyers could counteract. Moreover, in America, election of judges could not lead to tyrannical control by one group since election was "public" and not according to classes. Under these circumstances, if a justice wished to "connive" with the electorate he would have to intrigue with all, "that is with none." But Ogarev also found faults in the American

[3] Ogarev, "Razbor Osnovnykh Polozheni Preobrazovaniia Sudebnoi Chasti v Rossii," *Kolokol*, no. 153 (Jan. 1, 1863), pp. 1272–74. This was the fourth article in the series. The others appeared successively in the numbers of *Kolokol* for Nov. 15, Dec. 1 and Dec. 15, 1862, and Jan. 15, 1863.

system: the primary deficiency was that the courts were "swamped with work." Furthermore, he insisted, that when bribery did occur, it was the result of low salaries.

Deeper errors in the American system had arisen however, because higher state judges were in reality elected not by the public at large but by "legislative assemblies." Similarly, federal judges were chosen by the Senate and president. Ogarev therefore insisted that both state and federal justices were susceptible to political pressures on the part of legislators. "The colonies have broken away from the tradition of the mother country, but not entirely." "Public election," just as in England, was confined to the justices of the peace and to the federal Attorney-General. Yet, since the American franchise, unlike the English, was not based on economic class privilege, there was less political conniving with "rich men" in the United States than in England.[4]

Several of these ideas show the heavy influence of eighteenth-century thinkers; particularly of Montesquieu, who favored the independence of the judiciary for the salutary condition of the state. Here, of course, is the old idea of the separation of powers [5] (correlated perhaps with federalism), which Ogarev applied as a corrective to the autocratic government of Russia. His insistence upon untrammeled "public election" (by which he meant universal and direct election) reflected the somewhat Utopian idea that direct democracy is the ideal method for the choice of judges. However, Ogarev probably introduced his point of direct

[4] *Kolokol,* no. 153, p. 1273. Note that Ogarev mentions Russel's *America Compared with England* as one source for this series of articles; careful search fails to uncover this source.

[5] An idea under critical scrutiny by present-day administrative experts. Cf. Frank J. Goodnow, *Politics and Administration* (New York, 1900).

and popular election of judges to demonstrate further the necessity for universal suffrage in Russia.

Ogarev's analysis reveals careful investigation into the factual and mechanical workings of the American judicial system. And unquestionably he put his finger upon some of its main faults. He was quite correct in noting the insufficient pay of the lower levels of the judiciary, with resulting "fees" to justices of the peace,[6] and the evils involved in the choice of judges by state legislatures in those times. But Ogarev erred in believing that the Attorney-General was elected directly. He was also mistaken in thinking that "a strong guild" of lawyers was absent in America; in reality such a group had become influential even in the eighteenth century and had played a significant role as intellectual leaders of the American Revolution. Furthermore, he failed to observe that women were excluded from the "classless" American elections. Finally Ogarev was guilty of naïveté in imagining that popular election would automatically remove the possibility of the judiciary ever yielding to influence or bribery. Apart from these errors, Ogarev's article was reasonably competent in pointing a lesson to the readers of *Kolokol*.

The lesson was clear. Notwithstanding these faults of the American courts, the elective principle based on universal (manhood) suffrage was in force in the United States. Thus Ogarev inferred that Russian reformers might profitably study the American judiciary—a system superior to the English, although it still bore traces of the mother country's influence.

When finally consummated in 1864, the Judicial Reform by no means lived up to Ogarev's desires. The justices were appointed for life, and were not elected by the population at

[6] This criticism, as will be seen, was later developed by Lavrov in his broad attack against bribery in American public life.

all. Unfortunately, these life appointments, together with large salaries for the justices of the new law courts did not, as they might well have, germinate the independent judiciary that Ogarev had hoped for. This "most European" of the "great reforms" was vitiated by a system of rewards, honors, and titles by which the Minister of Justice might reach pliable judges: moreover, restrictions were placed, even from the beginning, on the competence of the courts; and, most disastrously, the reformed judiciary had to work outside the protective framework of a constitution.

Ogarev wrote in similar painstaking fashion when he appraised the new *zemstvo* institutions, local and provincial administrative councils established by Alexander II in his reform program. Ogarev declared that "they suddenly raise from the fog the elective principle native to the Russian mind." He believed that this favorable response to an elected institution indicated that despite other fundamental political and social disparities, "the Russian nation [was] much nearer to the states of North America than to any of the . . . European states." [7]

It is evident that Ogarev here transcended mere advocacy of the American elective principle for his own country. He now affirmed that this principle was organically rooted in the Russian "mind," and that this fact brought America and Russia onto common ground. If we grant the partial truth of his statement for Russia both historically and actually, in terms of the old Estates General, the *Zemski Sobor;* or of the then contemporary assembly of the peasant commune, we may well add this argument to Herzen's list of the points of contact between the two countries.

The United States in this period seemed to Ogarev as the

[7] Ogarev, "Polozhenie o Gubernskikh i Uezdnykh," *Kolokol,* no. 185 (May 15, 1864), pp. 1517–20; *Ibid.,* no. 186 (June 15, 1864), p. 1525.

best example of radical political and civil democracy—a model to be accepted by all those really interested in participating in the great work of transforming the old backward Russia of Nicholas I into something greater and better. The belief in the introduction of universal suffrage from above, and in a real self-limitation of autocratic powers, which is, for example, what an independent judiciary would have meant, was quite consistent in this brief period when hopes were raised high for the possibility of a "social" monarchy under Alexander II. The comparatively rapid dissipation of this enthusiastic hope and the shift to disillusionment and even despair is another story.

CHAPTER IV

Bridled Intransigence

MICHAEL BAKUNIN

MICHAEL BAKUNIN, "apostle of destruction" and Russian anarchist *par excellence,* had well-defined opinions of American life, and like Herzen's they were often penetrating. But although America exerted a constructive influence on Bakunin's ideas, the United States was far less a source of consolation to him than to Herzen.[1]

Michael Bakunin was born in 1814 at Premukhino, in the

---

[1] Edward Hallett Carr has written that "in 1872, Marx secured his [Bakunin's] expulsion from the International and thereby determined his exclusion forever from the Marxist calendar of revolutionary saints. No memorial to Bakunin will be found within the confines of the Soviet Union," thereby implying that Bakunin is somehow outside the evolutionary line of Russian socialism in the eyes of the leaders of the U.S.S.R. Yet by 1934, four volumes of his collected works and letters were published in Moscow, and it is stated that additional volumes have not appeared because materials in the possession of such followers of Bakunin as Max Nettlau have not been made available. Furthermore, the editor of these four volumes carefully defines Bakunin's contribution to the development of Marxian revolutionary theory and practice in Russia as seen by contemporary Russian Marxists. After noting that Bakunin's influence reached even to South America, the editor remarks that Bakunin was in a sense the teacher "of the first theoreticians of the proletarian revolution of Russia," and that even "in the struggle with the attempts of Bakunin and his adherents to carry out their program and tactics in the First International, there was advantage derived, since the Marxists were able successfully to formulate more precisely the program and tactics of revolutionary Communism. . . ." Cf. E. H. Carr, *The Romantic Exiles* (New York, 1933), p. 364, and M. A. Bakunin, *Sobranie Sochineni i Pisem* (Moscow, 1934), 4 vols., ed. I. M. Steklov, I, 5–6, 13, hereinafter referred to as *Soch.*-Bakunin.

Tver *guberniia* (now Kalinin), some one hundred and fifty miles north of Moscow. This future anarchist sprang from an illustrious noble family, as did Herzen. His father, Alexander Bakunin, a cultured and traveled aristocrat, was a liberal who participated in a minor way in one of the Decembrist societies; and his mother was a relative of Muraviev-Apostol, one of the five executed martyrs. The Decembrist uprising, however, seems to have made little impression upon Bakunin at the time when it happened.

In January, 1833, after three years in the Cadet School in St. Petersburg, young Michael was commissioned an ensign in the Artillery. But early in 1834, for "lack of progress and inattention throughout the whole course of instruction," he was dismissed from the Artillery and transferred to a post at a desolate spot on the Polish border.[2] Bakunin's sympathies for unhappy Poland, later so ardently displayed, did not stem from this period, for he was convinced that the crushing of the recent Polish insurrection was necessary and useful. It was mainly for personal reasons of temperament that he resigned from the service early in 1835.

Between 1835 and 1840, Bakunin lived in Moscow, familiarizing himself with the ideas of German romantic philosophy in the circle of Stankevich and Belinski. By 1838, he had embraced Hegelianism, although one-sidedly. In 1839, he first met Herzen and Ogarev, just returned from banishment, but their views were too discordant for satisfactory rapport with his own at this period. Although later on, in 1848, Bakunin wrote very respectfully of Pestel and Ryleev, in his youth he was considered rather conservative by his radical comrades.[3] Even Katkov, who later became a staunch

---

[2] E. H. Carr, *Michael Bakunin* (London, 1937), pp. 16–17.

[3] *Soch.*-Bakunin, III, 289; Carr, *Michael Bakunin*, pp. 59–93. In this same 1848 period, Bakunin wrote that "three large-scale events that are

pillar of the autocracy, probably stood to the left of him in Stankevich's circle.

Bakunin left Moscow in 1840, and after a brief journey to St. Petersburg traveled to Berlin to study German philosophy more intensively. In close contact with Ivan Turgenev, who was also currently under the sway of German philosophical thought, Bakunin became deeply preoccupied with the new logical theories of Hegel.[4] His aim was to return eventually to Russia and take a post in Moscow University. How really undeveloped Bakunin's theoretical views were, in relation to his mature *Weltanschauung*, even in 1840, may be illustrated by his belief in immortality. Such a belief, surprising from this quarter, was expressed in a letter to Herzen on the occasion of the premature death of Stankevich in that year.[5]

It was in Germany, however, closer to the fountainhead of philosophy, and also under the influence of Arnold Ruge, that Bakunin, too, began to sense the wider implications of Hegel's doctrines as "the algebra of revolution." And in 1842, he wrote his essay on the *Reaction in Germany,* in which appeared the celebrated sentence, "the passion for destruction is at the same time a creative passion." [6]

Very shortly afterwards, Bakunin announced to his brother Nicholas in a letter written from Dresden that he would remain in Western Europe and never return home, that he was "not fit for present-day" absolutist Russia. He was "spoiled for her." But in Europe, he sensed that he still

---

instructive . . . the starting point of the new Russian life, are: Pugachev's revolt, the burning of Moscow, and the unsuccessful uprising of 1825," *Soch.*-Bakunin, III, 392.

[4] *Soch.*-Bakunin, III, 40, 43.

[5] Carr, *Michael Bakunin*, p. 93.

[6] *Soch.*-Bakunin, III, 148.

could live and act—"for Europe," he still retained "plenty of youth and energy." [7]

As early as 1842, therefore, five years before Herzen abandoned his position in Russia, Bakunin voluntarily decided to sever his connections with his fatherland. Only much later did the Imperial government order him to return to Russia because of his radical activities abroad. The remaining years prior to the Revolutionary period were spent in Western Europe, in Switzerland and Paris for the most part. During this period of high faith in the nearness of the European Revolution, Bakunin wrote to the German revolutionary August Becker and opposed the idea of flight to America, a movement, which apparently had gained ground among certain Germans in the mid 1840's. "I am glad," Bakunin declared, "that you are not going to America and that you are remaining with us." A journey to America, he felt, could be regarded at that time only as an "abstract, cowardly way out; a kind of suicide." And he insisted that one had to have the strength despite everything "to stay and live in Europe in order later on to retain the right to act in Europe." [8]

[7] *Ibid.*, III, 121; A. A. Kornilov, *Gody Stranstvi Mikhaila Bakunina* (Leningrad, Moscow, 1925), p. 163.

[8] *Soch.*-Bakunin, III, 236 (June, 1844), and pp. 464, 466. In another letter, written in August, 1847, almost on the eve of the Revolutionary period, Bakunin expressed similar sentiments. "Simon Schmidt is here in Paris and wants to go to America. . . . I have tried to dissuade him with all my strength. It seems to me that this is a time when the best, most vital and forceful people are necessary since the moment is not far off when we will have to act. It is not good to leave Europe now"; *ibid.*, pp. 263–64, 477. These sentiments were quite understandable at that time and are strangely anticipatory of those expressed in the 1870's by Lavrov and by Stepniak. Yet it must also be noted that in his *Confession* to Nicholas I, Bakunin wrote that in 1843 he left Dresden for Switzerland with George Hervegh, the German political lyricist and "if he had gone to America, I should have gone there with him"; *Soch.*-Bakunin, IV, 104.

In Paris Bakunin came in contact with Proudhon, Georges Sand, Marx, and many Polish revolutionary exiles—whose cause he was later so ardently to espouse. He also renewed his acquaintance with Belinski, and with Herzen and Ogarev. After being exiled briefly to Brussels by the Guizot Government, Bakunin was back in Paris for a short time before the outbreak of the February revolution. He was a veritable storm center of insurrection in those crowded months, hurrying thence to Bohemia to take a conspicuous part in the Pan-Slav Congress at Prague, where he advocated radical views in opposition to Palacky's brand of Austrophile Slavic nationalism. After Bakunin's revolutionary rhetoric had stimulated the Czech peasantry to abortive revolt, he played a hero's role on the Dresden barricades (joined by Richard Wagner), where at last he was taken prisoner by the Saxon Government upon the suppression of this outbreak.[9]

The years 1849 to 1861 were a hiatus, a time of imprisonment and exile for Bakunin. He suffered terribly in Austrian and Russian prisons; but a bright event during these dark days was his marriage to a Polish lady. Upon the accession of Alexander II in 1855, amnesty was granted to many political prisoners, but the new emperor with his own hand struck Bakunin's name from the list of those to be pardoned. Indeed, Alexander II later informed Bakunin's mother, "Understand, Madame, that your son will never be free, as long as he lives." However, Bakunin's lot was somewhat ameliorated when he was transferred to Siberia, where he had close association with his cousin Muraviev-Amurski, Governor-General of Eastern Siberia, and later Count of the Amur.

[9] For a good analysis of the revolutions in the Hapsburg lands, the Slav Congress, and Bakunin's role therein, cf. A. J. P. Taylor, *The Habsburg Monarchy, 1815–1918* (London, 1941), pp. 60–79, and Oscar Jaszi, *Dissolution of the Habsburg Monarchy* (Chicago, 1929), pp. 86–99.

Since his was a life-time sentence of exile, Bakunin determined to escape. And he executed this plan successfully in 1861, making his way to San Francisco by way of Japan on an American vessel. After a short stay in the New World, he journeyed to London, once more to take up the stormy course of revolutionary agitation; at first working on *Kolokol* in association with Herzen and Ogarev, then rapidly moving to at least verbal participation in various revolutionary movements such as the Polish Rising of 1863. With the formation of his various "Internationals," Bakunin attempted directly to foment revolution in Lyons in 1870, in Russia (via intermediaries) in the great "going to the people" movement of the early seventies, and finally in Bologna in 1874. It was at this time that the fierce polemics with Marx and the German "centralizing" socialists occurred. As a result of these conflicts, Bakunin was expelled from Marx's First International in 1872. But since the International itself died for all practical purposes after the very Congress which condemned Bakunin, the expulsion was at best a Pyrrhic victory for Marx and his adherents. After this there ensued Bakunin's struggle with the disciples of Lavrov. Bakunin, anarchist to the very end, died just four years later, in 1876, a worn-out but emphatically not a forgotten man.

Bakunin's professional revolutionary activity was more important than his mature theoretical ideas of "anarchism, collectivism, and atheism"—aims to be realized in his belief through a universal uprising organized by small secret groups possessing a coördinating center. The "Anarchist pope" favored such tactics in part, possibly because they were peculiarly suited to his temperament. Bakunin himself acknowledged that he knew less than Marx of political economy and accepted Marx's criticism of himself as a "sentimental idealist." Furthermore, in a letter written from America, Bakunin granted that he did not "possess Herzen's talents . . . in the most extensive sense." [10]

There is no question that Bakunin's teachings have had a wide influence among the working classes, especially in the Latin countries of Europe and America. His most lasting theoretical contributions were those oft-reiterated negative critiques of church and state, his two constant hobgoblins.[11] An amusing illustration of Bakunin's "negativism" is found in a reputed reply to a question about his positive beliefs. He burst out: "I believe in nothing. I read nothing. I think of but one thing: twist the neck, twist it yet further, screw off the head, let not a trace of it remain!" [12] This rejoinder, though an extreme and perhaps unjust representation of the man, does underscore the volatile, iconoclastic personality of Bakunin—a dynamic revolutionary, who loved his vocation with an artist's love; an individual who knew little of method or order in either his life or his fragmentary writings. As Herzen once bitterly jotted down, Bakunin was a person who too often lived in a world of illusions. Perhaps he came

[10] Bakunin, however, did accuse Marx of being "vain," "perfidious" and "sneaky." Herzen's great deficiency was his "skepticism." To this Bakunin contrasted his own constant "faith in the realization of the socialist theory." For all citations, cf. *Oeuvres de Michel Bakounine*, ed. James Guillaume (Paris, 1907–13), II, xi, IV, 234; M. Dragomanov, *Correspondance de Michel Bakounine; lettres à Herzen et à Ogareff*, tr. (Paris, 1896), p. 125; T. G. Masaryk, *The Spirit of Russia*, tr. (London, 1919), I, 455.

[11] Cf. Samuel Rezneck, "The Political and Social Theory of Michael Bakunin," *American Political Science Review* (May, 1927), XXI, 270–96. In this superficial sketch, Rezneck contends that Bakunin's positive political and social ideology was surprisingly unoriginal, a badly organized composite of the leading radical ideas of the nineteenth century. From the former "official" Russian Marxian point of view, M. N. Pokrovski terms Bakunin's positive program "illiterate"; "Bakunin," *Entsiklopedicheski Slovar* (Moscow, 1926), IV, p. 515.

[12] Masaryk, *op. cit.*, I, 456–57.

closest to being the prototype of Turgenev's *Rudin*.[13] And it may even be true that this tempestuous personality loved ideas and not human beings, as Belinski once observed.[14] No one will deny though that Bakunin stormed through the nineteenth century with a giant's tread, and if his career so often appears to have been confused and chaotic, this was due in large measure to the chaos of a Europe seething with the new forces of bourgeois revolution, nationalism and socialism, which often converged and collided with each other as well as with the older feudal society.

Bakunin had the advantage of Herzen in that he had first-hand acquaintance with America. His brief visit to the States took place in the fall of 1861, after his escape from Siberia. He traveled to San Francisco on an American vessel and thence to New York and Boston via Panama. Even in the course of his journey to America, Bakunin came in contact with at least two presumably politically advanced American traders, one of them in Siberia, the other in Japan. With them he arranged for the distribution of several hundred copies of *Kolokol* among the sailors of the Russian flotilla in the Far East and among the traders of the area [15] —an indication that his activism was unflagging even after more than ten years of prison and exile. From these two Yankees, he may have derived valuable information about the United States. In Europe, "he had read much of American literature," including "James Fenimore Cooper's novels, all of which he had read in the German." [16] And while

[13] As Masaryk has concluded, *op. cit.*, II, *passim*, a view which has been expanded by recent Soviet researches.

[14] *Ibid.*, I, 432; Carr, *Michael Bakunin*, p. 72.

[15] Dragomanov, *op. cit.*, Letter to Herzen and Ogareff (dated "San Francisco, 15/3 Oct., 1861"), p. 122.

[16] Oscar Handlin, "A Russian Anarchist Visits Boston," *New England Quarterly*, XV (March, 1942), 107.

in Königstein prison in 1849, Bakunin recorded that he was studying English,[17] a language which in Boston he spoke "with fair facility." Bakunin's host in the New England capital, Martin P. Kennard, later wrote that his Russian guest's "knowledge of American affairs seemed intuitive." Kennard offered this tribute despite alleged misinformation about the Civil War with which the "rebel" ex-Senator Gwin of California supposedly had propagandized Bakunin on the voyage to Panama.[18]

There is little record of Bakunin's stay in America. He wrote that he knew no one in San Francisco,[19] and of his stay in New York nothing is known except the address of his residence in that city. That Bakunin was in contact with a group of German refugees who settled in New York after the 1848 debacle seems exceedingly probable, for his letter of introduction to the Abolitionist jeweller Kennard, his Boston host, was "from a valued friend, Reinhold Solger, Ph.D., a German, . . . a political refugee from . . . his fatherland . . . [after] the notable political events in 1848." [20] Reinhold Solger (1817–66) was a German radical writer, a colleague of Bakunin's in Western Europe during the early 1840's; he participated in the unsuccessful Baden uprising of 1848 and emigrated to America in 1853, where he ended his days as a bank director.[21] Such contacts would have been valuable sources of information about American conditions, explaining in great measure Bakunin's "intuitive" knowledge of the United States.

Only Bakunin's Boston visit seems to have been chronicled in detail. That visit "left significant impressions on both host and guest." [22] Bakunin carried letters of introduction to many

[17] Cf. *Soch.*-Bakunin, IV, 11.
[18] Handlin, *loc. cit.*
[19] Dragomanov, *op. cit.*, p. 121.
[20] Handlin, *op. cit.*, p. 105.
[21] *Soch.*-Bakunin, III, 467.
[22] Handlin, *op. cit.*, p. 104.

outstanding figures besides his host: to Governor Andrew of Massachusetts; to Henry Wilson, the later historian of the "Slave Power"; to General McClellan, who had been in Russia in 1855–56 observing the European armies at war;[23] to Samuel Longfellow, brother and biographer of Henry Wadsworth Longfellow; and to George H. Snelling, a prominent Bostonian partisan of the Polish Insurrection of 1831. Bakunin also spoke of his "old friend professor Agassiz," whom he intended to visit in Cambridge,[24] and there were several familiar references to Charles Sumner as well as to Lincoln, Grant, and Stephen Douglas.

The "Russian Bear" even went so far as to record a fleeting intention of becoming an American citizen while in Boston. But even though Kennard reflected "that under other circumstances he would have cast his future fortune with Americans," he recognized that Bakunin had no serious intention of becoming an American citizen at that time. Shortly thereafter, Bakunin departed for London, to rejoin his wife and to commence anew his revolutionary activities. To these ends, he relinquished a contemplated journey to Washington and contented himself instead with an autograph of George Washington. Bakunin also met many Americans after his return to Europe; men such as Andrew Cameron, the able delegate of the National Labor Union to the fourth Congress of the International in Basle, 1869. However, the nuclear source of the Russian anarchist's "American views" was most probably his visit to the United States.

The greater part of Bakunin's recorded observations and

[23] Cf. Anna M. Babey, *Americans in Russia* (New York, 1938), p. 6.

[24] Dragomanov, *op. cit.*, p. 124. For Bakunin's amusing and somewhat terrifying brusqueness during his stay with H. W. Longfellow at Craigie House, cf. Van Wyck Brooks, *The Flowering of New England* (New York, 1937), p. 510, and David Hecht, " 'Laughing Allegra' Meets an Ogre," *New England Quarterly*, XIX (June, 1946), 243–44.

judgments of American life falls within a span of twelve years (1860–72) coming either during or after his American visit. In contrast to Herzen, Bakunin's most complete and generalized sketch of the American scene did not possess a highly philosophical flavor but was rather of a broad social and economic category. In his famous essay entitled *Federalism, Socialism and Anti-theologism,* written seven years after the American visit, Bakunin discussed the deepening gulf between the classes and the steady impoverishment of the masses in the more industrialized European nations. He praised the United States for being "as yet" largely exceptional—an exception which pointed up the rule. The American worker never starved and was "better paid" than his European brother. In addition "class antagonisms" were "as yet" almost non-existent. The workers in the United States were "citizens" forming part of the "single body" of society. Elementary and even "secondary" education were "widely distributed among the masses there." Bakunin reasoned that these benefits were mainly attributable to that "traditional spirit of liberty that the first colonists imported from England," a liberty tested in "the great religious struggles." This idea of "individual independence and municipal and provincial *self-government* (in English and italicized in original) was further encouraged, because "transplanted to a desert," that "principle" could create a "new world . . . of liberty," free from "the obsessions of the past." And inspired by "liberty" alone, Bakunin rhapsodized, "in less than a century North America has been able to attain, and . . . today, even to surpass the civilization of Europe."

But almost in the same breath, Bakunin warned against unwarranted illusions. America owed her "marvellous progress" and "so enviable prosperity," above all, to the great advantage that she possessed in having an "immense quantity of fertile lands which for lack of hands remain uncultivated even today." Thus because of the liberty that exists nowhere else and this abundance, "hundreds of thousands of energetic colonists" have been attracted annually and ultimately absorbed. Concomitantly, the posing of the social question has been delayed. For an unemployed or ill-paid worker "can . . . as a last resource . . . always migrate to the *far west*" (in English and italicized in original). This possibility has worked to maintain wages at a high level and has offered the worker "an independence unknown in Europe." But a disadvantage has risen, for these high wages prevent American manufactures from competing with the products of European industry. From this inequality, "the necessity" of tariff protection has resulted. High tariffs, however, have tended to create a "host of artificial industries," and especially "to oppress and ruin the non-manufacturing Southern states . . . making them desire secession." Furthermore, protective tariffs have caused "masses of proletarian workers" to congest metropolitan centers such as New York, Philadelphia, and Boston. And this proletariat little by little has found itself in a position analogous to that of the working classes in the advanced industrial states of Europe. Bakunin concluded, "we indeed see the social question . . . posed in the Northen states as it has been much earlier among us." [25]

In this eloquent, well-reasoned and well-rounded sketch of social and economic conditions in *ante-bellum* United States, several leading ideas emerge. Permeating the whole is Bakunin's view of "American exceptionalism" as then related to the favorable political, educational, and economic status of the masses in America. This exceptionalism was

[25] *Oeuvres*, I, 28–29.

caused by specialized factors absent in whole or in part from the life of the European states. In this connection, Bakunin noted the beneficent stimulus which the new continent had given to English liberty transplanted thither—that process of "acculturation" so favorable for the growth of decentralized political institutions, which Herzen also had been quick to point out. Combined with this was Bakunin's shrewd if oversimplified analysis of the importance of America's vast tracts of free land. Here, actually, was Turner's famous "safety-valve theory," stated in explicit form twenty-five years before the presentation of the American historian's well-known argument.[26] The role of both American political freedom and abundant cheap land in drawing immigrants to our shores was somewhat distorted, for Bakunin inflated the numbers of yearly newcomers.

Bakunin was careful, however, to emphasize that the uniquely favorable position of the United States as contrasted with that of European nations was at best temporary. In future—indeed, even at that moment the process had already begun—the United States would be faced with the same social and economic maladjustments that confronted the advanced industrial states of Europe. Bakunin may be criticized adversely for failing to observe, as Lavrov did contemporaneously, that class stratification and conflict were by his time characteristic features of American life, and that Amer-

[26] Cf. Frederick Jackson Turner, *The Significance of the Frontier* (New York, 1920), pp. 1–39. For an historical sketch of the "safety-valve theory" and recent criticisms of Turner's frontier theses, cf. C. Goodrich and F. Davidson, "The Wage Earner and the Westward Movement," *Political Science Quarterly*, L (June, 1935), 161–86 and LI (March, 1936), 61–117. Also cf. F. A. Shannon, "The Homestead Act and the Labor Surplus," *American Historical Review*, XLI (July, 1936), 637–52, and a penetrating review of Turner's early writings by Herbert M. Morais, *Science and Society*, III (Summer, 1939), 406–9.

ica had for many years entered upon that path of commercial
and industrial life which engendered such cleavages and maladjustments. But in justice, it should be added that in 1872
Bakunin held the opinion that the United States was the
third greatest commercial and industrial power of the world
—following France and England. Such a view in a sense revealed an implicit recognition of this truth proclaimed by
Lavrov.[27]

Bakunin's analysis of the genesis of the protective tariff
in high wages, and again, the tendency of this tariff to ruin
the South, is certainly open to many objections. Presumably,
high wages in themselves should not be responsible for a
higher cost of production of commodities, if at the same time
the labor force receiving these wages is more efficient than
lower-paid workers. It may also reasonably be argued that
the slave system itself rather than any protective tariff turned
the South into a non-manufacturing area, especially when it
is recalled that the trend in American tariffs was steadily
downward between 1832 and 1862.[28] Although this section
of Bakunin's account tends to be artificial and schematic,
the main outlines—and his after all was a general sketch
—present a penetrating and unified summary of American
social and economic evolution. And the evaluation of trends
up to that moment was highly favorable to American life.
Many of Bakunin's observations of political, social, and economic tendencies in America to be noted later on will modify
and amplify these judgments.

A few philosophic generalizations about American na-

---

[27] *Oeuvres*, IV, 487.

[28] Cf. Charles A. Beard and Mary Beard, *The Rise of American Civilization* (New York, 1927), II, 3–13; Arthur C. Cole, "The Irrepressible Conflict: 1850–1865," *A History of American Life*, ed. A. M. Schlesinger and
D. R. Fox (New York, 1934), VII, 62–66, 68, 70.

tional characteristics in the manner of Herzen appear in Bakunin's writings but these are distinctly subordinate to the generalized economic and social view. In a letter to Herzen and Ogarev written from San Francisco in 1861, Bakunin deprecated "the banality of material welfare" in the United States, "where the heart" was "absent." He further observed that the "infantile national vanity" of Americans had helped to deprave this people.[29] Yet this by now familiar characterization of the less agreeable traits in American life was followed by the optimistic view that perhaps the Civil War—then just erupted—would be "salutary" in that it would cause America again to find her "lost soul."[30]

In light of this foregoing survey of American life, one would hardly expect Bakunin to omit detailed discussion of the nature of the state in his writings on America. But again one is agreeably surprised in finding no complete dismissal of the American political system and state apparatus in the generality of observations, despite Bakunin's usual tendency to damn all governments *in toto*.

Repeatedly, Bakunin characterized America as "the classic land of political liberty," or politically the freest country in the world, or as possessed of "the most democratic institutions."[31] Closely related to this was his frequently expressed preference for a republican form of government as opposed to the rule of kings. He was firmly convinced that "the most imperfect republic" was "a thousand times" worthier than "the most enlightened monarchy." For in a republic, there were "moments" when the people were not "oppressed," al-

---

[29] Dragomanov, *op. cit.*, p. 123. For derogatory comments on the role of money in America and the relation of property to social standing, cf. *Oeuvres*, III, 172–73.

[30] *Ibid.* For other expression of such hopes, cf. Handlin, *op. cit.*, p. 108.

[31] Cf. *Oeuvres*, I, 171, and IV, 183, for two of many examples.

though they were "continually exploited." In monarchies, however, both evils "always" prevailed.[32] Hence this Russian anarchist's fulsome praise of the February Revolution in Paris was entirely logical; "Long live France! Long live the republic! Long live democracy!"[33]

More specifically, Bakunin singled out the American federal system as worthy of emulation by European socialists. In a program offered to the League of Peace and Liberty in 1868, he demanded that the League oppose a new principle to the "monstrous and oppressive centralization of military, bureaucratic, despotic, monarchical, constitutional, or even republican states." And he insisted that this doctrine be the "great and salutary *principle of Federalism* (italicized in original), a principle in regard to which the recent events in the United States . . . have, moreover, offered us a triumphant demonstration . . . ."[34]

After this sympathy expressed for American federalism emerging triumphant from the Civil War and the attack on all centralized forms of government, Bakunin concluded with an overt plea in favor of American federalism. He declared that while all who really desired "the emancipation of Europe" could profitably retain their "sympathies for the great socialist and humanitarian ideas enunciated by the French Revolution," they "should reject" its centralizing "policy of state." In its stead, European radicals had resolutely to "adopt the policy of liberty of the North Americans."[35] In this instance we may unhesitatingly assert that American federalism enriched Bakunin's socialist ideas, just as it had Herzen's. Unfortunately, Bakunin's approbation of American federalism is vitiated by his failure to realize that precisely in this period, post-Civil War Reconstruction had

[32] *Ibid.*, I, 174.
[33] *Soch.*-Bakunin (March 13, 1848), III, 294.
[34] *Oeuvres*, I, 12.
[35] *Ibid.*, I, 13.

moved significantly in the direction of more centralized governmental controls, at least for the recently rebelled Southern states. Indeed, Bakunin was so captivated by his belief
in American federalism that in 1871 he used it as an argument favoring the existence of the then far from democratic
American Senate.[36]

The zenith of Bakunin's approval was attained a year later,
when he delivered a panegyric in favor of English and especially of American liberty. It is of great significance that
Bakunin dwelt upon the force and importance of public
opinion in the "only two great countries" where the people
"really" enjoyed "liberty and political power." Liberty in
England and the United States was "more than a political
right." It pervaded everyone's "social nature," was a prerogative inviolable by government. Even "the most disin-
herited and miserable foreigners" shared in it "as fully as the
richest and most influential citizens." Thus in Bakunin's estimation, English liberty constituted a *"veritable power of
public opinion"* (italicized in original), ever ready "to arise
and make itself felt beyond and above all the political forms
and rights explicitly expressed and consecrated by the English constitution . . ."[37]

Then, after affirming the power of contemporary mass
agitation in England and noting the passage of the Reform
Bill of 1867, Bakunin asserted roundly that the English
people had "no need" to struggle further for either "liberty
or . . . political power." It possessed them "already . . . in
the customs . . ." And Bakunin stated in conclusion that
these remarks about the "English people" referred "of course,
even more to the people of the United States." There, "liberty and . . . political action directly exercised by the

[36] *Ibid.*, III, 166.   [37] *Ibid.*, IV, 448.

masses ·have attained the highest degree of development known in history up till now." [38] The "apostle of destruction" appears tamed indeed!

Yet what Bakunin could concede with one hand he could qualify, if not retract, with the other. After some of these amazingly favorable and intelligent opinions about American political life and institutions, Bakunin did not hesitate to attack many aspects of the political apparatus in the United States. [39] After noting correctly the limitations of American federalism, which in itself lacked the ability to prevent the "overthrow and destruction" by the Civil War of the "most beautiful political organization that ever existed in history," [40] Bakunin began to sound a theme that was more familiar to the Russian radicals. This was the attack on what he considered to be the sham of universal suffrage, of parliamentarism, and even of political liberty *in toto*. In the very same essay where he penned such encomiums to American federalism, the Russian anarchist could pillory the workings of one of its most closely linked doctrines: the sovereignty

[38] *Ibid.*, IV, 449. Along the same lines, Bakunin also speculated that "Germany would have developed much more rapidly in terms of liberty and equality, if she had had the United States . . . as neighbors instead of the Russian Empire . . ."; *ibid.*, II, 413.

[39] Bakunin's modifying and negative comments fall within the same approximate time span as do the positive ones: 1868–72.

[40] *Ibid.*, I, 22. Bakunin affirmed that federalism could not resolve the "social" question of slavery. And although he believed that the Civil War was actually a slaveholders' conspiracy "fomented against . . . the North," he could nevertheless maintain that "the internal political organization of the Southern states was in certain aspects even more perfect, more completely free than was that of the Northern states." Southern federalism was unfortunately, however, tainted by the "black spot" of the "forced labor of slaves" which "sufficed to overturn the whole political existence of these States." The attempted vindication of American federalism, despite its limitations and even in the otherwise despised Confederacy is the important thing here.

of the people, and indeed, the very "public opinion" lately extolled. Because of "forcible" absorption in daily labor, and "very inferior" education, the people "is sovereign in law, not in fact," Bakunin insisted. They are "forced" to relinquish their "supposed sovereignty" to the bourgeoisie. And he averred sarcastically, that the only residual "advantage" which the people derived in the United States, lay in the fact that there "ambitious minorities, the political classes, cannot arrive to power otherwise than by paying court to them, flattering their transient passions, sometimes extremely bad ones, and most often, deceiving them." [41]

Of course Bakunin in attacking the mechanics of popular sovereignty in the American republic did so not from the point of view of damning democracy as a system but of improving it. This is amply demonstrated in the remainder of the passage just cited. These criticisms, interestingly enough, may be compared with those advanced by an equally famous countryman of Bakunin, Constantine Pobedonostsev, Procurator of the Holy Synod in Russia at the end of the last century, a man who shuddered at the word, "liberalism." This "philosopher of reaction" scorned the "dextrous manipulators of votes," who with their "placemen" were the "real rulers" in a "democracy." It was they who skillfully operated "the hidden springs" that moved the "puppets." Pobedonostsev contemptuously dismissed these gentry for being "ever ready with loud speeches" to laud "equality," when "in reality, they rule the people as any despot or military dictator might. . . ." [42] Certainly, after juxtaposing these two

[41] *Ibid.*, I, 173. Also cf. *ibid.*, I, 171; III, 54; IV, 183–84; 190–91; and *God and the State,* tr. (Columbus Junction, Iowa, 1896), p. 14, for repetitious and bitter amplifications of this critique of universal suffrage in the United States.

[42] K. P. Pobyedonostseff, *Memoirs of a Russian Statesman,* tr. (London, 1898), p. 27.

comments, we may say with justice that extremes meet.

Besides decrying universal suffrage and representative government for benefiting only the American bourgeoisie, Bakunin frequently went so far as to lump republics with monarchies, calling them equally evil. In fact, he asserted at one point, that a republic might be "more despotic," an even greater political menace than a monarchy. For, founded upon "universal suffrage," a republic, using "the pretext" of representing "the will of all . . . will press down the weight of its collective power on the liberty and the free movement of all its members." [43]

Here, one must remember, Bakunin was theorizing about the state in general, naming no *particular* republics. Yet it would be wrong to discount such statements for they are totally in keeping with his oft-repeated dictum "the State is the flagrant negation of humanity." The absolute character of this denial fades, however, against the background of Bakunin's positive views regarding American political institutions.

In venturing a summary of what Bakunin's "attitude" towards American political life really was, it may safely be said that there were several attitudes. Outstanding was his generally laudatory recognition of the workings of political freedom in the United States. This was a real concession of Bakunin's doctrinaire theorizing to the actualities of the American scene, although some of these actualities were far from pleasant in the politically "dreadful decade" of post-Civil War America.

In directing his attention to the "church" in America, Bakunin was anything but ambiguous. Launching a vigorous assault in 1870 upon that "elder brother of the State," he linked English and American "Protestant propagandism" to

[43] *Oeuvres*, I, 145 (these words were written in 1868).

the "propagandism of the material and commercial interests of those two nations." Bakunin further asserted that commercial penetration of colonial regions, accompanied by the "word of God," resulted in parasitic "exploitation" of those areas to the benefit of "certain classes" which "in their own country" aimed similarly to exploit the masses.[44]

Certainly we are familiar in recent times with the role of various churches as passive (and sometimes even quite active) agents of exploitation at home and of imperialism abroad. But to describe the American Protestant churches of that era, many of which were imbued with traditions of militant aid to numerous causes on behalf of the common man (for one outstanding example, the Abolitionist tendencies in the Unitarian Church), as Bakunin did, was surely incorrect. Bakunin himself expressed the belief that such resurgence of "manifest destiny" as did occur in post-Civil War America—that is, the "imperialist" tendencies described above which the American "church" supposedly aided—was not normal but aberrant in that period. He reflected that "a political and social milieu" frequently produced a result "quite opposite to its real nature." And thus were explained away the "singularly impassioned tendencies to imperialism in the bosom of the American democracy . . . manifested today."[45]

Much more shrewd was Bakunin's demonstration of what he regarded as the *necessary* tie-up of even the "freest states" with some formalized religion. He pointed out that "divine Providence, that superior sanction of all States," played "an important part . . . in all official discourses. . . ." And cynically he remarked that whenever the head of a state,

[44] *God and the State* (tr. 1896), p. 22. These views were repeated; *Oeuvres*, III, 74.

[45] *Oeuvres*, V, 244 (written in October, 1869).

whether "the German Emperor or the president of any re-public whatever," mentioned "God," one could "be sure" that he was "preparing to shear his . . . flock once more." [46] We may not go all the way here with Bakunin, but there is enough truth in the first part of his argument to make us ponder.

Bakunin was prolific in his observations on the "social question" in America. Under this rather amorphous heading, he discussed slavery and the Civil War, the American labor movement and the education of the masses in the United States.

As has already been recorded, Bakunin was a firm op-ponent of American slavery and unwaveringly supported the North during the Civil War. This attitude, shared by Herzen (also by Belinski, Chernyshevski, and Lavrov), was to be expected not only in light of Bakunin's general *Weltan-schauung* but also in view of his specifically Russian experi-ence of opposition to serfdom. While in America he wrote to Herzen and Ogarev that in "the struggle between the North-ern and Southern United States . . . of course . . . the North . . . has all my sympathies." But, Bakunin continued, "alas! . . . up till now . . . the South . . . has acted with the most force . . . wisdom and solidarity, for which it deserves the triumph that it has had in all the clashes." [47] Despite his ardent sympathy for the North, Bakunin could still condemn what he considered to be Northern blunders

---

[46] *God and the State*, p. 40. Cf. *Oeuvres*, III, 128, for an almost verbatim repetition of this passage, with the significant change (in the year between the two) that the phrase, "Grant, the president of the great republic," is substituted for "the president of any republic whatsoever." Pobedonostsev is again instructive in this connection. Cf. his informed comments on the rela-tion of religion to the American state—almost an elaboration of Bakunin's views, *op. cit.*, pp. 18–19.

[47] Dragomanov, *op. cit.*, p. 123.

and vacillation. Above all, he censured the North for being "taken by surprise" by the South.

Seven years later, in 1868, Bakunin attacked the Southern slaveholders "and all their Northern partisans" for daring to call themselves "democrats." [48] In more intense tones, Bakunin declared that "the Southern States . . . have lately drawn to themselves the reprobation of all the partisans of liberty and humanity in the world." And he denounced them for "the iniquitous and sacrilegious [sic] war which they fomented against . . . the North." [49]

After the Civil War, Bakunin retained great interest in the fate of the liberated Negroes, and favored the politics and program of the "Radical" Republicans as the solution of this vexing problem. He upheld the "really intelligent and liberal minority" in the Republican party in its fight against President Johnson and the pro-Southern elements in Washington. Bakunin hoped for the "triumph" of this minority "of great and generous . . . principles," but at the same time was aware of the limited possibilities of the "revolution by consent" (as we would call it today), once this minority achieved power. For "popular self-government" really to become "a reality . . . another revolution . . . far more profound . . ." would be necessary. [50]

Beyond expressing an attitude shared by his American Northern contemporaries in regard to the "Radical" Republicans (as a glance through the pages of the *Atlantic Monthly* will confirm), Bakunin here expressed a rather profound analysis of the process of crystallization of political power. Moreover, Bakunin, again far from totally rejecting the American state, was heartily in favor of certain measures

---

[48] *Oeuvres*, I, 21–22.

[49] *Ibid.* Also cf. *ibid.*, I, 172, for even more vituperative comments on this subject.   [50] *Ibid.*, I, 172–73.

which could be taken to improve it. Accordingly, this support of Republican party policies bears a connection, although unspoken, between the immediate and ultimate (maximalist) goals in Bakunin's mind. Once more, the American example militated against too abstract theorizing. What one of the immediate goals was that Bakunin favored is indicated in the following passage:

Even in America, has not socialism completely dawned in the proposition of an eminent man, Mr. Charles Sumner, Senator from Boston, to distribute lands to the emancipated Negroes of the Southern States? [51]

This interpretation of the status of socialism in America was over-optimistic and misleading, just as was Bakunin's elaboration of his views on the American labor movement.

As already pointed out, Bakunin believed that wage-labor was, in the socialist sense of the term, "exploited" in America as it was in Europe. Commenting on the historical continuity of such exploitation, he wrote in 1868 that "in general, no state" could ever do without "the forced labor of the masses." Such "wage laborers or slaves" were an "indispensable necessity for the leisure, liberty and civilization of the political class: the citizens." And in this regard, Bakunin declared, "The United States of North America do not as yet form an exception." [52]

The very fact that Bakunin felt compelled to single the United States out as also fitting into his preconceived pattern of thought, revealed a certain doubt on his part. Exploitation certainly did exist in America, but how important was it in relation to the ameliorating factors that Bakunin himself noted from time to time? There was an ideological hesitation here.

Touching on the subject of the actual strength of Amer-

[51] *Ibid.*, I, 50.   [52] *Ibid.* I, 157. Also cf. *ibid.*, IV, 187–88.

ican trade unionism in 1870, Bakunin allowed his revolutionary enthusiasm to blind his judgment completely. He asserted boldly that there were "800,000" trade unionists "last year and they have certainly passed the figure of a million today." [53] His oversanguine attitude towards the strength of American labor was revealed even more clearly in his estimate of the position in 1871 of the National Labor Union (the American section of the International). He insisted that since the suppression of the Paris Commune, the International was stronger than ever "in Europe and America." The International "exists, . . . agitates, and publicly propagates" its program "in America and in the rest of Western Europe except for France." [54]

When one recalls that the National Labor Union collapsed

[53] *Ibid.*, IV, 205; at this point M. Guillaume (editor of *Oeuvres*) interposed to shield Bakunin by reporting that "when at the General Congress of the . . . International at Basle in 1869, president Jung . . . introduced the American delegate, Cameron, sent by the *National Labor Union* [in English and italicized in original] . . . , he announced that this delegate 'represented 800,000 brothers from beyond the Atlantic.'" A modern estimate of the *total trade union* membership in the United States just before the Panic of 1873, made by Selig Perlman is 300,000, conservatively, and certainly no higher than 600,000 in 1869. And the National Labor Union was not synonymous by any means with all of the organized workers of America in those years. Selig Perlman, *A History of Trade Unionism in the United States* (New York, 1929), p. 44.

[54] *Oeuvres,* VI, 363–64. This passage also reveals Bakunin's constant view that the American labor movement was to be considered as an integral part of the European labor movement embraced in the First International; that is, that American labor was, in a sense, mature enough to work with the parallel movements across the Atlantic. To that extent the American "exceptionalism" was belied. For corroboration of this point, cf. *Oeuvres,* I, 3; IV, 161, 301, 412. These citations range from 1868 to 1872. For a good study of the National Labor Union (1866–72), cf. J. R. Commons, *History of Labor in the United States* (New York, 1926), pp. 85–155, esp. pp. 86–87, 131–32. Bakunin's attitude to the American labor movement (or at least its radical wing) may have been intensified by the fact that the American section of the International was Bakuninist rather than Marxian.

only a few months afterwards, and that the International itself was destined shortly to perish, Bakunin's exaggerated optimism can only be interpreted as a symptom of the desperation of a leader seeing his cherished goals receding ever further into the unattainable future. This psychological *malaise* was to occur again.

Among the other "social" questions closely related to the American labor movement with which Bakunin grappled, was workers' education. In a lecture delivered to a group of Swiss working men in 1871, Bakunin was willing to concede, as he had three years earlier, that popular education had made great strides in the United States. However, even though America and Switzerland had done "more than all others" in this regard, equal education did not exist in these two countries. According to Bakunin, only the "children of the bourgeois" enjoyed higher education. The children of "the people" received "primary education only, and on rare occasions, some mite of secondary education." [55]

Despite the general correctness of this accusation of class privilege in the American educational set-up, there is a certain narrowness in Bakunin's disregard of such facts as the authorization by law of the system of state "land-grant" schools. These dated from 1862 when the Morrill Act was passed by Congress. And while it was mainly true as Bakunin asserted a little farther on that "the workers" had not "the means . . . of feeding, clothing, and lodging their children for the whole duration of their studies," yet the progress of free public education in the United States was unquestionably moving beyond that of "a mite of secondary education" for the people. [56]

[55] *Oeuvres*, V, 324–25.

[56] *Ibid.* Also cf. Cole, *op. cit.*, pp. 208–9, 242, and Allan Nevins, "The Emergence of Modern America, 1865–1878," *A History of American Life,* ed. A. M. Schlesinger and D. R. Fox (New York, 1927), VIII, 15–16.

Bakunin's utterances on this subject two months later were even more ill-founded. "In the most democratic countries," he insisted "the great majority of the children of the people" attended school for only "two or three years at the most." After this brief period they were forced to "earn their livelihood, and . . . once entered upon conditions of wage labor, the proletariat is forcibly obliged to renounce learning." [57]

Bakunin was certainly on dubious ground in thus denouncing this aspect of American social life. The severity of his attack was undoubtedly attributable, in part, to the "agitational" nature of the polemic in which it occurs, a form of propaganda which inevitably led to over-drawn conclusions. Yet both here and in Bakunin's earlier remarks on popular education in the United States, the outstanding fact remains his acknowledgment that America (sometimes coupled with Switzerland) had done the most for this cause. Such approval outweighed his criticisms of the American educational system.

Bakunin summed up his views on the "social" question by renouncing the "fatal" concept of patriotism in favor of complete internationalism. He declaimed that "patriotism" was "the negation of human equality and solidarity." Hence, the "solution" of the "social question" which European and American workers had posed was "possible only through the abolition of state frontiers." And Bakunin concluded hopefully that the "social question" tended "necessarily to destroy this traditional custom" of patriotism "in the conscience of the workers of all countries." [58]

This typically nineteenth-century vision of a world without national boundaries (the obverse of the then immedi-

[57] *Oeuvres*, VI, 98.
[58] *Ibid.*, I, 243 (citation written in 1869).

ate issues of nationalism) was augmented by Bakunin's confident prophecy of a great proletarian federation of Europe and then of the world. Here, in a sense, was extended political federalism, with socialist content of course. The "future," he believed, "a long future," belonged "foremost to the Europeo-American Internationality." And later on, "this great Europeo-American nation" would be "organically merged with the Asiatic and African groupings." [59]

Notwithstanding these grandiose and optimistic dreams of proletarian internationalism, it is significant that Bakunin at least once gave overt expression to a feeling of despair for the prospects of socialism in Europe. On this occasion Bakunin's disillusionment forced him at least briefly to look to America for solace. He insisted dolefully that if the Prussians were to triumph over France in 1870, there would be nothing left for "us old folk but to die." And in that case,

> Alas! I will have to acknowledge that my deceased friend, Alexander Herzen, was right after the ill-omened June days of 1848 . . . when he proclaimed that Western Europe henceforward was dead, and that for a renewal, for a continuation of history, there remained no more than two sources: . . . America, and eastern barbarism.[60]

[59] *Ibid.*, VI, 392 (citation written in 1871). M. Guillaume has added a somewhat apologetic note that "in 1871, the Australian States had not yet entered . . . into the preoccupations of the socialists of Europe." Also cf. *ibid.*, V, 14.

[60] *Ibid.*, IV, 233. By "eastern barbarism," Bakunin was, of course, referring to Russia. But it would be a great mistake to underestimate Bakunin's nationalist ("Slavophile") feelings for what, after all, remained his native land—despite the seemingly paradoxical rejection of patriotism in favor of proletarian internationalism expressed earlier. Besides frequently referring to his "love for the fatherland" (e.g., *Soch.*-Bakunin, III, 194), Bakunin once prophesied, in 1845, of the Russian people that, "knowing it, it is impossible not to be convinced that before it there stands a great mission to be fulfilled in the world"; *ibid.*, III, 242. Cf. also *ibid.*, III, 222–31. It is also interesting in this connection that Bakunin, writing to Herzen

This passage may well be compared in sentiment to Herzen's bitter eloquence in the post-1848 years. It was written following the failure of the 1870 Lyons rising, which Bakunin organized. The Paris Commune, however, was to maintain itself **some** months more. These deeply pessimistic sentences collated with the desperate note of optimism in regard to the health of the International after 1871, gain more than momentary significance when fitted into the framework of Bakunin's predominantly enthusiastic appreciation of America; the despairing mind reached across the Atlantic for hope. America, despite all faults of a bourgeois republic as Bakunin had catalogued and judged them, might, on the basis of her long history of political liberty and federal government, her reserve of free land, and her successful abolition of Negro slavery, be the first country to take the next step towards realizing the beatific vision of socialism.

In general, it can safely be asserted that Bakunin helped familiarize his **European followers with United** States history and institutions—albeit, occasionally in distorted form. And finally, American democracy (especially American federalism) had a lasting influence upon Bakunin's thought, although it was perhaps not quite so distinctly delineated as in Herzen's case. To what extent Bakunin's 1848 program of Slav federation was influenced by American federalism is difficult to estimate. It is, of course, possible to speculate that Bakunin had the United States in mind when he wrote that "finally we proclaimed the indissoluble solidarity of all Slavic nations." In future they would have to "comprise one large political organism, constructed on a federal basis,

---

from Irkutsk in 1861, was able to extol the work of Siberian colonization then under the administrative direction of Muraviev-Amurski. Here was a specific example of what could be accomplished even under the hated autocratic Russian government; *ibid.*, IV, 321.

upon the democratic principles of nationality, freedom, equality and fraternity." [61] In any case, knowledge of American institutions helped partly to qualify Bakunin's schematizations. And it offered this deracinated Russian radical some consolation for the future, even if he never quite permitted this to beguile him into advocating a theory of "American exceptionalism."

[61] *Ibid.*, III, 311 (written in 1849).

CHAPTER V

The Land of Promise

NICHOLAS CHERNYSHEVSKI was unquestionably the outstanding representative of "that generation of middle class" intelligentsia which during "the twenties and thirties of the nineteenth century . . . emerged into the limelight from the roots . . . of . . . mother Russia."[1] Of all the Russian radical intellectuals of that time who remained within the confines of their native country, Chernyshevski was the most significant individual.

This Russian "revolutionary-democrat" was born in the quiet town of Saratov, along the Volga, in July, 1828. Unlike Herzen, Ogarev, and Bakunin, his origins were plebeian and clerical; and with this man the great generation of *raznochinets* intelligentsia came into its own.[2]

Until the age of fourteen, Chernyshevski remained at home studying under his father's guidance for the priesthood, then was sent to a Russian Orthodox seminary, where he amazed his teachers and fellow students by his knowledge. It was hoped that one day the precocious youth would be a shining adornment of the Church, and indeed Chernyshevski was quite inclined to religion in his adolescence. During these teen years he read avidly in the fields of secular

[1] N. G. Chernyshevski, *Polnoe Sobranie Sochineni,* ed. B. P. Kozmin (Moscow, 1939), I, 567; hereinafter referred to as *Soch.*-1939.

[2] Cf. Chapter I, *supra,* for discussion of the *raznochintsy,* or men of different classes.

philosophy and history, and also gained familiarity with the works of such authors as Pushkin, Georges Sand, and Schiller. All of these interests along with great linguistic talent undoubtedly advanced him beyond a mere theological outlook and helped to shape his future course. Priestly education ceased to satisfy him, and in 1846 he entered St. Petersburg University to specialize in historical and philological studies.

During his first four-year sojourn in St. Petersburg, even while Chernyshevski anticipated a professorial career, he was being subjected to revolutionary influences. In the northern capital, he joined the literary circle of Vvedenski, who introduced him to the study of Belinski (whose mantle in literary criticism Chernyshevski was to assume). The neophyte persevered in familiarizing himself with the main currents of contemporary European thought and was at first greatly interested in Guizot's historical writing. His general reading at that time was astonishingly wide, including the works of the Utopian socialists and the economists, Proudhon, Louis Blanc, Fourier, Saint Simon, and Adam Smith. Of particular significance was Chernyshevski's study of Hegel. He acknowledged that the German's *Philosophy of Right* moved him—but only his head, not his heart; indeed after a brief reading of Hegel, he "fell asleep." [3] Though this sounds exaggerated, it illustrates the fact that Hegelian philosophy exercised no such sway over Chernyshevski as it had over Herzen, Bakunin, and other "men of the forties" in Russia. Hence although Chernyshevski knew Hegel's doctrines well, and distinguished clearly between his principles and conclusions, the decisive influence over his intellectual development came from Ludwig Feuerbach,

[3] N. G. Chernyshevski, *Dnevnik* [Diary], 1848–1849 (Moscow, 1931), *passim;* p. 236 for citation.

whose materialist philosophy was greatly valued and utilized by the radical Russian opposition of the 1860's.[4]

The 1848 revolutions in the West evoked a sympathetic response in Chernyshevski similar to that of Herzen and Bakunin. The young student closely followed the turbulent events of that stormy time, rejoicing privately in his diaries over the gains of the democratic and revolutionary parties. He extolled Ledru-Rollin and Louis Blanc as "great men" and excoriated the bourgeoisie as "the beast of prey."[5] In that period, too, Chernyshevski defined himself as "a red republican and socialist."[6] Democratic revolution (a regime of democratic reforms attained if necessary by revolution), and Utopian socialism, with a peasant emphasis (emancipation of the peasants with adequate land allotments, and preservation of the communal system), were accordingly to be the cardinal points of Chernyshevski's mature views of life. These beliefs superseded his earlier conviction that an absolute, hereditary and centralized monarchy, acting as a

[4] Feuerbach's influence is most clearly visible in Chernyshevski's study, *The Anthropological Principle in Philosophy.* For a concise exposition of Feuerbach's materialist, anthropomorphic, and anti-religious philosophy, consult Frederick Engels' *Ludwig Feuerbach,* tr. (New York, n.d.). This work also contains Marx's eleven brief *Theses on Feuerbach.*

[5] *Dnevnik,* pp. 97, 102; entries for September 8, 12, 1848.

[6] *Ibid.,* July 11, 1849. At the same time, Chernyshevski confided in his diaries: "If the power were now in my hands, I would immediately proclaim the liberation of the peasants" and "dismiss over half the army. . . . I would limit administrative and general governmental power as quickly as possible, . . . I would . . . attempt . . . to give political rights to women." In regard to immediate practical affairs, Chernyshevski called himself a friend of the Hungarians in their struggle for independence under Kossuth, "wished for the defeat of the Russians there and for that would be prepared to sacrifice much," pp. 315–16. This last point may be compared with an earlier insertion, "I respect Russia very little and hardly think of her at all," p. 109. Here is a lack of that "patriotic" feeling for Russia held by Herzen and Bakunin.

supra-class regime, might in certain circumstances be the best agency for improving the conditions of the masses, and simultaneously might reduce the power of its presumed natural enemy, the landed nobility.[7]

After his stay in St. Petersburg University, Chernyshevski returned to Saratov in January, 1851, to teach Russian literature in the town *gymnasium*. Now, at the age of twenty-three, which for so many men seems to have been crucial, Chernyshevski stood for the destruction of monarchy and expected a revolution in Russia in the near future; he asserted, "without convulsions there has never been one step forward in history." [8]

In Saratov, Chernyshevski met Kostomarov, who was living in enforced exile. Around this noted historian of the Ukraine, a circle of intellectuals sprang up, and Chernyshevski soon became one of its leaders. In 1853 he had married Olga Vassilieva, daughter of a local physician, and he appears to have confided in her that he would take part in the uprising which he felt was impending in Russia.[9] Also, during his engagement, his fiancée had heard Chernyshevski praise Herzen in almost adulatory manner, and prophesy for himself "a similar destiny" of governmental persecution and exile.[10]

Saratov society soon palled, and Chernyshevski returned to

[7] *Ibid.*, p. 109.

[8] Quoted by I. M. Steklov, *N. G. Chernyshevski* (Moscow, 1928), I, 89–92; citation on p. 90. Two years earlier when the famous Petrashevski circle was uncovered by the secret police, Chernyshevski wrote in his diary that there was never any doubt that he eventually would have become "mixed up in their society"; *Dnevnik*, Aug. 25, 1849, p. 288.

[9] Valerian Polianski, *Tri Velikikh Russkikh Demokrata* (Moscow, 1938), p. 114.

[10] *Soch.*-1939, I, 419. Herzen likewise esteemed Chernyshevski highly, despite serious differences of opinion on many issues. Cf. *Soch.*-Herzen, XIX, 39, 128.

St. Petersburg in 1853. The bulk of his work appeared in the decade that followed. Among it was the rejected thesis *The Aesthetic Relations of Art and Reality,* which really launched the offensive. Here Chernyshevski expounded Belinski's social dicta of literary criticism and decisively condemned the theory of an autonomous art. *What Is to Be Done?,* the novel written in prison, and the Bible of two generations of Populist thought, closed this productive period. In his nine years of journalistic activity, first in association with the *Annals of the Fatherland,* and then on the staff of Nekrassov's *Contemporary,* both outstanding radical-democratic publications of the period, Chernyshevski was responsible for over five hundred published articles, which included the very important *Sketches of the Gogol Period* and the *Studies of Lessing and His Time.* This was indefatigable labor on a uniformly high level of achievement. And it was accomplished in the face of more or less rigorous governmental censorship,[11] constant attacks by reactionary elements, and even sharp criticism by the "older generation" of the Left, in the persons of Herzen and Turgenev.

So illuminating are the relations between Chernyshevski and the older generation of the Left that some notes about them are worth repeating. The quarrel of Chernyshevski, Dobroliubov, and the group directing *Contemporary,* with Herzen and Turgenev revealed the fundamental cleavage between the aristocratic revolutionary generation of "fathers" and the new *raznochinets* generation of "unwashed seminarists." Herzen, defending the "superfluous men" of Pushkin and his followers—"superfluous men" who have had

---

[11] After the death of Nicholas I in 1855, the severe censorship regulations were somewhat relaxed. They became more rigorous again after 1859. Cf. V. Evgenev-Maksimov, *"Sovremennik" Pri Chernyshevskom i Dobroliubove* (Leningrad, 1936), pp. 7–12, 421–22.

a long career in Russian literature—considered the *Contemporary* group "very dangerous," and applied the term *zhelcheviki* (the bilious set) to them. Turgenev, a man of lesser caliber in such situations, was attacked by Dobroliubov for the political inadequacies of *On the Eve*, and by him and Chernyshevski for caricaturing Bakunin in *Rudin*. In retort, Turgenev called the editors of *Contemporary* not simply a "nest of snakes" but of "cobras." Chernyshevski, however, journeyed to London in 1859 to arrange a reconciliation with Herzen (then publishing *Kolokol* in the British capital). Although no real reconciliation did or could take place, Chernyshevski holding firm to his position, Herzen backtracked somewhat and indirectly apologized in print for his attacks on *Contemporary*. Herzen had, as it were, two souls, one of which, as already seen, was capable of a very high regard for Chernyshevski.[12]

A series of repressive activities in the tense days of the great St. Petersburg fire and the threatening Polish insurrection were directed against *Contemporary* and its editors by the autocracy, and rapidly the Third Section moved against Chernyshevski himself. In 1862, he was imprisoned in the fortress of SS. Peter and Paul, in St. Petersburg, and his magazine suppressed for eight months. This imprisonment lasted for two years, following which, a farce trial sentenced this "dangerous revolutionary" to the Siberian mines. His fourteen years' term, finally commuted by the tsar to seven, was to be succeeded by a lifetime exile in remote Asia.[13] Thus Chernyshevski's career came abruptly to

[12] Cf. *ibid.*, pp. 375–421, for further discussion of this controversy; also Steklov, *op. cit.*, II, 13, 27, 34, 48–60.

[13] For Herzen's unwitting role, his "fatal blunder" in this trial, cf. Steklov, *op. cit.*, II, 361–65. Also cf. Brandes, *op. cit.*, pp. 263–67, for details of the trial and of the untenable position of the Third Section in its attempt to use "legality" to silence Chernyshevski.

a tragic standstill, and his life and writings from then on were practically without significance except as the symbols of a martyr. In 1883, he was allowed to return to Astrakhan, although under police surveillance, mainly because of the government's lingering fear of the terrorist *Narodnaia Volia* group—some members of which had previously made spectacular attempts to rescue the exile. Six years later, in 1889, the government permitted its aging and now broken victim to revisit his native Saratov, where he died within a few months.

Chernyshevski was then, after the death of Belinski, the outstanding representative of the Russian radical intelligentsia who stayed to work in their native country. Possessing an inclusive knowledge of history, philosophy, sociology, economics, European literature, ancient and modern languages, Chernyshevski was an avowed "Westerner," a revolutionary man of letters. His Western orientation is perhaps best seen in his view that the history of other Slavic peoples has by no means the "importance for our public" that the history of Western Europe and America has.[14] Within the narrow limits of freedom defined by the relatively inefficient absolutist government of the mid-nineteenth-century Russian autocracy, he was a brilliant critic of society and the guiding spirit of the most radical tendencies possible in a Russia

[14] *Contemporary* (June, 1857), in *Polnoe Sobranie Sochineni*, ed. M. N. Chernyshevski (St. Petersburg, 1906), III, 318; hereinafter referred to as *Soch.-1906*.

In terms of such a central issue as the *mir*, Chernyshevski had more realistic views than did the Slavophiles, certain later *Narodniki*, or even Herzen; conceiving it to be something not peculiarly Russian, but the survival of an agricultural institution once common to most European peoples. He did agree with Herzen, however, that Russia could skip stages of social and economic development. But Chernyshevski wanted the *mir* preserved in Russia, partly to prevent the proletarianization of the peasant masses. Cf. J. Hecker, *Russian Sociology* (London, 1934), pp. 70–71.

where, as yet, Populism and "scientific" socialism were not strongly differentiated. Thus Chernyshevski could, especially through the rationalist cult of the strong, principled, and socially conscious individual, presented in *What Is to Be Done?*, be the greatest influence upon the Populist youth of the sixties and seventies. At the same time, through his realism and materialism, he could be one of the important precursors of Marxism in Russia. Indeed, Lenin was a great admirer of Chernyshevski and his famous tract of 1902, symbolically enough, takes its title from Chernyshevski's novel. Finally both radical groups could properly unite in paying homage to the exiled Chernyshevski as the immolated martyr, the greatest perhaps of the victims struck down by the power of the autocracy.

In estimating Chernyshevski's significance and contribution to the Russian revolutionary opposition, it must constantly be borne in mind that he did not enjoy the freedom that Herzen possessed abroad. Hence, if Chernyshevski was a less active participant in revolutionary activity than Bakunin for example—of whom he had a fairly high opinion —his influence was at least as lasting and profound. Certainly, Dostoevski, who in his post-Siberian exile period constantly defended Russia against the corroding influences of the radical "devils," believed that it was Chernyshevski, even more than Turgenev, who was the "father of lies." [15] And perhaps Chernyshevski was regarded as a more dangerous opponent by the Slavophiles and the autocracy because he lacked the mercurial quality that so strikingly characterized the temperaments of Herzen and Bakunin. Chernyshevski's stature as a revolutionary publicist has always remained high, and outstanding recognition has been offered

[15] For Dostoevski's attacks on Chernyshevski, cf. notably *The Possessed,* originally published in 1870–1872.

to him by succeeding generations of revolutionaries, and, in our time as well, in the U.S.S.R.[16]

Of all the Russian radicals here under consideration, Chernyshevski offers us the most complete documentation of his sources of information on America, secondary ones, of course, since he never crossed the Atlantic, but sufficient to lay the groundwork for his copious and remarkable observations on America.

A talented linguist, Chernyshevski painstakingly studied English at St. Petersburg University, and eventually developed an excellent command of the language. His method of study was to read diligently the novels of such writers as Maria Edgeworth, looking up every word in the dictionary "even when not necessary."[17] The English language was to be his invaluable tool, especially for keeping up with current events in the United States reported by the British and American press.

The main sources of information on America at Chernyshevski's disposal and those whose context he himself indicates as having utilized may conveniently be summarized as follows: Western European and English magazines and newspapers, American newspapers, books by Europeans and Americans on America, and American literature. None of these seems to have been used uncritically; in fact they frequently served more as a springboard for the expression of views previously held than as simple sources of factual knowledge.

The *Allgemeine Zeitung, Indépendance Belge, Revue des*

[16] The new sixteen-volume Soviet edition of Chernyshevski's works (of which only two have so far appeared) contains a long preface of laudatory comment on Chernyshevski by Lenin and others; *Soch.*-1939, I, 5.

[17] *Dnevnik,* January 23, 1849, p. 234.

deux Mondes, Revue Brittanique, L'Annuaire de l'Économie Politique, The Edinburgh Review, The Athenaeum, and the London *Times* were the important European and English periodicals which Chernyshevski consulted in seeking news and information about the North American States. Although Chernyshevski was familiar enough with the names and trends of the important American newspapers, the *New York Times* and the *New York Herald* were apparently the only two that he managed to obtain even at irregular intervals.

For studies of American institutions by European observers, he turned to the writings of John Stuart Mill, Macaulay, Lyell, John Robert Godley, and especially those of de Tocqueville. American sources, apart from newspapers, included the census reports of 1850 and 1860, Carey's economic treatises, and the descriptive writings of Olmsted and John Abbott. In American literature, Chernyshevski, like most Russian boys of that period, read James Fenimore Cooper, and he was also familiar with the works of Hawthorne, Prescott, Emerson, and Harriet Beecher Stowe. Among these literary figures, Mrs. Stowe especially served as a valuable source.

Chernyshevski undertook only one journey outside of Russia, his visit to Herzen in London in 1859, and it was of the shortest duration and accomplished in secret. Few records of the journey are extant,[18] and they do not indicate that during this trip he met any individuals who supplied first-hand impressions of the United States. It is almost unnecessary to add that Chernyshevski read industriously all contemporaneous Russian publications and periodicals— whatever their worth may have been in building up his

[18] Steklov, *op. cit.,* II, 48–50.

knowledge of and attitudes towards America.[19] Finally
Chernyshevski mentioned using the telegraph several times
as the transmitter of news dispatches on American affairs;[20]
this was surely an indirect source routed through London,
and though adding nothing to information derivable from
the English press, it did speed the reception of his news.

Chernyshevski's observations on American institutions appeared almost entirely during the fruitful years of his life,
1848–62. From them, one gains a striking impression of his
detailed and highly diversified knowledge of American life.
On the whole, these views were favorable. To Chernyshevski
the United States was a country with "a glorious past."[21]
And its "progressive" character demonstrated the inadequacies of a geographical interpretation of history. "It is
impossible to explain by any sort of geographical conditions
why Brazil should lag so far behind the North American
States."[22]

Chernyshevski's appreciation of America was set down in
detail when he wrote an article explaining the events that
led up to the American Civil War—published in *Contemporary*, February, 1861. In a manner reminiscent of Herzen
during his period of sympathy with America, although in
more guarded language because of the exigencies of the censorship, Chernyshevski wrote that "progressive people in
Western Europe" pointed to "North America" when told that

---

[19] Consult V. Popov, *Ukazatel Statei 1830–1884* (St. Petersburg, 1885),
for a systematic index of articles which appeared in twelve leading Russian
periodicals (and also in the *Revue Brittanique* and the *Revue des deux
Mondes*) for the years indicated. There are a fair number of articles dealing
with American literature to be found; for example, cf. 230–233.

[20] Cf., for example, *Soch.*-1906, VIII, 436 (April, 1861), and IX, 199
(January, 1862).

[21] *Ibid.*, VIII, 387.

[22] *Ibid.*, III, 514.

their ideas were "impractical." Contrariwise, Western European "conservatives" pointed out "the bad things in American life as death to the theories defended by the progressives." Both groups, Chernyshevski continued, considered "North America . . . a model" whereby their convictions might be verified. "A bad opinion of America" was utilized as "an argument in support of the existing Western European relations; a better opinion" was awakened by the wish "to reform those relations."

Chernyshevski insisted that the impending "crisis" of the Civil War could not but have "a very strong influence upon the destiny of the civilized world." If this crisis were to lead to "the result now predicted by almost everyone in Western Europe," one party would become discouraged and "public opinion" would shift to the "other." If the outcome were different, then "the course of events in Western Europe" would be "hastened considerably." In any case, Chernyshevski argued, the influence of "North American history" upon the history of Western Europe was pervasive, and not the mere impinging of some "one . . . isolated . . . American event." The "connection" lay in the "general disposition of Western European thought either to cling to old times or to strive ahead." Hence the North American "example" was "a constant force" which had either to "draw Europe onto the well-known path or repel her from it."

The effects of "the present North American crisis" upon Western Europe perhaps would be difficult to evaluate in the short run. There was, however, no doubt that it would "affect the trend of the history of Western Europe for whole decades," just as the "very founding of the North American Union" had in an earlier age. And now, Chernyshevski asserted, "the example" was offered "not by a sparsely numbered people, weak in comparison with the states of Western

Europe, but by a powerful nation" that already occupied "one of the foremost places among all states." Chernyshevski concluded with a plea for thorough understanding of this crisis since its outcome was "highly important for the evaluation of the future movement of the political ideas" by which "the events" of the present, and possibly the "succeeding . . . generation" would "be determined."[23]

This apotheosis of America becomes even clearer when a critic not restricted by a censor may make certain emendations and changes. Where Chernyshevski used the term Western European, he unquestionably did not wish to exclude Russia from his observations; he might even have intended the reader to substitute "Russia" in place of this phrase. And later on it becomes evident that Chernyshevski was also using the expression "the bad things in America" most loosely; for to him these "bad things" were almost completely attributable to, and corollaries of, the slave system. "The result now predicted by almost all in Western Europe," was, of course, the defeat of Northern arms and the sundering of the Union should the secession issue go to the extreme. In using the phrase, if "the outcome" were "different," then "the course of events in Western Europe" would be "hastened considerably," Chernyshevski meant that if the free North triumphed, democratic development would be hastened everywhere. And, as will be demonstrated, the objective tone which characterized his opinions here was camouflage for a most intense and partisan pro-Northern interest. Finally, Chernyshevski himself must be placed in the foremost ranks of those very European "progressives" of whom he wrote. The Russian publicist's admiration for what he considered the best in American life was manifest. Similarly his consciousness of the salutary and growing influence

[23] *Ibid.*, VIII, 389–90.

of the American "example" upon the Old World was delicately sensitive—a covert assertion of American "exceptionalism" in the world of capitalist nations.

Chernyshevski emphasized these thoughts of the present and rising significance of America by singling out the day of Lincoln's election, November 6, 1860, as a date marking a new epoch for "the great North American people." The date was a turning point from which the American people would march to heights "not attained since Jefferson's time." And this was exemplary since "the good repute of the North American nation" was "important for all nations with the rapidly growing significance of the North American States in the life of . . . humanity."[24]

Following to some extent Bakunin's general analysis of American economic and social conditions, Chernyshevski criticized Macaulay's sweeping condemnation of American democracy, stated by the latter shortly before his death in 1859. In a famous letter to Henry S. Randall, the American biographer of Jefferson, Macaulay had noted the general distress, unemployment, restlessness, and other familiar symptoms of the state of the masses in Western Europe during mid-Victorian times. Thereupon Macaulay asserted that only the vast expanse of fertile and unoccupied lands, which siphoned off the cities' surplus populations and thus acted as a "safety valve" for dangerous social ferment, had saved America temporarily from these disorders of the high noon of industrial capitalism. But, he affirmed, a time would come when these lands would be exhausted, and with them the principles of Jeffersonian democracy. Then in the new Manchesters and Birminghams of New England, the inherent leveling tendencies of American democracy would at last function unchecked, and America in the twentieth cen-

[24] *Ibid.*, VI, 730–31.

tury would succumb to her own inner "Huns and Vandals," as
Rome presumably had succumbed to external barbarians.
Therefore, Macaulay had concluded, "I cannot reckon Jefferson among the benefactors of mankind." He remained
more than ever convinced of the necessity of government
by an aristocratic few to control this process.

The interesting thing here is that Chernyshevski agreed
by and large with this prognosis of general economic and
peculiarly American development. Reviewing the Whig
historian's vivid argument, Chernyshevski wrote that it was
superfluous to disagree with Macaulay's contention that institutions could not operate "well" where the position of the
masses was "calamitous." However, "the sense of Macaulay's
letter" was "different." For in Macaulay's view, with the
exception of "savage" lands, the "masses in all countries" had
"inevitably" to "live in great poverty." Moreover, if this
"law of necessity . . . not to be averted by human strength"
were true, only one conclusion was possible: the masses,
dwelling in "poverty," and ever susceptible to the blandish-
ments and easy promises of "charlatans," had to be "de-
prived of influence over public affairs." Then Chernyshevski
skillfully fired his broadside. Even though he dared not make
his own radical judgments explicit, he did not hesitate to
denounce "all this" as "entirely" in line with the "system" of
"present day Whiggism," indistinguishable "in any essential
from Toryism." [25]

It was clear that Chernyshevski firmly believed that the
worsening condition of the masses could "be averted by
human strength," and that the continuation of democratic
political institutions in America or any similar region was

[25] *Ibid.*, VI, 380–83. Macaulay's letter is reprinted in full in *What
Did Macaulay Say about America?* ed. H. M. Lydenberg (New York, 1935),
pp. 23–25.

not simply dependent upon available unused tracts of fertile land to drain off "surplus" population. Chernyshevski's program for the radical alteration of society, which, in his estimation, would preserve democratic political institutions, could only be hinted at, naturally, within the pages of *Contemporary*. In this respect his position differed from that of Bakunin, who could and did express a fully developed program of anarchy as the solution for such appalling conditions.[26]

Chernyshevski pointedly displayed warm sympathy for the democratic attributes of the American people when he characterized the psychological attitude of Americans towards the "hero." Writing in January, 1862, he flatly denied the possibility of General McClellan's becoming a dictator in the course of the Civil War; in the first place, the Northern military chieftain, unfortunately, had not won sufficient victories. But there existed a deeper cause, as Chernyshevski felt that Americans attached "almost the entire merit" of military achievement to "themselves . . . , to the mass of the army and . . . to the whole nation." Moreover, the "riotous scenes" and "enthusiastic ovations" which this "impressionable people" arranged in honor of an "illustrious hero," were intended "for their own satisfaction." Americans thus never forgot that a "distinguished" person was "their own creation and all his importance derived only from the fact that they took a fancy to make him their darling." [27]

This close link of the "hero" with the masses was perhaps somewhat over-idealized. It was, however, surely an

[26] Our criticisms applied earlier to Bakunin for too over-simplified an application of the "safety-valve" theory are relevant also for Chernyshevski. We may note, too, that Chernyshevski, following Macaulay, also anticipated Turner by several decades.

[27] *Soch.*-1906, IX, 198.

American trait not to lean to the deification of an outstanding individual. Furthermore, the relation between an outstanding public figure (especially a military leader) to the very numerous group of semi-anonymous followers who make his achievements largely possible is recognized even today, at least theoretically, when the separation of the populus from the leaders or the heroes is much greater than it was in the mid-nineteenth century.

Towards the end of *What Is to Be Done?*, an American character, Charles Beaumont, suddenly appears on the scene. As a literary creation, he is wooden and lusterless; but as spokesman for Chernyshevski's own views of America, Beaumont is notable. By "America," Chernyshevski meant "of course . . . only the free Northern states." The author first informed his readers that young Beaumont was neither "overpowered by the greatness of the mind that could make . . . millions" nor deeply concerned about "the failure which left sufficient means to maintain a good cook. . . ." The reason for his indifference probably lay in "the American custom of not seeing anything extraordinary either in a rapid accumulation of wealth or in a failure." [28]

There is little doubt that Chernyshevski approved not only of this American energy and social mobility but, even more so, of the American and democratic trait of "not being impressed." Beaumont himself observed that "loneliness" was in "fashion" among the English. But, he insisted, "we Americans know nothing about it; we have no time to be melancholy. We have too much to do to allow of it." [29]

[28] *A Vital Question; or What Is to Be Done?*, tr. (New York, 1886), 425–26.

[29] *Ibid.*, 425. Cf. Arthur M. Schlesinger, "What Then Is the American, This New Man?" *American Historical Review*, XLVIII (January, 1943), 225–45 for a suggestive listing of this and similar psychological traits of Americans.

Chernyshevski here came perilously close to advocating a rather uninspired cult of practicality—of feverish activity for its own sake—to the neglect of broad social purposes, generated both in the ethics of individualism and on the American frontier. But it was not quite that. For this presentation of the American "doer" was immediately contrasted with the picture of the "gloomy" sensitive Russian intellectuals who "have to sit and fold their hands." Katerina Vasilevna (Beaumont's fiancée) cried out, "Give me something to do and the chances are that I shall not be melancholy." Beaumont's call to arms followed directly: "You want something to do? . . . you see all around you such ignorance . . . there are great opportunities." And when Katerina wanted to migrate to America to "accomplish something," Charles replied definitively that one could "find something to do in Petersburg."[30] Thus Chernyshevski's message was really an appeal for thoughtful use of this energy for social purposes. His was in the end a program of earnest work in Russia. It differed somewhat from the "Let us, then, be up and doing, With a heart for any fate" of Longfellow's *Psalm of Life*. Nonetheless, there lurked in Chernyshevski's phrases a certain admiration for a country where individual energy and power, even when *not* used continually for social ends, had free expression though they nurtured a pragmatic philosophy of shallow optimism.[31]

It is evident that Chernyshevski touched upon the important things in American life: the democratic system, the economic and social order, the people's psychology, and the nation's rising importance for Europe both in the present and in time to come. The over-all impression derived from these generally intelligent and skillfully phrased observa-

[30] *Ibid.*, pp. 426, 428.
[31] For further confirmation of this point, cf. *ibid.*, p. 431.

tions is that of one long paean of praise for American life in the "free Northern states." The Russian publicist's enthusiasm was sufficient for him to overlook in large measure the evil effects of unbridled individualism in the young democratic republic across the ocean—the land that, except for slavery, was almost the living embodiment of his desires.

CHAPTER VI

"Social Despotism"

AMONG all the questions to which Chernyshevski devoted his tireless pen in regard to the United States, the issues of Negro slavery and the American Civil War assumed the greatest magnitude. The American slave system was the one serious blot on an otherwise unsullied record of democratic achievement; with it removed, European radicals might look to America with no reservations as source of inspiration for their own democratic (if not socialist) goals. Many Russian radicals of the period of course held the same view.

In his famous review of Lavrov's work, *Outlines of the Questions of Practical Philosophy* (St. Petersburg, 1860), Chernyshevski acknowledged the undoubted fact that the Russian *Narodnik* sociologist was "a progressive thinker." He next seized upon a formulation that Lavrov had borrowed from John Stuart Mill: "the social despotism in the United States." This "social despotism," so called, frowned upon expenditure for luxuries. Chernyshevski criticized Lavrov adversely for not qualifying such phrases as that one, which, though understandable to the English public, would not be so to the Russian.[1] Then followed a three-pronged refutation: "Social despotism" existed only in New England and chiefly in Boston, not throughout the United States. And far from being a universal phenomenon, it was simply

[1] *Soch.*-1906, VI, 183, and Mill, *On Liberty* (London, 1859), p. 157.

a remnant of Puritanism, which grew weaker each year.
Nor did it stem from North American institutions, as superficial observers erroneously inferred. Indeed this "Puritan
constraint" was now almost a sham, useful only as another
pretext for the accumulation of worldly goods among the
miserly descendants of the Puritans.[2]

After having disposed of this issue, Chernyshevski arrived at his main point. He insisted that the real "social
despotism" existed in the slave states where the Southern
planters ruled with an iron hand, permitting no word in
favor of abolition and subjecting to spoliation, exile, and
criminal punishment all who dared to raise their voices
against the slave system. Power in the South was concentrated in the hands of a few ten thousands of rich planters,
who kept not only their Negroes in ignorance and poverty but
also the mass of poor whites as well. These planter magnates
were the descendants of the earliest aristocratic Cavalier
settlers of Virginia and the older Southern states. They maintained their power by accretion and the creation of new
slave states. And "in general," Chernyshevski declared, "the
contrast between Naples and Switzerland" was "not so great
as the contrast between the Southern and Northern halves
of the United States." Heretofore this Southern aristocracy,
under the paradoxical guise of the "Democratic" party had
dominated the American government. The fundamental

[2] It would be tempting to engage in a long analysis of this "saving,"
quality of the descendants of the New England Puritans. We may confine
ourselves, however, to the following observation: that there was *some*
connection between the Puritanism of Massachusetts and the ethics of
capitalism which arose in colonial America is not to be denied. This is the
real issue which Mill, Lavrov, and Chernyshevski have sensed and hit upon
here. It remained for Marx, and after him Max Weber and R. H. Tawney, to
draw the coördinates of this problem. An outstanding modern work which
treats this subject comprehensively is H. M. Robertson's *Aspects of the
Rise of Economic Individualism* (Cambridge, Eng., 1933).

struggle between the Southern magnates and the abolitionists then raging was taking place because the true democratic elements ruling in the Northern states wanted "to wrench political hegemony over the Union from the hands of the aristocrat-planters." [3]

Such was Chernyshevski's succinct delineation of the Southern slave system as "social despotism." By and large it was a correct picture of the balance of power in the South on the eve of secession.[4] These broad sketches were filled in many times over in almost exhausting detail for Chernyshevski repeatedly recurred to this question. Here the Russian publicist presented the highlights: the description of the Southern planter aristocracy; its relation to the Negroes, the poor whites, the anti-slavery elements, and to the rest of the country; and discussion of the deeper nature of the sectional conflict.

Chernyshevski went astray in explaining the origins of the planter aristocracy, stressing too much the continuity of aristocracy from England to America. Today it is known that no such group settled colonial Virginia, but in the main large numbers of middle-class individuals.[5] But Cherny-

[3] Soch.-1906, VI, 184.

[4] Cf. Arthur C. Cole, "The Irrepressible Conflict: 1850–1865," A History of American Life, ed. A. M. Schlesinger and D. R. Fox (New York, 1934), VII, pp. 34–58, for the economic structure and class striation in the South in the last years before secession. For persecutions of anti-slavery elements in the Old South, cf. Jesse Macy, The Anti-Slavery Crusade (New Haven, 1920), pp. 65–84, and A. B. Hart, Slavery and Abolition (New York and London, 1906), pp. 205–6. The role of Chernyshevski, Dobroliubov, and other contemporary Russian radicals as opponents of the Southern slave system is recognized in recent Soviet historiography; cf. Z. Eggert, "Otmena Rabstva v S. Sh. A. i Otkliki v Rossii," Istoricheski Zhurnal, no. 8–9 (Moscow, 1943), pp. 69–75, esp. 74–75.

[5] Cf. Thomas J. Wertenbaker, Patrician and Plebeian in Virginia (Charlottesville, Va., 1910, pp. 2–3: "But few men of high social rank in England established families in Virginia . . . the larger part of the aristocracy of

shevski may be pardoned for this inaccuracy since this belief was a common misunderstanding of his time. Chernyshevski, in his desire to uphold the "free North" against the slave-owning South, also exaggerated the over-all democracy "which rules" the Northern states.

In elaboration of some of these issues, Chernyshevski distinguished first the economies of the North and South, then discussed in detail the nature of the two systems. He next reviewed the historical genesis of slavery in the United States, its repercussions in political and intellectual life, secession, and the events and personalities of the Civil War. Lastly he commented upon such subsidiary problems of the slavery question as expansionism and the tariff.

In the February, 1861 number of *Contemporary*, Chernyshevski wrote a long, informative essay on the whole question of the relation of the North and South in America. His main arguments were the following: First, the basic differences between the North and South, he contended correctly, arose not from the time of the enormous expansion of cotton cultivation. That development only widened already existing differences and extended the peculiarities of life in the South. If it had not been cotton, then tobacco, sugar, and coffee would have been cultivated under the same regime—in fact, sugar and tobacco were so cultivated, but not as extensively because of certain special factors, such as the shortage of labor power in the South.

The North, Chernyshevski stated, was settled by simple

---

the colony came directly from merchant ancestors . . . the leading planters of the 17th century were mercantile in instinct and unlike the English aristocrat of the same period." Also cf. Wertenbaker, "The First Americans: 1607–1690," *A History of American Life*, II, ed. A. M. Schlesinger and D. R. Fox (New York, 1927), 22–49, for a valuable discussion on land holding in seventeenth-century Virginia and disproof of the idea of the prevalence of great *latifundia* in the early colonial period.

freedom-loving people who had fled from England. Land was generally occupied in family-size holdings because of the need of an area adequate for supporting a family and because of a limited labor supply. In most cases, only the head of the family and his grown sons were available to work the land. "The North from the very beginning was, as it now remains, a country of independent farmers before whose mass all other estates disappear." [6] The growth of mining and manufacturing in Pennsylvania and in New England and the commercial development of New York originated and developed, for the most part, among these same small farmers. In turn their children or grandchildren would move westward once more to become settlers and farmers; for, Chernyshevski declared, wealth in the North did not long remain stable nor was it retained for posterity. However, even if "small groups of families" in certain large cities could still cling to a position "comparable to the higher and middle classes of European society," that, too, was insignificant. Not only did they "disappear" in the totality of the "urban" population but also "the cities themselves" were unable to "acquire hegemony over the political life of the North." Such power depended upon "the farming population." [7]

To clinch this last point, Chernyshevski cited the results in New York State of the 1860 presidential election. New York City went Democratic by a large majority; the farmers, however, voted Republican. Hence, in the total count, the preponderance of votes remained with the Republicans despite the fact that over twenty-five percent of the voters lived in New York City. Therefore if the "huge city" of New York did not "possess hegemony over the political life of New York State," the importance of "the farmers' power

[6] *Soch.*-1906, VIII, 390.   [7] *Ibid.*

in the political life of the whole North" could readily be judged.[8] And the Russian publicist again insisted that each Northern farmer was an independent cultivator, neither serving as a working man nor possessing one.

It is quite true that the Northern United States formed, even in 1860, a basically agricultural region, settled by small farmers (by no means originating solely in England) and cultivated in family size farms; true, too, that the political power of these independent cultivators was large. But again Chernyshevski has idealized the equality, fluid class lines, and mobility of wealth in the North. The true historical picture was not quite so Arcadian. Large tracts of land were still held by speculators, that constant element in American life, and the decade, 1850–60, was "an era of speculation." [9] Feudal remnants of land tenures persisted in New York State (the very example which Chernyshevski chose) even as late as the 1840's, where in the Hudson Valley, great landed domains, a standing menace to democratic practices, still fiercely resisted the encroachments of the farmer and speculator. Furthermore, in the colonial period these inequalities had been even more pronounced. It is, however, true that this feudal resistance was doomed in the face not only of democracy and anti-rent riots, but of "advancing capital and business enterprise" as well.[10]

In industrial and commercial life, trade unions, strikes, business slump and depression, poverty and starvation were

[8] *Ibid.*, pp. 390–91.

[9] Cole, *op. cit.*, p. 112. Cole asserts: "While farms in general were decreasing in size, successful and ambitious individuals competed in accumulating ever larger tracts" in this period; p. 103.

[10] Dixon R. Fox, *The Decline of Aristocracy in the Politics of New York* (New York, 1919), pp. 437–38. For the dramatic story of the anti-rent riots of the 1840's in New York State, cf. Henry Christman, *Tin Horns and Calico* (New York, 1945).

by no means uncommon, all following in the path of modern industrialism, which the North had embarked upon many years earlier. When Chernyshevski wrote, this section had just emerged from the Panic of 1857, whose occurrence, it may be remarked, tended to make Southern extremists increasingly intransigent since the South was far less affected than the North and West by this economic setback.[11]

Chernyshevski's over-drawn picture of the North's virtues must, of course, be viewed in relation to his extreme concepts of the aristocratic social structure in the Old South.

The Russian publicist first postulated the historical origins of the Southern states in grants to courtiers by the Stuart kings. He observed the fact of great inequities in landholding even in colonial times with the great mass of whites a pitiful mob in utter moral dependence upon the rich slave-owning planters. And when new states were founded in the South, Chernyshevski declared, the traditional civil life of plantation economy was carried over by the older settlers. Only in recent years had an inflow of settlers from the North begun to introduce the civil *mores* of freedom into the northern rim of the Southern border states and on the western bounds of the Southern settlements (Virginia, Kentucky, Tennessee, Missouri, Texas, and Kansas). But the land system in the remaining expanse of the South was comparable to that which had existed in medieval Europe. The social structure corresponded with ten or fifteen thousand great planters at the top, a secondary layer of about one hundred or two hundred thousands of middling owners, and—lowest in the scale—the poor whites. This depressed

[11] Cf. Philip Foner, *Business and Slavery* (Chapel Hill, 1941), pp. 143–47, and T. C. Smith, *Parties and Slavery: 1850–1859* (New York and London, 1906), pp. 179–81, for good discussion of the effects of the Panic of 1857.

group, he wrote, lived in the same state of dependence upon the Southern grandees as had the middle and poor nobles of old Poland towards the topmost magnates of that unhappy country.[12]

According to Chernyshevski, the Southern planters cultivated their estates themselves, unlike the great English landlords, who let out their estates to capitalist farmers. In the South, such agricultural capitalists did not exist; moreover, a large supply of unsettled land in the West beckoned to anyone with initiative and capital.

From their peculiar position of supremacy, Chernyshevski declared, these great Southern planters had assumed all the psychological traits of an aristocracy. They were proud of their descent from medieval English lords and felt themselves superior to most contemporary English peers because of the relatively recent ennoblement of this class. In general they considered their true equals to be found only in the *faubourg* St. Germain; this ancient branch of the French nobility had not known, however, how to conserve either its rights or political power. The Southern magnates thus considered themselves the last guardians of that aristocratic prerogative which flourished in Western Europe before 1789. And imbued with such an attitude, slavery was a "necessity" to them. Under a regime of "free labor," the great estate would become a kind of "agricultural factory," requiring the owner constantly to be concerned with "tracking down each penny." Southern planters were constitutionally incapable of such diligence; their "habits of life" determined that they conduct their affairs only "in a care-

[12] Hart estimates that only 350,000 out of 1,800,000 white families owned slaves in the South in the last years before the Civil War: 77,000 owners possessed 1 slave apiece, 200,000 owned between two and ten slaves; only 2300 families owned more than 100 slaves; *op. cit.*, pp. 67–68.

less fashion"—a way which demanded neither "bustle, cal-
culation, nor commercial acumen from the master." [13]

It was evident, Chernyshevski summarized, that the North
American Union from the earliest times was divided into
two parts, differing in social structures even while retaining
the same political forms. [14]

These reflections on the social and economic order of the
Old South are interesting and picturesque if, again, not quite
accurate. It has been noted already that Chernyshevski
erroneously assumed that the great estate run by dependent
slave labor characterized the South from its colonial incep-
tions. And it is certainly not true that the original settlers
of the area from Maryland and Virginia southward were an
aristocracy. What happened in reality was that many of the
more fortunate settlers, especially those of mercantile origin,
tended to *become* such a ruling class through the accumulation of acres and slaves, as, for example, the Byrd family
in Virginia. And this occurred notwithstanding the destruction of primogenitures and entails during the Revolutionary
period.

Chernyshevski's attempt to equate the heterogeneous
group of even the top slave-owners with the French Bourbon
aristocracy is little less than bizarre. [15] Furthermore the poor
whites had not always been the "pitiful mob" he described,
as the history of the frontier in the eighteenth century, and
even of certain areas such as Virginia, during the early
nineteenth century, amply demonstrated. Finally, slavery
was necessary to the Southern planters not only because of
their alleged non-capitalistic attitude towards life but also
because the great plantation was worked under an "advance

[13] *Soch.*-1906, VIII, 391–92.
[14] *Ibid.*
[15] Cf. Cole, *op. cit.*, pp. 34–36.

system" of credit. Its lands, buildings, equipment, and slaves tied up great amounts of capital in a relatively fixed cycle of production, and this frozen investment was too huge for the planter to disturb by any such drastic shift as slave emancipation. Yet could the slave owners have peered into the future, emancipation, even without compensation, might have appeared, in the long run, to be more profitable and salutary than the enforced system of *latifundia*.[16]

Chernyshevski next developed his concept of the political conflicts which colored American history from the time of the establishment of the Constitution. The first and most significant of these conflicts concerned states' rights. The group which stood for subordination of the states to the national government (roughly compared to the subservience of the English counties to Parliament), Chernyshevski generically called "Whigs." To those who opposed to this tendency the principle of the greatest development of state self-government, Chernyshevski applied the generic term "Democrats." This struggle over states' rights, he contended, continued up to about 1845. At that point the Whig group, never able to develop its concepts fully but ever desirous of increasing central power at the expense of the states, was utterly defeated. With this crisis past, all danger to a state's right to full independence in its internal affairs disappeared. Then, Chernyshevski declared, the great questions of civil life, hitherto veiled by the political issue, emerged. For while it was true, he asserted, that Northerners had previously spoken out against slavery, they had done so as Whigs or Democrats. In many other respects they had continued to coöperate with "Southern Whigs or Democrats," a fact which showed that their "aversion to slavery" had "remained a private . . . a literary, or religious feeling," di-

[16] Cf. Hart, *op. cit.*, pp. 62–63.

vorced from any "program" of social reformation for the South.[17]

This practical national harmony, which continued despite conflicting idealistic attitudes towards slavery, was presently abruptly shattered. For the Democratic Party, having exhausted its political program, and with its opponents scattered, itself divided more and more into two halves over the crucial questions of slavery—into a Northern wing and a Southern wing which reflected two different modes of life. The ruling class in the South was forced onto the horns of a dilemma in regard to slavery. For to abolish the "peculiar institution," Chernyshevski asserted, would have meant either a painful shift from the Southerners' "aristocratic-feudal" outlook to a commercial one, or the sale of their lands.

Was it possible, however, to refute the enemies of slavery? No, Chernyshevski thundered; the Southern aristocrats could only force these elements to silence—and this they did within their own states by means of censorship, forced expulsions, and other punishments. Such procedures, however, destroyed the basic civil rights of American citizenship, and thereby the South inevitably revived Northern opposition to the slave system. But it was hazardous to rule in the South if in the North there was freedom to speak against slavery. Thus the South was forced to strive for the constraint of free speech in the North, too. And Chernyshevski condemned, as Herzen had, the brutal attack by the "cut throat" Brooks upon Senator Sumner. He termed this action a typically desperate tactic of a group sensing its own impending destruction. Herzen, it may be recalled, considered this incident sufficient justification for a blanket condemnation of the American Congress. Chernyshevski makes no such in-

[17] *Soch.*-1906, VIII, 392–94.

dictment.[18] Gathering up these points, he asserted that a system of dynamic repression developed—a system that reached its peak under the distinctly pro-Southern administration of President Buchanan.

In summary then, Chernyshevski declared, the Democratic Party failed to realize that the peaceful autonomy of each area—i.e. "states' rights"—was possible only when each area lived in harmony with the other, when "the basic tendencies of the regional governments" had "an identical goal." Thus it was urgently necessary to harmonize Northern and Southern civil relationships. To this end, the "general course of civilization" left "not the slightest doubt as to which system" would be "altered." Northern institutions would not "become identical with contemporary Southern ones." On the contrary, slavery would be "annihilated" in the South.[19]

Here in measured yet bold terms Chernyshevski had offered his readers a brief history of the slavery controversy in the United States for the seventy-odd years preceding Lincoln's election. The main facts are clearly organized, and although Chernyshevski was an avowed opponent of the slave system, they are presented without the *extreme* prejudice towards the South which Bakunin, for example, would surely have expressed. Unfortunately, however, Chernyshevski distorted history somewhat by placing the "states' rights" and slavery conflicts in two distinct periods. In reality these two issues were often intertwined. The issue of "states' rights" was by no means *finally* settled in 1845, as will be discussed more fully later on. Then, too, if the resurgence of the anti-slavery question as a burning issue were

[18] *Soch.*-1906, VIII, 392–94, also 32–35. Here, too, may be found detailed and lurid repetitions of Chernyshevski's opinion that "of all the difficulties and insufficiencies of the United States, slavery is the main cause, and in great part, even the unique cause."

[19] *Ibid.*, VIII, 392–94.

to be dated, 1831–32 would probably be far more accurate than 1845. For it was at the earlier time that William Lloyd Garrison's *Liberator* first appeared. And 1831–32 also encompasses Nat Turner's revolt as well as the famous debate on slavery in the Virginia legislature.[20]

Chernyshevski's estimate of the constitutional inability of the planters to adjust to a regime without slavery was, of course, questionable. The experiences of serf-owners in his native Russia, where serfdom (slavery in practice) was abolished and adjustment made, seem to belie the Russian's contention. Moreover, coercion and terrorist opposition were by no means the only weapons of the Southern landowners and their adherents. These men also constructed a vast arsenal of "arguments"—a rationale of slavery to which all outstanding Southerners subscribed in whole or in part.[21] Apart from these errors, Chernyshevski displayed remarkable acumen in analyzing the facts at his disposal concerning *ante-bellum* American affairs as they hinged on slavery; and he demonstrated a superior ability in historical synthesis of trends, which, after all, he never knew at first-hand.

The effects of slavery were also visible in America's external relations with her neighbors. One may observe, in passing, how contumaciously Chernyshevski treated such alleged agents of the "slave power" as the filibusterer, William Walker.[22] Chernyshevski ascribed American expansionism and aggressions against her "weak neighbors" squarely

[20] For these aspects of the anti-slavery movement, cf. Hart, *op. cit.*, pp. 202–15; Macy, *op. cit.*, p. 54; and Herbert Aptheker, *American Negro Slave Revolts* (New York, 1943), pp. 293–325. For corroboratory material on Buchanan, cf. Hart, *op. cit.*, pp. 68–69.

[21] Hart, *op. cit.*, p. 137. Cf. William S. Jenkins, *Pro-Slavery Thought in the Old South* (Chapel Hill, 1935) for a comprehensive study of this rationale.

[22] Cf. *Soch.*-1906, VIII, 396.

to the slave-owners, who wished to acquire lands from which new slave states could be carved. "Who then does not know whose cunning was active in this respect? All this was done by the planters." [23] Elsewhere he advanced the hypothesis that one of the principal reasons for Canada's refusal to join the United States (apart from possible English refusal to give up Canada) was her "European or abolitionist aversion to slavery." He also accused those Washington and New York newspapers which urged peace upon the warring sections in order that they might jointly march on Canada, of being "organs of the Northern allies of the planters' party." As such they endeavored "as much to provoke war between England and America as Lord Palmerston who seeks popularity by his threats against America." [24]

One may pardon Chernyshevski for his inadequate explanation of the dynamics of American expansion southward when so many of his American anti-slave contemporaries passionately confused Southern imperialism with America's "manifest destiny." [25] Although there were unquestionably excellent economic and political reasons for the Southern planters' desire to acquire Texas, Cuba, and other territories, there were other significant factors at work making for expansion: the interests of land speculators and free farmers in new lands, "manifest destiny," and other psychological forces. In regard to Canada, the Russian publicist's reasoning is open to serious question in view of the heritage of distrust between the United States and her northern neighbor, fitfully continuing from Revolutionary times when many thousands of American Tories had migrated to Canada. Cer-

---

[23] *Ibid.*, VIII, 31.   [24] *Ibid.*, IX, 193–94.

[25] Cf. Thomas A. Bailey, *A Diplomatic History of the American People* (New York, 1941), pp. 247–81, 294–95, for a good discussion of these aspects of American foreign policy.

tainly Canadian uneasiness was not mollified by the several Fenian raids across the unprotected border from the United States. And the idea of a great unifying crusade against Canada was proposed to Lincoln more than once by men who could hardly be called Southern partisans, for example Secretary of State, William H. Seward.[26] Hence in his eagerness to attribute every American shortcoming ultimately to the "slave power," and to believe (as Bakunin later did) that "imperialism" was incompatible with the true nature of a democratic country such as the United States, Chernyshevski inevitably fell into misconceptions concerning the dynamics of America's relations to her immediate neighbors.

Finally, Chernyshevski insisted, the slave system not only exerted a baneful influence upon Northern life and upon American foreign relations, but was ruining the Southern economy as well. Using the *Edinburgh Review*'s quotations from Frederick L. Olmsted, the trained American observer of the Cotton Kingdom, Chernyshevski emphasized first the inhibitory and devastating effects that slavery had wrought upon the "productive forces" of the Southern economy. Free, hired labor, as it existed in the North, was of relatively greater efficiency than a regime of imposed labor, and it avoided the necessity of maintaining "whole hordes of people, from whom labor is wrung by fear of the whip." Furthermore, slavery encouraged "the most energetic resistance" in the form of organized uprisings.[27] In conclusion, Chernyshevski stated that a minority of slaves in comparison with the total population of the slave states was sufficient "to annihilate . . . every element . . . of free labor." Here he marshaled facts and statistics which not only strengthened his case against Southern slavery but had the further

[26] *Ibid.*, 340–41.   [27] *Soch.*-1906, VI, 160, 171.

end of demonstrating the pernicious effects of serfdom upon the development of free labor in Russia.[28]

The issue of secession, the possibility and later the actuality of civil strife in the United States increased the attention which Chernyshevski devoted to American political affairs in *Contemporary*. More importantly, they had a qualitative effect on Chernyshevski's thinking; he quickened to the realization that at last the great opportunity for solving the slavery issue was at hand. Without a break, from the time of Lincoln's election to the moment of Chernyshevski's arrest, the pages of *Contemporary* carried long reviews of "affairs in America" written by Chernyshevski. Indeed, as early as November, 1859, he had described John Brown's raid upon Harpers Ferry as "very significant." The Russian observer commented to the readers of *Contemporary* that until this stirring event the abolitionists had been on the defensive in relation to the adherents of slavery. And though their first offensive was unsuccessful as were "almost all first attempts," Chernyshevski staunchly affirmed that "the struggle" would begin "gradually to assume a new character," and that the abolitionists would "shortly be avenged for their first martyrs." [29]

After a silence of one year, Chernyshevski jubilantly took cognizance of Abraham Lincoln's triumph at the polls. He wrote enthusiastically: "this fact hardly yields in significance to the Italian events of the last two years," referring to the imminent proclamation of the unified Kingdom of Italy in Turin. He hailed the Republican victory as the coming to

[28] *Ibid.*, IV, 67, 76, 79–80. Chapter VII, *infra*, elaborates these ideas.

[29] In the same article Chernyshevski reprinted from the London *Times* a sympathetic outline of Brown's career as well as two documents of the latter's military society for the liberation of the slaves. *Soch.*-1906, V, 440–42; 444–46; citations from p. 441.

national power "of the Northern and Western ploughmen."
And this was a victory gained at the expense of the Southern
planters' party, "now called democratic, but . . . in actuality . . . oligarchical." [30]

Chernyshevski unwaveringly asserted that the Southern
"fire-eaters" and adventurers had fomented the war. They
had used Buchanan as their pliant agent in the White House
and had managed by every unscrupulous means to carry
along most of the Southern white population. He did concede that the mass of poor whites in their ignorance had accepted the secessionists' propaganda and pardoned them in
the face of the even greater credulity of "almost all in
Europe" who believed in the great power, wealth, and
superiority of the South in relation to the North. Furthermore he excoriated ninety-five percent of the European
press for disseminating beliefs that "without slavery it is
impossible to grow cotton." At the same time, Chernyshevski
correctly noted the vital differences between the cotton and
sugar states on the one hand and the border slave states
of the South. [31]

The North, Chernyshevski insisted, had to accept the
challenge of the South. War or even peaceful secession were

[30] *Soch.*-1906, VI, 730–31. Chernyshevski's observations on the nature of
the Democratic Party in the South in this period are corroborated in
R. F. Nichols' *The Democratic Machine: 1850–1854* (New York, 1923).
Cf. also A. M. Schlesinger, Jr., *The Age of Jackson* (Boston, 1945),
pp. 486–90.

[31] *Soch.*-1906, VIII, 380–81. For a slight shift in Chernyshevski's view
of the degree of mass allegiance to the extremist Southern leaders, cf.
ibid., VIII, 194 (in a long review of de Tocqueville's *Democracy in
America*). The "impudence" of the Southern leaders of the Democratic
Party "became so unbearable that the masses began to forsake them. Then
they started the war." Chernyshevski's most significant error was to be the
prediction of lack of "vitality" in any Southern Confederacy. On this score
he repeatedly indulged in wishful thinking.

the only alternatives, but a complete rupture was necessary and compromise would have to be prevented at any cost. The war, in Chernyshevski's opinion, was, of course, a class conflict as well as a sectional one, with slavery as the central issue. But the great enthusiasm of the Northern masses at the outbreak of the war carried the upper classes with them. Finally, he believed in the "inevitable" triumph of the North and that the duration of the war would be only a matter of months.

Developing the first of these assertions, Chernyshevski declared, "compromise would be incomparably worse . . . than civil war, worse even than a peaceful severance of the Union." In both the latter cases, the Union would "rapidly" be reëstablished "with slavery destroyed" or, at least, with laws "leading to its destruction." Compromise, however, "would only delay the issue." Therefore, Chernyshevski objected to the "charity" that the North allegedly was "too, too ready" to have for the extremist leaders, "Buchanan, Cobb, Floyd, their fellow champions, Davis, Yancey, Perkins, Brooks and their praetorians." [32]

The Russian critic's argument that a peaceful division of the Union would accrue almost immediately to the advantage of the North because rapid disintegration of slavery in its native milieu would ensue, developed as follows: Not only was slavery deserting the border states because of such economic factors as soil exhaustion and inefficiency of the labor force in tending uncongenial crops, but it was maintained in the border states (e.g. Kentucky, Virginia, Maryland) mainly for breeding progeny to be sold to the cotton, sugar, and rice planters of the deep South. Peaceful secession would set the border states against the other slave states because a Southern Confederacy would inevitably reopen

[32] *Soch.*-1906, VIII, 387 (January, 1861).

the African slave trade, to the detriment of the interests of the slave breeders. Furthermore, the upper tier of the South would rapidly lose what slaves it possessed, either through their desertions to the Northern federation or through the migration of fear-stricken slave-owners themselves to the deep South. Within a comparatively short time, if not at once, the border states would be lost to the Southern Confederacy. This process would be repeated to its inevitable conclusion of extinction of slavery. Whether by war or by peaceful secession, slavery was doomed.

Such was the extreme abolitionist view. And as it happened, the border states of Delaware, Kentucky, Missouri, and Maryland did swing to the North, although not without a struggle in the latter three.[33]

Chernyshevski's formulation of the class character of the Civil War was positively and clearly stated: "The enmity of the South for the North is a class enmity—the hatred of patricians for dark-skinned plebeians, the enmity of a higher social estate for a republican social order. The Southern gentlemen would like to become courtiers." [34] And in moments of greatest insight, Chernyshevski was able to perceive Northern society in its complexity and not in oversimplified terms of "ploughmen" as opposed to "Southern oligarchs." He readily grasped, for example, the reality of the interdependence of the South and the port of New York. It was from New York City that the bulk of the cotton trade

[33] Chernyshevski's line of reasoning was derived principally from a book by an American anti-slavery writer named John Abbott, *South and North* (New York, 1860), pp. 307 ff. (quoted by Chernyshevski, *Soch.*-1906, VIII, 371 ff.). It was advocated by many extreme abolitionists, although Abbott himself was no extremist. For other expressions of Chernyshevski's persistent opposition to any compromise proposals or solutions of the secession issue, cf. *Soch.*-1906, VIII, 403, 435–36, 454–56, 495, and IX, 195–246.

[34] *Soch.*-1906, VIII, 452 (May, 1861).

export moved—its value totaling about $200,000,000 per year. Well could Chernyshevski fear, therefore, the possibility of New York merchants granting concessions to the secessionist South. He declared bitterly that "the New York merchants always kept the part of the Southern states." [35] Then in a flash of tactical wisdom, Chernyshevski, a firm believer in free trade, conceded the political necessity of supporting the protectionist demands of the New England states in the face of the greater necessity of supporting the latter in their abolitionist tendencies. Very possibly "protective tariffs are really not necessary for them," but, he asked, "what is to be done?" The "path of history" is "not the sidewalk of Nevski Prospect." Quite the opposite. It winds "wholly through fields, now dusty, now muddy, through bogs and debris." And he who fears "to cover himself with dust and to soil his shoes ought not to participate in social activity." [36]

Chernyshevski's confirmed faith in the Northern masses was expressed in the confident assertion that "when the federal government had to turn to the masses of the nation for aid, it received such patriotic support that even the higher classes were carried along by the general trend." [37] In support of this view, the Russian publicist observed that "counting only half of the Northern states, in the course of some ten days," contributions for the army and the war had mounted to "more than fifteen million silver roubles ($11,239,000)." [38]

Although Chernyshevski's faith in the North was unshake-

[35] *Ibid.*, VIII, 368. For statistics on the cotton trade and New York City in the decade prior to the Civil War, cf. Foner, *op. cit.*, p. 7. It may be added that at the crucial testing time, despite pre-war waverings, the New York merchants remained loyal to the Union.

[36] *Soch.*-1906, VIII, 36–38.

[37] *Ibid.*, VIII, 439.

[38] *Ibid.*, VIII, 447, 480–81.

able, his belief in the swift triumph of Northern arms was progressively altered during the actual course of the fighting. In May, 1861, he predicted optimistically: "if the rebels fight to their last gasp, the war will not end very soon—probably no earlier than next spring." In July he wrote that the early ineptitude and defeats of the Northern armies at the hands of the Confederates only seemed to spur the North to greater efforts. Indeed, with "such unbounded patriotism and . . . inexhaustible resources as the correspondent of the London *Times* reveals to us, the triumph of the North over the planters is inevitable." [39] However, after the rout of Bull Run, McClellan's promise to finish the war "by spring" met with Chernyshevski's revised opinion that it was "not possible to share such a hope." In fact the realization grew that to defeat the Confederacy would be no easy task. For the resolution of "the ruling party in the South" was "so great" that despite "lack of money and provisions," it would "probably find the means to continue the war" beyond "a single campaign." [40] At the same time Chernyshevski even conceded a certain grudging admiration to the South for the military sacrifices undertaken by this section in proportion to its population.[41]

In March, 1862, Chernyshevski predicted the "unconditional surrender" of the South within "two or three months" if the Northern armies continued to press "the insurgents" as they had. And in April, his final prognostication was that "no isolated victories" would "save the South now from the necessity of humbling herself." She would be "defeated" unless "the secret partisans of the planters in New York and Washington" succeeded in "bending the Northern government" to ill-advised "concessions." [42]

[39] *Ibid.*, VIII, 456, 481.   [41] *Ibid.*, VIII, 517–18.
[40] *Ibid.*, VIII, 508.   [42] *Ibid.*, IX, 225, 246.

Chernyshevski fiercely denounced all intimations of foreign intervention and European incursions in the New World such as in Mexico and in Santo Domingo during the Civil War. And he firmly asserted that the North had to thank the English working classes above all for their pressure upon the hated Palmerston Government, which prevented hostile intervention on at least one occasion—the *Trent* affair.[43]

The ferocity of Chernyshevski's attacks against reactionary foreign intervention was paralleled by his constant support of the abolitionist wing of the Republican party in its most radical measures. He continually predicted the necessary "radicalization" of the Republican party's platform if its triumph over the secessionist planters was to be insured. Especially was this true after the outbreak of actual hostilities. From prohibiting extension of slavery to the territories, the Republicans would have to move to total extirpation within the confines of the United States. In November, 1861, Chernyshevski did not hesitate to urge upon the Northern government the necessity of activizing the Negro slaves to revolt against their masters. This was indeed a dreadful slogan to raise—from a Southern planter's viewpoint. In January, 1862, he supplemented this opinion by advocating the formation of free Northern Negro detachments to fight against the South. On the question of compensation, however, Chernyshevski was more moderate. He suggested immediate emancipation of slaves in the conquered areas with remuneration to those planters who remained loyal to the Union but not to those in rebellion.[44]

The Russian publicist criticized Lincoln, and even Seward,

---

[43] *Ibid.*, VIII, 482–86, and IX, 186–90, 195, 200–2. For Chernyshevski's view of the role of English popular support in the *Trent* affair, cf. *ibid.*, VIII, 528–29.

[44] *Ibid.*, VI, 756; VIII, 507–9; 529–30; IX, 197.

adversely for what to him seemed a too extreme moderation and he was quick to turn upon McClellan when that commander did not live up to his expectations. At the same time he retained, of course, consistent aversion towards the Confederate leaders.[45]

Finally, Chernyshevski was alert not only to the military issues involved, grasping, for example, the great tactical significance of the *Monitor-Merrimac* incident, but also had well-informed opinions on such relatively technical subjects as the financing of the war.[46]

We may conclude therefore that, just as in regard to the other aspects of the slavery question with which he dealt, Chernyshevski brought a vast amount of well-chosen factual knowledge to bear upon the issue of secession and Civil War in America. His abolitionist and anti-Southern views, of ne-

[45] For Seward, cf. *Soch.*-1906, VIII, 425. For Lincoln's "moderate" views, cf. *ibid.*, pp. 377, 379–80, 435. Severe criticisms of Lincoln for weakness in the conduct of the war appear in *ibid.*, p. 509, and *ibid.*, IX, 197. Although Chernyshevski looked favorably upon old General Winfield Scott, *ibid.*, VIII, 488, when the latter retired early in the war, the Russian's admiration for McClellan, the new commander-in-chief, was extreme at first; *ibid.*, pp. 491–92 (August, 1861). By September, after Bull Run, this attitude became more restrained (p. 508), and in January, 1862, even somewhat sarcastic. By March, the shift was complete, with McClellan openly attacked as either a "traitor" or a "not very skillful strategist. If he did not deceive the Northern government, then the enemy generals deceived him." Finally, in a kind of caustic rebound of faith in Lincoln, Chernyshevski added that "at least the president is no traitor"; *ibid.*, IX, 226–27. For one example of Chernyshevski's animosity towards the Southern leaders, cf., his condemnation of Jefferson Davis, *ibid.*, VIII, 452–54.

[46] Almost every issue of *Contemporary* from May, 1861 (when the news of Fort Sumter reached St. Petersburg) carried résumés of military news and reviews of the fighting from Chernyshevski's pen. He always tried to relate military considerations to questions of over-all political aims and strategy on the part of the Northern government. For his intelligent appraisal of the *Monitor-Merrimac* encounter, cf. *Soch.*-1906, IX, 231 ff. Chernyshevski's reasoned defense of Northern paper money issues early in the war may be found in *ibid.*, p. 196.

cessity cautiously advanced, were, in their totality, clear
and unequivocating. In communicating these views to *Contemporary* readers, he had always the sense of acting both as
guardian and *pioneer*. Illustrative of his protective attitude
are Chernyshevski's frequent warnings against the pro-Southern European press, the London *Times* and especially the
New York Herald, "the *Moniteur* of secessionists." His pioneer attitude was softened down by constant repetition of
the phrase, "*chitatel znaet . . .*" ("the reader knows . . .").
This stylistic device was often used to present what were
probably unfamiliar facts of the slavery controversy to his
readers. For sheer amount of space devoted to the slavery
question, Chernyshevski far outdistanced such representative Russian radicals as Herzen and Bakunin; while his general insight into the fundamental issues involved was on a
level with that of his radical Russian contemporaries and
substantially in agreement with their views. Inaccuracies
there were, yet they were common to all American abolitionist spokesmen of those times.

Chernyshevski's commentary did not end with his arrest
and imprisonment. In a sense, it was continued within the
pages of *What Is to Be Done?*. Here was a kind of perpetual
reminder to Chernyshevski's revolutionary heirs: of the intrinsic importance of the issues involved in the American
Civil War and of his own passionate attitude towards them.[47]

[47] Cf. the ardently expressed abolitionist views of Charles Beaumont, the
American, in *A Vital Question; or What Is to Be Done?*, tr. (New York,
1886), pp. 426, 445.

CHAPTER VII

Democracy Triumphant

CHERNYSHEVSKI devoted almost as much interest to the American governmental system as he did to the question of slavery in the United States—the problem of democracy and governmental centralization being, of course, a fundamental issue to this Russian observer.

In his diary, he characterized Karamzin, the court historian and belle-lettrist of Alexander I's time, as "a very wise and conscientious man," though he disapproved of Karamzin's "many obsolete and worthless concepts"; above all, Chernyshevski criticized the author of the *History of the Russian Empire* for opposing "centralization," for wishing "to strengthen the power of the provincial governors," and for desiring that "certain posts . . . be given to the gentry nobility, whom, in general, he loves." [1] This entry is quite understandable, as Chernyshevski leaned heavily at this time towards the idea of absolute, hereditary, and *centralized* monarchy. Such a monarchy was the natural enemy of the gentry nobility whom Karamzin allegedly favored, and would be the advocate of the common people in the best traditions of enlightened absolutism.

His support of these ideas was not long-lived, however, especially in regard to America. In a review written in 1859, where Chernyshevski discussed the relations of democracy, federalism, and a centralized administrative bureaucracy, he

[1] *Dnevnik*, Oct. 10, 1848, pp. 137–38.

asked his readers: "What centralization and bureaucracy" does one find "in the North American States"? Without pause he went on to maintain that democracy and federalism did not warrant the presence of bureaucracy. Of this, the United States was the prime example. "Democracy," he declared, "demands self-government and impels to federation." In the United States, "democratic government . . . is formed of several . . . levels of republican union." Every "village is a specialized republic," and when several are joined to- gether, "the township is formed . . . once again . . . an independent republic." The union of "several townships" forms "a new republic, . . . the county; from several coun- ties," in turn, "the republican state" derives. Finally, "the State itself" is formed "from a union of the states." Is this system in any way "related to bureaucracy"? Chernyshevski asked.[2]

In this generally accurate sketch of the hierarchical levels of the United States, Chernyshevski was correct in pointing out the absence of a top-heavy national bureaucracy at that time. An equally important aspect of his presentation was the coupling of democracy with federalism—typical in the radical-democratic trend of thought in the mid-nineteenth- century. These ideas were prominent in the thinking of Her- zen and especially that of Bakunin, both of whom also em- ployed America as prime illustration. Chernyshevski's em- phasis upon the importance of public opinion in relation to the process of American political democracy strikes a familiar note: "In America public opinion leads rapidly to the power of people who are considered the most disinterested and honorable."[3] As Chernyshevski further discussed the Amer- ican federation, he approved "separation of powers" in the national government, just as Ogarev had; and he showed his

[2] *Soch.*-1906, IV, 471–72.   [3] *Ibid.*, VIII, 30.

familiarity with the precise functions and relations of President, Senate, and House of Representatives.[4]

Two years later, Chernyshevski made light of the attacks directed against the spoils system by Henry Charles Carey, American economist. The Russian admitted that there were certain evils in the too intimate relations of the victorious political party with its appointed officialdom. But whatever evils did exist, he declared, were on the agenda of reform announced by the victorious Republican party. In any case, government service was "the least profitable of all careers in the United States." It was possible to "get rich there in any career, but there has not yet been one example of anyone who got rich through government service."[5]

This winking at the evils of the spoils system and this blithe inability to foresee anything but progress in the victory of the Republicans so far as the Civil Service was concerned were shallow. It was obviously part of Chernyshevski's endeavor to present his readers with only the best side of the Northern governmental apparatus, especially when its great ordeal was so close upon it.

Chernyshevski continued his argument even more obstinately in rebutting the charges of corruption leveled by Carey against the American Congress. He insisted that in any "society of three hundred men . . . three or four" less than "pure" individuals would "always be found."[6]

Similarly charges of municipal corruption in America were lightly waved away. New York City, Chernyshevski declared, was really the only corrupt municipality—principally because it was "under the influence of highly exceptional circumstances. It serves as the commercial center for the plantation states." Aside from this, Chernyshevski asserted, Carey ought to have realized that the coming to power of

[4] *Ibid.*, pp. 196–97.   [5] *Ibid.*, p. 30.   [6] *Ibid.*

the anti-slavery party would put an end to the bad management of New York City's affairs by the "swindling agents of the planter party." [7]

In his carefully analytic review of de Tocqueville's *Democracy in America*, Chernyshevski again referred to the subject of democracy and federalism. He objected vigorously to de Tocqueville's view that democratic governments possessed a special affinity for centralization. In support of his objection, the Russian cited the case of America, insisting that there the reverse was true. He further asserted that although the reconstruction and relief functions which the central government would have to undertake in the defeated South would undoubtedly extend the scope of its activities, "this work would not have the slightest resemblance to centralization." Indeed, "the Northern states . . . wage war according to the principle of self-government." [8] Expanding upon this bold prophecy, Chernyshevski expected greater decentralization of governmental functions than ever before, once the Civil War was over. And this development, he thought, would aid greatly in cleansing American life of remnants of institutions incompatible with the nation's basic democratic principles. [9]

How over-sanguine such prophecies were is clear today. In writing on the same subject, de Tocqueville was shrewder than his critic, although he himself was manifestly wrong in using such an all-inclusive phrase as "the conceptions of Democratic Peoples are naturally Disposed to the Centralization of Power." What neither Chernyshevski nor de Tocqueville foresaw was the subsequent vast growth of American industry and finance which, coupled with the more immediate influence of undisputed rule of the Republican party in the post-Civil War period, were greatly to encourage tendencies

[7] *Ibid.*, p. 31.   [8] *Ibid.*, p. 194.   [9] *Ibid.*, pp. 191–95.

towards federal centralization and bureaucratic controls.

Once again, the desire to uphold the institutions of the free and democratic United States led Chernyshevski into something little short of self-deception and indeed even ludicrous error despite his detailed knowledge of the factual material involved.[10]

Chernyshevski's observations on the more purely economic aspects of American life are of importance even though not so abundant as those about American government. In his critically annotated translation of John Stuart Mill's *Principles of Political Economy,* the Russian utilized America for a rather successful refutation of Malthus' pessimistic theory of the disproportionate relation between the increase of food and of population. Chernyshevski's familiarity with certain economic aspects of American life is of interest in this connection. On the question of American agriculture, he correctly noted the abundance of land and the scarcity of labor. Related to this was "an extensive cultivation whose inefficiency hits one in the eye." Indeed "the agricultural methods of Americans in relation to those of Englishmen are as the ordinary methods of Englishmen to those used in Flanders or Tuscany." [11]

As pointed out earlier, Chernyshevski not only was aware

[10] In this review, entitled, "Disrespect for Authority," Chernyshevski was very critical of de Tocqueville, an indication of knowledge of America previously gained from other sources; cf. *ibid.,* pp. 189–206.

[11] *Ibid.,* VII, 231. Also cf. an incomplete translation of this text, *L'Économie Politique Jugée par la Science* (Brussels, 1874), pp. 353–54. Chernyshevski's sources here were primarily English: John Robert Godley's *Letters from America,* and *Travels in North America* by the eminent geologist Charles Lyell. He also probably used Carey's important economic treatises. In his *Principles of Social Science,* the American economist staunchly opposed Malthusianism, principally on the basis of American abundance of arable land. Cf. P. T. Homan, "Henry Charles Carey," *Encyclopaedia of the Social Sciences,* II, 226–27.

of the prevalence of the family-size farm in the North, but also approved of this institution. In fact, he had the highest esteem for the federal system of reserved lands and for the relatively wide distribution of these lands in private holdings. In favoring this system, he diverged from his theory that communal possession was the most salutary form of land holding, at least as far as Russia was concerned.

In 1857 the Russian publicist wrote that the basic difference between Western Europe and the Northern and Western states lay in the fact that every American in those states had "a territorial inheritance"; he could "take a section of sixty acres of state lands" that were "available . . . to each," and still there would be "enough for tens of millions of families." Private possession of land under these conditions of vast abundance and easy means of settlement was most wholesome. Indeed, such a guarantee of "participation in a secure life" imposed a healthy stamp upon the "character of national life." Hence, Chernyshevski declared, "among all the nations with a highly developed economic life, the Northern States" were "closest to approaching that position for whose attainment common possession" of land served. This situation explained "the unexampled prosperity of their population." [12] Russia too was fortunate in possessing a large quantity of state-held lands, he observed. But in America wider distribution of such lands was possible because of a superior transportation system and the absence of previous settlers on vacant areas. In consequence, Chernyshevski concluded, the American westward movement differed significantly from Russian "colonization." [13]

[12] Soch.-1906, III, 502–03. Note has already been made of Chernyshevski's exaggerated stress upon the "significance of the frontier," supra, pp. 92–93. For a vivid description of an American colonist in the "Far West," cf. Soch.-1906, III, 745.

[13] Soch.-1906, III, 503.

The lesson which alert Russians were to draw from his somewhat idealized description of Northern land tenures was that "state lands" had to "predominate in a country, over those distributed in private property." [14] What Chernyshevski was really proposing was the preservation of the peasant commune in any scheme of serf emancipation. The North American land system proved useful in serving his subtle purpose. "Only by such preservation," Chernyshevski contended, would "the chief feature" that Russia shared "with America be retained: the predominance of fertile state lands over private landed property." [15] By using the American example—including the American "prosperity"—Chernyshevski undoubtedly hoped to influence a change of the widest scope in Russian life; thus these passages possess significance far beyond simple recognition on Chernyshevski's part of intrinsic value in a particular American economic institution.

In regard to the tariff issue, Chernyshevski was willing to make exception to his own free-trade theory because of certain highly specialized factors at work in the United States. First, relatively high tariff duties were a necessary source of revenue for the federal government. But of greater importance was a fact already discussed; the New England states, which demanded protection, served as the chief support to the party which aspired to destroy slavery. Moreover, Chernyshevski made his own theoretical position quite unmistakable by insisting that Russia had "no need for a high tariff." In this connection, the Russian took his American mentor, Carey, severely to task for advocating high protectionism for the United States not because of "special circumstances," but for reasons of "economic theory." [16] As in the question of land tenures, Chernyshevski overtly recog-

[14] *Ibid.*   [15] *Ibid.*, p. 504.   [16] *Ibid.*, VIII, 35–36, 38.

nized the impossibility of fitting the United States into his general ideological pattern.

The American system of transportation, mentioned by Chernyshevski as fostering a wide distribution of land, impressed him greatly. He asserted that the railroads, those "exceedingly convenient means of communication" between the North and West, were superior to the Russian in terms of the traffic they bore.[17] The reasons for this were numerous: plans for the American network had not bogged down in administrative or strategic considerations as they had in Russia despite similar abundance of land and relatively small population density. Moreover, in the United States, a high productivity of labor prevailed in conjunction with an enterprising national character. In Russia, however, Chernyshevski declared, "these conditions do not exist"[18] largely owing to the dead weight of serfdom. But "the great expanses of land in the [American] West awaited only the railroads in order to be settled by colonists."[19]

Chernyshevski was again overlooking such aspects of the American situation as the role of speculation in railroad enterprise, which often led to collapse and panic. Besides, certain of the American railroads to be constructed were partly intended to meet strategic needs. Certainly this was true in the case of trunk lines to California and Oregon, whose remoteness from the rest of the North was soon to be realized sharply in the Civil War. One may note, too, Chernyshevski's glaring omission of any reference to turnpike, canal, or river facilities as conveyors of "colonists" westward in this period, except for one observation that the state of the American roads was "generally bad."[20]

[17] *Ibid.*, III, 502.   [19] *Ibid.*
[18] *Ibid.*, 117–18.   [20] *Ibid.*, IX, 243.

Chernyshevski believed that when the American railroads were first constructed, "industry" had already developed to "an enormous extent." [21] In terms of the America of the 1830's, this was utterly mistaken. Chernyshevski did not err, however, in pointing out that "the London Exchange" served "as a source of capital for all powers that lack it . . . even . . . America." [22]

Allied with these economic issues were certain sociological topics which drew the Russian critic's attention to America. These were typically problems of immigration and acculturation, women's rights, and the daily press.

In discussing the adaptation of newcomers to America, Chernyshevski wished to demonstrate that the "drunkenness" of Irish immigrants was primarily a function of their previous social environment. He cited first the terrible social and economic conditions prevalent in Ireland under British domination. Next he described the dynamics of acculturation and noted the beneficial effects of American society upon the Irish newcomer in the flood-tide period of immigration from the Emerald Isle. We are concerned only with the latter part of this argument. Chernyshevski asserted that from the point of view of the Irish immigrant, the new American life soon became quite enviable.

Chronicling the Irishman's transition to a model citizen, Chernyshevski vividly depicted him upon arrival in New York as an "ignorant, filthy and lazy drunkard." But upon discovering that he is not swindled out of his "surplus" earnings by a grasping "landlord," and that American governmental agencies settle disputes between his employers and him in a seemingly "just and impartial" way, "he begins to work more diligently." The Irish immigrant "ceases to fear

[21] *Ibid.*, III, 118.   [22] *Ibid.*, V, 133.

injustice and in a short time, a year or a year and a half," he becomes "regenerated." He is now "industrious and thrifty and the habit of drunkenness has completely disappeared in him." In fact he has even accumulated "a small capital, migrates to the Western states, acquires a tract of land, builds a house, and becomes a model farmer." Furthermore, he "sees that his children get an education, and despite his own forty or forty-five years, even teaches himself to read." [23]

That the general condition of the Irish who emigrated to America did eventually improve, often somewhat in the manner described by Chernyshevski, is not to be denied. But the rapidity of the transformation, "a year or a year and a half," is again illustrative of Chernyshevski's tendency, by now familiar, to magnify the virtues and attractions of Northern life to the detriment of conditions either in the South or in Russia.[24] The frequent plight of the pauperized Irish immigrant upon arriving in America, his long years of ill-paid labor at heavy canal and railroad construction, or in the dockyards—these are completely overlooked by the Russian.

Chernyshevski also commented in glowing terms upon the capacity of American civilization for assimilating European peoples as well as the Irish. From the end of the eighteenth

[23] *Ibid.*, IV, 253.

[24] Within these passages there is one seemingly curious contradiction: "We do not wish to decide whether American laws are, in general, good or not; whether American civil life is enviable or not. Many people find that an odious anarchy exercises dominion in America; perhaps such is a just opinion; we even share the opinion—but the Irishman does not share it," *ibid.* Here is the one place where Chernyshevski appears to have expressed thorough disapproval of American life. This, however, seems more a rhetorical device to please the censor than a genuinely held opinion. Therefore, within the context of the other passages here dealt with, it may probably be safely discounted.

century, he pointed out, "hardly a year passed" without some new territorial addition to the "young North American state." And as the "enlightened and vigorous" pioneers carved "flourishing states" out of the wilderness, the "pitiful tribes" of Indians "who did not wish to accept civilization" were constantly driven before this advance. Contrariwise, the Americans "have already . . . incorporated" the French of Louisiana and the Spaniards of northern Mexico. Indeed, "within a few years," these peoples have been so "permeated by the spirit of the new society . . . that they are not to be distinguished from the descendants of Washington and Jefferson." In like manner, just as "millions of drunken Irishmen" have been transformed by American society, "no fewer miserable Germans have become a prosperous and good lot of people in the Union." [25]

Chernyshevski's presentation of the scope and energy of the American westward movement, while grounded in fact so far as the plight of the Indians was concerned, is otherwise an exaggeration of America's solvent power during those times. The qualities of the "melting pot" have become so potent, in his view, as to leave nothing but a uniform, gray mass. This was certainly not the case, at least so far as concerned such national groups as the French or Spanish.

It has already been pointed out that as early as 1849 Chernyshevski had favored granting political rights to women.[26] But his well-developed views on the "emancipation of women" were formulated in *What Is to Be Done?*, and certain of them had reference to America. For example,

[25] *Soch.*-1906, VI, 208. Cf. also *ibid.*, II, 649, where Chernyshevski drew a parallel between the successful American advance upon the "redskins" and the retreat of the Tartars before the Russian pioneers. He attributed both of these achievements to the "*superior cultural level*" of the Americans and Russians in relation to their foes.

[26] *Dnevnik*, 315–16; cf. *supra*, p. 80, note 6.

the heroine, Katya Polozova, inquired of her American
suitor, Charles Beaumont, whether it was "true" that a girl
had more freedom of action in America than in Europe.
Beaumont replied, "Yes . . . what a contrast between us
and you Europeans! All that you have been told about the
emancipation of women [in America] is true." [27] On another
occasion, Katya, after calling Beaumont a "panegyrist of
women," added half-jokingly that in his views on "the
woman question," he resembled Harriet Beecher Stowe. For
Mrs. Stowe proved that "the Negroes are the most talented
of all the races, that they stand above the white race by their
intellect." [28]

Chernyshevski's discussion of the status of women in
America did not range beyond the level of these generalities, and what he did have to say about the "emancipated" American women was not quite true. Until even the
middle of the nineteenth century the inferior position of
women actually yielded but slowly to change, as witness
the experience of the feminist movement under the leadership of Lucretia Mott and Elizabeth Cady Stanton. Yet conditions did improve, and "in the exciting decade preceding
the Civil War the influence of women continued to be felt
in all forward-looking movements." At this time, too, "women
were . . . emboldened to make their initial appearance in
the professions." [29]

But if the position of women in American society at that
time could serve even as a second-rate model for the treatment of women in Continental society, Chernyshevski was
greatly mistaken in thinking that Russian women, at least

[27] *What Is to Be Done?*, p. 427.
[28] *Ibid.*, p. 441.
[29] A. M. Schlesinger, *New Viewpoints in American History* (New York, 1922), pp. 140–41.

of the upper class, were still maintained in the patriarchal seclusion customary in the days before Peter the Great. But in this case, too, the American example was Chernyshevski's ideal.

Wherever the actual American situation did furnish serviceable illustrations, Chernyshevski skillfully utilized them. Hence the Russian publicist expressed high regard for American freedom of the press, although this was an extremely delicate subject to broach within the pages of *Contemporary*. In 1859, he asserted that freedom of the press did not exist in France "in comparison with the freedom of the printed word in England, Switzerland, Belgium and the United States." Indeed, "the printed word in France is hardly freer than in Prussia." [30]

Three years later, Chernyshevski contrasted the press laws in England, Switzerland, and the United States with those prevalent in other European states. In the countries first enumerated, he found "no special significance or exceptional position . . . attached" to the press. In the second group, the press was subservient to varied types of censorship. Chernyshevski's covert conclusion, of course, was that the system of freedom was preferable to that of official control. [31]

The Russian was in a position to judge this American freedom of the press "in action," since he knew of all the important American newspapers and was acquainted with at least one at first-hand. In May, 1861, for example, he complained bitterly of his dependence upon European newspapers and the "meagre sources" of his "information on American affairs." The one American newspaper which he

[30] *Soch.*-1906, IV, 566. Perhaps "Russia" may be substituted for "Prussia" in this passage.

[31] *Ibid.*, IX, 128–32, esp. pp. 128–29.

could sometimes procure was the *New York Herald*. However, it usually arrived "two or three weeks late" and then "only" in a condensed "weekly edition," from which Chernyshevski said it was difficult to glean "much sense." This, he declared, might "be endurable" if the *Herald* were "only decent." But, "unfortunately," this newspaper was "the most vulgar of the five or six thousand American newspapers." [32]

At the same time Chernyshevski castigated the *Herald* as secessionist. It was worse than a "Charleston newspaper"; it was the lackey of the New York Stock Exchange. And, Chernyshevski declared cynically, it finally threw its support to the North once the war had commenced because "the Stock Exchange understood that the North had to wage the war energetically." [33]

Some years earlier, in 1856, Chernyshevski had compiled a table of the principal American newspapers for the subscribers of *Contemporary*. The brief identifying notes were cast in terms of the newspapers' political attitudes, especially in relation to the slavery issue.

He first noted that the "main newspapers . . . were those published in New York, the political and commercial metropolis of North America." He identified the *New York Herald* as the most important "newspaper of the conservatives and the defenders of slavery." Formerly a constant advocate of the ideas of the Democratic party, it was currently opposed to the Democratic Administration because President Pierce had refused a diplomatic post to its editor-in-chief. Second in Chernyshevski's listing was the *New York Tribune*, with its abolitionist policy. The *Daily Times* (*sic*) was "distinguished" from the *Tribune* "by the rougher character of its polemics." The *Courier and Enquirer* of General James Watson Webb leaned heavily towards the "Know-Nothing"

[32] *Ibid.*, VIII, 437.   [33] *Ibid.*, pp. 438–39.

camp because of its policies of anti-Roman Catholicism. The *Evening Post*, oldest of the current New York papers, was directed by the poet Bryant, a "veteran American journalist," and was inclined towards union with the Democrats. The *Journal of Commerce* was a purely commercial paper, but when it did express opinions they were usually in favor of the Democrats and of Protestantism. Last among the New York papers that Chernyshevski mentioned was the *Express and Commercial Advertiser*, which now supported the pro-slavery wing of the "Know-Nothing" party.

Concerning provincial journals, he declared that only those originating in the state capitals and Washington possessed more than local significance. The *Union* was the organ of the Administration; and the *National Intelligencer*, he remarked somewhat vaguely, was the organ of the conservatives.

Chernyshevski also wondered why the moderate Democrats never had a really official organ in New York City after 1832, especially since the Democrats had been at one time a ruling power there. Then he presented the reverse situation: the *Boston Post*, "one of the most well-known New England newspapers," was "famous . . . for the stubbornness" with which it defended "the Democrats . . . and . . . slavery," and managed to do this "in a city permeated with Whiggism" and having "a population opposed to involuntary servitude." [34]

Chernyshevski's summary characterization of American newspapers is significant because it again illustrates how central the slavery issue was in the totality of his attitudes

[34] *Ibid.*, II, 453–54, for all citations in this listing. Chernyshevski was careful to note the sources of his information when he did not have actual copies of the newspapers at hand. These sources were principally: *Allgemeine Zeitung*, *Athenaeum*, *Indépendance Belge*, *Revue Brittanique*, and *Revue des deux Mondes;* cf. *Soch.*-1906, p. 456.

towards America. More specifically, one notes that the Russian not only selected the most influential and widely circulated American newspapers for his list but was also surprisingly accurate in his evaluations of their political attitudes. This was particularly true for the *Herald,* the *Tribune,* and the *Times.*[35] Where Chernyshevski erred most seriously was in his political characterization of the liberal *Commercial Advertiser,* which actually was anti-slavery; in fact it was one of the few New York newspapers which remained "measurably loyal to the Administration" during the Civil War.[36]

[35] Cf. W. G. Bleyer, *Main Currents in the History of American Journalism* (Cambridge, Mass., 1927), Houghton Mifflin Company. Bleyer asserts that the *Herald's* "avowed sympathy" for the South "before the outbreak of the Civil War" brought it into "open opposition to the outstanding Republican newspapers . . . , the *Tribune,* the *Times,* and the *Courier and Enquirer.*" Because of the *Herald's* circulation among 100,000 readers and its influence upon the London *Times,* which considered it representative of "the substantial commercial interests of this country," the Northern leaders were extremely apprehensive about the *Herald's* attitude when the war broke out, *ibid.,* p. 204. Bleyer notes further that during 1850-60, "throughout the North and West, the *Tribune* was undoubtedly the most powerful of all forces in crystallizing public opinion against slavery," *ibid.,* p. 228. These judgments corroborate Chernyshevski's opinions of the *Herald* and *Tribune.* Cf. *ibid.,* p. 248, for confirmation of Chernyshevski's evaluation of the *Times.* Bleyer, however, does not concede polemics "rougher" than those of the *Tribune* to the *Times.* For the *Courier and Enquirer,* cf. *ibid.,* pp. 146-47. There is no mention, however, of the relation of this paper to the "Know-Nothings." Cf. *ibid.,* pp. 143-44, for Bryant and the New York *Evening Post;* and *ibid.,* pp. 147-48, for the *Journal of Commerce,* although Bleyer is silent on political attitudes of this paper. Cf. *ibid.,* p. 114, for the *Commercial Advertiser.*

As for the *National Intelligencer* and the *Union,* Chernyshevski is generally corroborated by Frank Luther Mott, *American Journalism* (New York, 1941), who identifies the *Union* as the official organ of the Polk, Pierce, and Buchanan administrations, *ibid.,* pp. 256-57. The *National Intelligencer* was "presidential organ" from 1800 until the election of Andrew Jackson in 1828. And Mott terms the Boston *Post* "a great Democratic journal," *ibid.,* pp. 178, 259.

[36] Mott, *op. cit.,* p. 339.

In line with his approval of a free press, Chernyshevski also favored the advanced degree of religious freedom in the United States. He expressed this attitude by protesting against persecution of the Mormons in the name of the "basic principle" of American religious freedom. While the Americans should not be "blamed for Mormonism," he declared, they could be censured because "the noble sentiment of indignation against the savage principle of Mormonism swept them into violence" that had "no inherent justification." [37] Such views, while flattering to Americans, are surely extreme in characterizing Mormonism as "savage."

Chernyshevski's familiarity with American literature and historiography, noted earlier, gave rise to some interesting evaluations of American writers. These commentaries, while by no means comprehensive, are occasionally striking in their literary and sociological references. His opinion of James Fenimore Cooper was decidedly negative; "Again read Cooper," he scribbled in his diary. Cooper's novels were "rubbish in . . . their . . . analysis of the human spirit." There was "nothing—except for local types of those places and of that time." Chernyshevski dubbed Cooper's work "a kind of . . . ethnographic novel" and concluded emphatically that he was "*not so developed*" as to be able "to read this trash easily." [38] In conformance with these caustic views, the Russian criticized the *Last of the Mohicans* adversely because "nothing" was "there." It possessed "no characters . . . nothing but quaint, queer people. . . . There is naught that we can term Gogol." [39]

Such estimates of Cooper are eminently acceptable today and parallel Mark Twain's famous evaluation of Cooper's

[37] *Soch.*-1906, VIII, 32.
[38] *Dnevnik* (Oct. 23, 1848), p. 148.
[39] *Ibid.*, p. 154.

worth.[40] Beyond this, Chernyshevski's record of his early interest in Cooper reveals that American author as having widespread penetration among the Russian radical intelligentsia at this time. Herzen and Bakunin also read Cooper contemporaneously.

In 1860, a lengthy review of Nathaniel Hawthorne's *Wonder Book for Boys and Girls* appeared in *Contemporary*.[41] To Chernyshevski, Hawthorne was "a writer of great talent," and "since Hoffmann, there has been no storyteller with such a bent for the fantastic as Hawthorne." This American's talent was "so enormous" that no one "among our [Russian] artists" could "equal . . . him." [42] Chernyshevski, nonetheless, evaluated these tales, too, as "rubbish." Their main faults lay in Hawthorne's failure to rework them (as Goethe, for example, had done) in such a way that they would reflect the leading ideas of the century. In addition, they were seriously handicapped by their "moral" character, that is, by inadmissible distortions committed for the sake of prudery. Finally they suffered from false artistic devices such as prolixity of "poetic diction." The Russian critic then devoted some detailed analysis to the question of artistic form (a subject too frequently neglected in Russian sociological criticism). Chernyshevski's criterion of form was derivative of Goethe, the mature classicist, and was summed up in the aphorism, "without compression there is no high artistic value." [43] The review concluded

---

[40] Cf. S. L. Clemens, "Fenimore Cooper's Literary Offenses," *Collected Works*. Mark Twain calls the Leather Stocking Series the "Broken Twig Series," and describes the Indians as wooden as those in front of a cigar shop.

[41] *Soch*-1906, VI, 274–85. Chernyshevski rendered this title as *Wonders and Fables Borrowed from Mythology*.

[42] *Ibid.*, pp. 274–75.

[43] *Soch.*-1906, VI, 284–85.

with an attack upon those Russian artists "who turn to us as Hawthorne to children, who either hide the truth from us or who bother us with idle talk." [44] This last was apparently aimed at Turgenev. It is also illustrative of Chernyshevski's tendency to use the book review as a medium for expressing his thoughts on many issues.

In a highly appreciative review of Granovski's historical works,[45] Chernyshevski mentioned Prescott and placed him on a higher level of achievement than Guizot, whom he also esteemed. He criticized the American historian, however, for his "almost exclusive attention to political history." Such an accusation was certainly unjust and can be readily refuted by anyone who has read even a small part of either *The Conquest of Mexico* or *The Conquest of Peru*.[46]

Chernyshevski believed that Emerson's thought had exerted a healthy influence on Granovski; nevertheless he considered that the American Transcendentalist did not possess Granovski's stature as an historian. For "in Emerson the sense of the meaning of history is far from having that importance ascribed to it by Granovski." To Chernyshevski, it was Granovski's addition of the "popular element" to the political and intellectual elements of history which opened a new epoch in historiography. But Emerson was deficient in this regard as well as lacking in a strict methodology.[47]

---

[44] *Ibid.*

[45] Timothy Granovski (1813–55), a contemporary and friend of Herzen, is little known outside of Russia. He exercised substantial influence on students of his history courses at Moscow University; many of them later became radicals.

[46] *Soch.*-1906, II, 416.

[47] *Ibid.*, p. 417. For a highly appreciative note on the substance and style of Granovski's public lectures delivered at Moscow University in the 1840's, cf. I. Ivashin, "Rukopis Publichnykh Lektsi T. N. Granovskogo," *Istoricheski Zhurnal* (Moscow, 1945), no. 1–2, pp. 81–84. Chernyshevski's remarks on Granovski are generally borne out there.

Of all the American writers with whom Chernyshevski had familiarity, Harriet Beecher Stowe and her *Uncle Tom's Cabin* impressed him most. In *What Is to Be Done?*, he portrayed the girls in the co-operative sewing establishment as eagerly seeking information about "the life of Mrs. Beecher Stowe whose novel we have all known" and who was a "great" woman.[48] She was also mentioned with great praise by Chernyshevski in an unfinished story begun in 1863, which was named after Alfieri in tribute to that great Italian patriot.[49]

In analyzing these conglomerate observations of American life, one is primarily impressed by a relatively greater devotion to and interest in America on Chernyshevski's part than was evinced even by Herzen. The extent of Chernyshevski's factual knowledge of America was very great. And it may safely be stated that he would have had no favorable words for any American institution that did not reflect what he considered the progress of democracy, or which was not conducive in some way to the extermination of slavery. Chernyshevski—with his bifurcated view of America—ascribed almost if not all of the evils and shortcomings of American life to slavery. This accounts for his exaggeration of Northern virtues often to the point of idealization, and in contrast also accounts for his presentation of the culture of the Cotton Kingdom as little short of malign. With this in mind, one can understand Chernyshevski's short-sighted predictions in regard to the trend towards political centralization in the post-Civil War period.

The evils which Chernyshevski observed in American life were usually far more concrete than the abstract shortcomings and insufficiencies (e.g., "social despotism") noted by

[48] *What Is to Be Done?*, p. 222.
[49] *Soch.*-1906, vol. X, part II, *Alferev*, p. 44.

the older generation of "romantic exiles" like Herzen. But more important, these evils did not alone receive attention; the radical democrats of the new age of "unwashed seminarists" always had Chernyshevski's very favorable opinions of American life before them. In the pages of *Contemporary* and in *What Is to Be Done?*, the Russian undoubtedly was educating the intelligentsia about America—and it was an America which not only frequently marked an exception to his generalized theories, but which also represented a land of hope for democratic and radical Europe.

Of all the Russian radicals thus far discussed, Chernyshevski had the most comprehensive observations and opinions of the United States, and their influence upon his contemporaries and upon future Russian revolutionaries—at any rate, until the views of Peter Lavrov came into prominence —must have been extensive. The reasons for this may be found in Chernyshevski's enforced exile and martyrdom; in his remaining in Russia rather than emigrating to work abroad; in his plebeian origins; and finally in the fact that he was never discredited in revolutionary eyes as Bakunin or even Herzen unfortunately sometimes were.

CHAPTER VIII

"The Republic of Humbug"

PETER LAVROV

PETER LAVROV was one of the most important social philosophers of the Populist movement (*Narodni-chestvo*) during the seventies and eighties of the last century. He was one of the several great Russian radicals whose lives were patterned after the turbulent career of Belinski in their devotion to humane ideals.

Lavrov's well-developed opinions of America often differed sharply from those held by Chernyshevski, his contemporary and friend. Unlike him, Lavrov was not a seminary *raznochinets,* but a man whose upbringing shaped him more to the tradition of Herzen and the "men of the forties." Lavrov lacked much of the passion and color that Herzen revealed in his prose, but in his own way he was as intransigent in his views as Bakunin.

Lavrov was born in 1823, the son of a wealthy landowner of Pskov, a retired colonel married to a Russianized Swedish woman. His youth showed little promise of the revolutionary tendencies that were later to be so characteristic. As a child, he read omnivorously, if unsystematically, and learned both French and German. At the age of nineteen, after finishing the course in the Artillery School, he became an army officer, and in 1849, was promoted to the rank of colonel. From 1844 to 1866, he taught higher mathematics at a military academy in St. Petersburg.

During this period, Lavrov familiarized himself with German philosophy and French Utopian socialist thought along the same general lines as his contemporaries with whom we have already dealt. The Crimean War influenced him to more revolutionary views; and his opposition to the Russian government in the era between the humiliating defeat and the epoch of the "Great Reforms" found expression in topical verse, which circulated both in manuscript form and in Herzen's *Kolokol*. These experiences led this scientifically minded country gentleman to join the *Zemlia i Volia* group in 1862, and brought about his friendship with Chernyshevski shortly before the latter's arrest.[1]

The vast learning which Lavrov accumulated in mathematics, the exact sciences, sociology, philosophy, history, and literature served him well in his work of writing and editing technical and literary and philosophical publications of liberal tendency. More importantly, this learning was crystallized in the famous *Historical Letters* written for the most part in Vologda between 1867 and 1869. Lavrov had been banished to this provincial capital after his dismissal from the academy, one of the many repressive incidents following Karakozov's attempt upon the life of Alexander II in 1866. The main sources of the *Historical Letters* were Comte, Kant, Hegel, Feuerbach, and Proudhon. All these were synthesized and transformed into what has been called "the first and most important system of Russian subjective sociology," [2] and "the

[1] Cf. "Lavrov o Chernyshevskome," *Literaturnoe Nasledstvo* (Moscow, 1933), VII–VIII, ed. I. Knizhnik-Vetrov, pp. 95–116. According to this author, Lavrov had read Chernyshevski's articles, and his political development was greatly influenced by them before he actually met Chernyshevski in 1859. Chernyshevski had not read one of Lavrov's essays before this meeting.

[2] Nicholas Rusanov, "Lavrov," *Encyclopaedia of the Social Sciences*, IX, 201.

first work which drew the attention of the general Russian public to him."[3]

In 1870, Lopatin, Marx's Russian translator, aided Lavrov in escaping abroad. The *Narodnik* sociologist made his way to Paris, too late, however, to meet Herzen, who had invited him thither but who had died in the interim. Lavrov was in time, however, to make an important contribution to the Paris Commune and even journeyed to Belgium and London on behalf of the besieged Communards.

Lavrov was now forty-seven years old, and at this relatively advanced age his mature socialist period began. Indeed 1870–71 was probably a nodal point for Lavrov in much the same way that 1848 had been for Herzen and Bakunin. It was then that he met Marx and Engels in London and read *Das Kapital* for the first time.

In the thirty years of enforced exile (for he never returned to Russia), Lavrov assumed a leading role in many centers of revolutionary activity, principally London, Paris, Geneva, and Zürich. From 1873 to 1876, he edited the militantly socialist review *Vpered!* (Forward), which occasionally was Marxian in flavor.[4] But despite the importance of this journal, it never achieved as wide readership as *Kolokol* had in Herzen's time. It did, however, circulate now and again in America.[5]

During the early 1880's, Lavrov associated with Plekhanov in literary activity of a revolutionary nature. Later on he was an editor of the *Messenger of the People's Will*,[6] devoting

[3] L. A. Tcheskis, "La Philosophie Sociale de Pierre Lavroff," *Revue de Synthèse Historique* (Paris, Oct., 1912), XXV, 129.

[4] Cf. the program of this paper, mentioned in Lavrov's "Gosudarstvennyi Element v Budushchem Obshchestve," *Vpered! Neperiodicheskoe Obozrenie* (London, 1876), vol. IV, part I, p. 7; hereinafter referred to as *Vpered, Nep.*

[5] *Vpered*, no. 39 (Aug. 15, 1876), p. 513.

[6] It is of interest to note that Nicholas Chaikovski (to be discussed in Chapter X, *infra*) was contemporaneously London agent of this journal.

much time towards the end of his life to the attack against the Russian monarchy. Along with these propagandizing activities, he continued to write with erudition on generalized sociological and historical questions. He died in Paris in 1900.[7]

The *Historical Letters* were written while Lavrov was under arrest, in circumstances similar to those of Chernyshevski, when he composed *What Is to Be Done?* They expressed Lavrov's reaction to Pisarev's advocacy of egotistical and individual freedom; for in these *Letters* Lavrov enunciated an idealistic doctrine of the "critically thinking individual," whose effect upon human "culture," so prone to stagnate, was to "civilize" it, to be the motive force of "progress."[8] The critically thinking, sensitive individual had an ethical duty to the mass of society (in Russia, the peasantry). Specifically, this duty was to awaken and direct the inert masses onto the path of progress and revolution by education and propaganda; and this concept was to have a striking influence upon the *Narodnichestvo* of the early 1870's, and, in a different way, upon their terrorist successors at the end of the decade. Along with Herzen's slogan, "To the people!," Bakunin's agitation, and Chernyshevski's teaching, the *Historical Letters* acted as a stimulus to almost immediate activity among the peasantry. The great movement of the intelligentsia to the countryside in the early 1870's owes much to them.[9]

Lavrov, although anything but a "reformist" in the Western European Social Democratic sense, contented himself

[7] *Deiateli Revoliutsionnogo Dvizheniia v Rossii* (Moscow, 1930), vol. II, parts 1–2, pp. 729–30.

[8] Lavrov, *Izbrannye Sochineniia* (Moscow, 1934), I, 252; hereinafter referred to as *Soch.*-Lavrov.

[9] Turgenev's last novel, *Virgin Soil* (1876), depicts the "simplification" movement of "going to the people" in critical as well as unflattering terms.

in his teaching with an emphasis upon education, despite his expectations of "maximalist" results within a generation at most. Tactically, his views thus clashed with the emphasis upon agitation of Bakunin and his followers. Bakunin's group, of course, advocated "the propaganda of the deed." This meant stirring up sporadic risings (*bunty*) among the peasantry, an "active minority" seemingly privileged to utilize any means and any opportunity for achieving its purposes.[10]

Detailed discussion of Lavrov's over-all philosophical and sociological outlook is not germane to this book,[11] but brief reference to it will facilitate understanding of his attitudes towards American institutions. For the *Narodnik* sociologist, the "economic question" was primary. It emerged as the central evil in society, which had to be overcome ultimately by violent revolution.[12] Lavrov was also firmly opposed to Christian dogma and believed at least for a time that Christ was mythical; [13] "We are enemies of religion and allies of science," he declared.[14] The Darwinist theories of struggle for existence and survival of the fittest, Lavrov interpreted as guarantees of the socialism he so much desired.[15] The "Slavic question," which disturbed so many of Lavrov's contemporaries, notably Bakunin, was part of "the general human question." And in line with the pronounced pro-Polish sentiments of Herzen and Bakunin, Lavrov stoutly defended

[10] *Vpered*, no. 47, p. 771.

[11] Cf. the excellent studies of Masaryk, *The Spirit of Russia*, II, 89–92, 115–36; Hecker, *Russian Sociology*, pp. 75–102; Tcheskis, *op. cit.*, XXV (Oct., 1912), 129–42, and XXVI (Feb.–April, 1913), 64–81.

[12] *Vpered, Nep.*, vol. III, part I, pp. 119, 142.

[13] *Ibid.*, 128n.

[14] *Soch.*-Lavrov, III, 103.

[15] *Vpered*, no. 17, p. 526.

the idea of a democratic resurrection of that martyred nation.[16]

About his Russian revolutionary contemporaries, he commented in glowing terms. On the occasion of the reprinting in 1875 of some of Herzen's writings in *Vpered*,[17] he wrote that there "was a *man* in the fullest sense of that word." He also declared that if any one epitaph were to be sought to characterize Herzen's life, that ought to be the first stanza of the poem that Ogarev, "his closest friend," dedicated to him in 1858:

> When I was a placid and delicate boy,
> When I was a passionately rebellious youth,
> Both in maturity and in advancing age,
> Throughout the whole of life, anew, and ever fresh to me
> Resounded one unalterable word;
> Freedom! Freedom! [18]

Lavrov was shrewd enough to add that Herzen never celebrated mere abstract freedom, devoid of "content." [19] Clearly enough, Lavrov felt warmly disposed towards Ogarev, and he printed his verses in *Vpered* "with pleasure." [20]

For Chernyshevski, there was high praise for his stand on the question of serf emancipation.[21] But above all, Chernyshevski was to be regarded as having "engraved an . . . indelible image upon the history of Russian thought." [22]

Even Bakunin, his ideological opponent of many years'

[16] Cf. *Soch.*-Lavrov, II, 40; *Vpered, Nep.*, vol. III, part II, pp. 101–3; *Vpered*, no. 3, p. 89, no. 24, p. 757.

[17] *Soch.*-Lavrov, IV, 116–33, esp. pp. 119–20, 123, 127, 132–33.

[18] *Ibid.*, 119–20.

[19] Other laudatory notes on Herzen and his work may be found in *Soch.*-Lavrov, II, 48, 50, III, 367; *Vpered, Nep.*, vol. V, part I, p. 85, part II, p. 137.

[20] *Vpered*, no. 10, 298 n. Also cf. *Soch.*-Lavrov, II, 48, 50.

[21] *Vpered, Nep.*, vol. V, part I, pp. 85–86.

[22] *Soch.*-Lavrov, III, 169.

standing, had a measure of appreciation from Lavrov who referred to him as "our well-known agitator," and on one occasion even reprinted a long letter of Bakunin's in *Vpered*.[23] Fittingly enough, upon the "agitator's" death in 1876, Lavrov published a sympathetic eulogy of Bakunin's career.[24]

It is evident that there was significant evolution in Lavrov's intellectual life. One may reduce the most important aspects of this process to Lavrov's contact with Marx and Engels, and his readings in Marxism.[25] These led him away from orthodox *Narodnik* thought to the extent of believing that a capitalist development was present in the Russia of the mid-seventies. And he even reasoned that this trend prepared the way for a socialist revolution in Russia as well as in the rest of the civilized world. Indeed *Vpered* was undoubtedly launched with the propagation of Marxian ideas as one of its fundamental goals.[26]

But in the late 1880's Lavrov apparently turned away from Plekhanov's *Emancipation of Labor* group and became alienated from Russian Marxism. The *Narodnik* sociologist reverted to his earlier Populist beliefs, adding to them, however, the concept of terrorism as a justifiable weapon of struggle. This entailed renewed faith in the peasant commune and in the *artel*, activized by the "critically thinking individual." Thus he relinquished the Marxian belief in the proletariat as the prime bearer of socialism for Russia.[27]

[23] *Ibid.*, II, 326–29; for citation, cf. p. 329.

[24] *Vpered*, no. 37, pp. 437–39.

[25] Tcheskis, *op. cit.*, XXVI, 77.

[26] *Bolshaia . . . Entsiklopediia* (Moscow, 1937), XXXV, 639; Tcheskis, *op. cit.*, XXV, 131.

[27] Cf. Tcheskis, *op. cit.*, XXVI, 77. Some authorities assert that Lavrov never mastered Marxism at all: *Bolshaia . . . Entsiklopediia*, XXXV, 639; and Tcheskis, *op. cit.*, XXVI, 75.

Lavrov had reverted to a political position and program which were eminently defensible during the seventies, when the state of capitalist development in Russia was still confused. But in the eighties and nineties, when industrial development forged ahead more rapidly, such views became more vulnerable. For this reason Lavrov justly bears the onus of being regarded by many as a great eclectic or a "petty bourgeois socialist," and by others as a man who "in spite of his democratic convictions and his socialist ideal . . . remained at bottom an intellectual aristocrat and a convinced individualist." To be sure, Lavrov's exclusiveness was "moral and intellectual" rather than haughty.[28] Bearing these reservations in mind, one may agree with the verdict of one group of commentators that "up to his death," Lavrov was "the most authoritative interpreter of the views of *Narodnichestvo*." [29]

Fortunately, the sources of Lavrov's knowledge of America, as in the case of Chernyshevski, have been recorded —for the most part, by Lavrov himself. Like Chernyshevski, the *Narodnik* sociologist never visited the United States. But in the course of his long residence in Russia and his many years of exile abroad, he read copiously about Amer-

[28] *Bolshaia . . . Entsiklopediia,* XXXV, 646. Gorev, in this résumé of Lavrov's life and work, goes too far in condemning Lavrov on Leninist grounds. Lenin carefully differentiated the militant revolutionary *Narodniki* of the seventies from their transformed descendants of the nineties and had much respect for the former. Cf. Lenin, *Selected Works,* "What the 'Friends of the People' Are," tr., I, 408–9, 428. Cf. Tcheskis, *op. cit.,* XXVI, 75, for the second citation.

[29] Lenin, *Soch.* (Moscow, Leningrad, 1935), I, 518. The commentary is the editors'. One may also concur with the verdict expressed by another author: "What would Lavrov be today? A communist? An anarcho-syndicalist? A left or a right S.R.?—I do not know and I do not want to know, but I do know that he would be a maximalist socialist." R. Ivanov-Razumnik, "Petr L. Lavrov i Kommuna," *Sbornik Statei Posviashchennykh Petru Lavrovichu Lavrovu* (Petrograd, Moscow, 1920), ed. P. Vitiazev, p. 47.

ica and came in contact with individuals who knew the United States at first-hand.

It should first be noted that Lavrov followed in the long tradition of linguistic cosmopolitanism exampled by Herzen. He not only knew Russian, French and German, but also Polish. He knew English, although he seems not quite to have mastered the language, as indicated by his odd mistakes in spelling and capitalization.

Besides reading most contemporary Russian journals such as the *Messenger of Europe* and the *Week,* Lavrov also read the *Revue des deux Mondes,* the London *Times, Le Nord,* the *Vienna Daily Press,* and other representative European publications.[30] More specifically, Lavrov had read with enthusiasm Tom Paine's *Common Sense;* he knew of the American economist Carey, and referred to Charles Sumner as "the famous American." He was also well acquainted with the work of Emerson, Longfellow, Lowell, Whitman, and Whittier.[31] For background knowledge of American institutions, de Tocqueville's *Democracy in America* seems to have been one of the mainstays, as in the case of most mid-century Russian radicals.[32] The channels which transmitted information to him on the state of the American working class and the struggle for socialism in the United States were several: such workers' journals as *Vor-*

[30] Cf. *Vpered, Nep.,* vol. III, part III, p. 64; vol. V, part I, p. 6; vol. II, part I, pp. 209–13.

[31] These last Lavrov apparently read mostly in Russian translation. Charles Waite's *Sketch of the History of American Literature* is also mentioned as a source. For Carey, cf. *Vpered, Nep.,* vol. III, part I, p. 3; for Paine, cf. *ibid.,* vol. IV, part I, p. 194; for Sumner, cf. *Etiudy o Zapadnoi Literature* (Petrograd, 1920), ed. A. Gizetti and P. Vitiazev, p. 141; for the men of letters, cf. *infra,* pp. 185 ff.

[32] *Soch.*-Lavrov, II, 128. Lavrov was also acquainted with the writings of Harriet Martineau, who had spent two colorful years in America in the 1830's; *Vpered, Nep.,* vol. II, part I, p. 176.

bote, a German language newspaper published in Chicago and an organ of the American section of the First International; the *Volksstaat* in Philadelphia; and in New York the *Arbeiter Zeitung.*[33] Other important sources of information for this central aspect of Lavrov's interest in America were the alert communications of William Frey, a founder and leader of a Russian Utopian Socialist Colony in Cedar Vale, Kansas, in the mid-1870's. Lavrov may also have received the publication of this group, the *Progressive Communist.*[34] His information on the state of the social struggle in America was further augmented (whether accurately or not, we cannot be sure) by contacts with American delegates to various meetings of the First International.[35]

The bulk of Lavrov's observations on America (found in his as yet unsatisfactorily collected writings), fall within the decade of the seventies. More specifically, they may be dated from 1868–69, when the first chapters of the *Historical Letters* were drafted, to 1891, when this work received final revision.[36] It is important to notice that these writings appeared after the time when Herzen, Chernyshevski, and even Bakunin were active. Thus Lavrov's attitudes towards America supplement in a very real sense those of his Russian radical contemporaries who were his precursors in their attention to America. At the same time, it is not impossible that the *Narodnik* sociologist not only supplements but also takes over as his own some of their impressions.

Lavrov's notes on America are abundant and furnish a

[33] *Vpered, Nep.,* vol. III, part III, p. 53; *Vpered,* no. 1, pp. 29–30, no. 40, pp. 549–51.

[34] Cf. *Vpered, Nep.,* vol. III, part I, pp. 120 ff., for a very valuable letter by Frey on America. Also cf. *Vpered,* no. 2, p. 58. William Frey is treated in Chapter X, *infra.*

[35] Cf. *Soch.*-Lavrov, II, 258; *Vpered, Nep.,* vol. III, part III, p. 96.

[36] Cf. Tcheskis, *op. cit.,* XXVI, 77n.

clear view of his over-all impression of the United States. In an article entitled, "Unavoidable Enmity," [37] after declaring firmly that "no governmental measures, no purely political methods" could "better the condition of the worker by themselves," Lavrov asked sarcastically whether the North American republic, "that model product of political liberalism, rescued the American people from economic panics and crises whose magnitude even old Europe might envy." Did it perhaps save the American people from "venality in the courts, the legislative assemblies, the states, Congress or the Senate [sic]"—a venality so widespread as to "evoke astonishment" among European business men of "present and former times?" [38]

The answer was obviously a resounding "No!" This fragmentary passage written in the wake of nine years of post-Civil War misrule by the Republicans clearly expressed Lavrov's deep disillusionment with contemporary America. It denied in undertone the "unique" position of the American republic in the world of nations which Herzen and, on occasion, Bakunin had attributed to this country. Missing, too, was Chernyshevski's glowingly optimistic faith in the American democracy. As shall be seen, Lavrov was wont repeatedly to attack both what he considered the maladjusted American economic system and the corruption in American public life due to the rule of money. But his profound dissatisfaction with "the republic of humbug [English in original] and the empire of dollars" did not prevent him from viewing American life with historical perspective and thus acknowledging that the present state of affairs had not always existed. [39]

[37] Vpered, Nep., vol. III, part I, pp. 26–27.
[38] Ibid.
[39] Cf. Vpered, no. 41 (Sept. 15, 1876), pp. 561–62, for citation.

In an essay written to commemorate the centenary of Pugachev's revolt (1773),[40] Lavrov drew certain parallels between the great popular uprising which so shook Catherine II's throne and the contemporaneous American Revolution. He considered the outbreak of the American Revolution a blow for the liberty not only of Americans but for the rest of humanity as well. He declared that after deciding upon their "Tea Party," the "Bostonians did not recoil," for they knew that "the most remarkable, the most cautious and the most penetrating minds in America" were "on their side." Further, they knew that "law" was "lawlessness" and "force a duty before the firm will of the nation." Hence, "the revolt attained the significance of a revolution." And "that revolution . . . inaugurated the beginning of the North American States."[41]

More than that, Lavrov asserted that the American Revolution introduced "a period in the history of mankind," which, "after the Washingtons and the Hamiltons," brought into being the "Dantons and Robespierres." Similarly in the wake of our revolution followed the whole series of other nineteenth-century political and social revolutions, of which the Paris Commune was not only the most recent but certainly one of the most significant.

The Declaration of Independence, built upon the theories of the eighteenth-century philosophers and promulgated in 1774 [sic], was fulfilled in reality, according to Lavrov, only after six years of hard fighting. And such fulfillment was possible solely because of the "rare historical combination" of the necessary "individuals" and the correspondingly "satisfactory social environment." Hence the "historically pro-

[40] Soch.-Lavrov, II, 123–40.
[41] Ibid., pp. 125–26. Bakunin similarly considered the American Revolution "the cause of liberty against despotism," Oeuvres, IV, 289.

duced ideal" could be "achieved almost exactly as it was conceived." [42]

But, Lavrov noted with some emotion, "other dangers threatened the young state": the financial disorders of depreciated currency—the heritage of the Revolution—and the peril of military seizure of whatever state apparatus existed. There was "a moment in 1783," Lavrov declared, when the army was "prepared" to "revolt," and the "conquering leader" in a position to make himself "dictator . . . with the help of the army that was devoted to him." Here, however, "Washington's personality had a definitive, if not a decisive influence"; "he stopped the rebellious passions of the army by persuasion" and "calmly took leave of the troops who had been prepared to march with him." Lavrov insisted that Washington uniquely demonstrated the possibility of holding "a dictatorship in one's hands" and yet not abusing it. The Russian believed that America was fortunate in having such a man "in command" and an army capable of such restraint in that most difficult moment.[43]

However, apart from these abortive schemes of disgruntled army officers gathered at Newburgh, other troubles of this new nation still persisted. There were even greater difficulties in the years following the Peace. Tensions were enormous in the relations between the Congress of the Articles and the states. Further dangers of revolt and of dissolution loomed on the horizon. But at that moment, too, important "representatives of American thought"—Washington, Franklin, Madison, and Hamilton—"emerged with the project of a new constitution. After "Congress" had "de-

[42] *Soch.*-Lavrov, II, 126.
[43] *Ibid.*, pp. 127–28. Cf. Schlesinger, *New Viewpoints in American History*, pp. 185–86, for general corroboration of Lavrov's presentation of the financial and military problems of the new United States.

clared its lack of power to the nation in 1787 . . . the nation thoughtfully responded to this appeal in opposition to the ruling classes." Between 1787 and 1789, the new constitution was "worked out" and "exists to this day." Lavrov asserted that "this constitution placed the North American States in the first rank among the states of the world," for "it developed in them that political attractiveness" which has caused men "of all countries who are 'tired of Europe' " to migrate thither "to forget their nationality and their local problems . . . and to become simply Americans." Furthermore, the new constitution "produced in America tremendous political power and a high development of economic forces in the form of . . . free competition." More recently, it enabled the "Union republic to endure without difficulty the bloody war against the separatist slaveholders and the burdensome monetary crisis that stemmed from it." In summary, Lavrov declared, the constitution "caused" the United States "to approach the ideal of a constitutional state" as closely as is possible to "a . . . political entity with . . . inevitably coercive forms." [44]

Nevertheless, Lavrov went on to say, these splendid achievements of the heroic age of the American republic were now "exhausted" owing to the rise of a new factor. This was "the social evil" before which the "state form" revealed its impotence. As "constitutions and codices" were transformed into "empty formalities . . . the descendants of Washington and Adams . . . opened a public market place in the legislative chambers. . . ." And "the social question smashed, destroyed and buried the political creations of the revolutionary period." [45]

By contrast to the "program" of mere "political revolutions," the *Narodnik* sociologist found deeper satisfaction in

[44] *Soch.*-Lavrov, II, 128.   [45] *Ibid.*, p. 132.

the Cossack Pugachev's demands on behalf of the people for "liberty," "eternal freedom," and "the destruction of the landlords." For this revolutionary's manifestoes contained "more vital social elements, more . . . inevitably menacing prophecies for the future" than did "all the liberal and radical homilies directed against throne and altar" that were "circulated" along "the Thames, the Seine and the Delaware." And in Lavrov's estimation, the cardinal deficiency of "the warriors of the Enlightenment in Europe and America" was their failure "really" to "think of the needs and rights of the majority, . . . of the suffering masses." Lavrov concluded his comparison by asserting that "the Pugachev rising was an event with wider and more enduring meaning for the future than the Bostonian revolt." [46]

These passages form a well-rounded generalized view of America from the developmental and historical aspect. Apart from certain inaccuracies of dates (e.g., 1774 for the Declaration of Independence; 1787–89 as the years of the Constitutional Convention), Lavrov's essay offers an instructive parallelism between two contemporaneous events in the revolutionary history of Russia and the United States. The force of Lavrov's belief in the crucial historical importance of the idea and of the individual is revealed in his treatment both of the struggle for American independence and the personality and role of Washington in the immediate post-Revolutionary period. The identification of the American Revolution as the first violent overturn useful as an example for the "progressive" elements in nineteenth-century Europe is accurate if one overlooks the English Puritan Revolution.

What is perhaps surprising in a man who castigated latter-day America so scathingly was Lavrov's almost uncritical

[46] *Ibid.*, pp. 135–36, 139.

acceptance of the American constitution as a force for democratic progress and his almost casual placement of Franklin, Hamilton, and even Washington in a group which opposed the "ruling classes." One may certainly agree with Lavrov's assertion that the work of the Convention in 1787 really did open the door to great economic development in nineteenth-century America and did come to be regarded by most as the symbol of the greatest political liberties. Nonetheless the constitution was framed to oppose no "ruling class" (unless "King Mob"). And even with the addition of the first ten amendments it was still looked upon as a bulwark against the "danger" of that very spirit of "revolt" in the 1780's to which Lavrov so condescendingly alludes.[47] This viewpoint is startling in one who revered such elemental revolts as Pugachev's. In fact, it is almost superfluous to repeat that those who framed the new instrument of government for the United States were themselves the new ruling class of America, after having expelled by force of arms and with great sacrifice both the foreign overlord and the domestic Tory.

Hence the Russian's tribute to the origin and significance of the American constitution exhibits a certain political naïveté and over-generalization. This attitude may well be contrasted with his pessimistic extremism towards the America of the 1870's. To Lavrov's credit, however, the main facts of this story are present (if not always too accurately) and are dramatically unfolded. The theme of opposition to American slavery is also struck. Beyond this, Lavrov's dwell-

---

[47] Cf. Charles A. Beard, *An Economic Interpretation of the Constitution of the United States* (New York, 1914), for the classic confirmation of our view. Also cf. Merrill Jensen, *The Articles of Confederation* (Madison, Wis., 1940), who, writing in the Preface in defense of the Articles, insists that they "can be understood only in relation to the internal revolution in the American States."

ing upon the "social question," so reminiscent of Bakunin, will recur persistently. Finally his conclusions as to the greater social and historical significance of the Pugachev revolt in comparison with the American Revolution, from the point of view of a radical *Narodnik* of the 1870's, are not to be denied.

Lavrov looked upon post-Civil War America as a rather ugly place, characterized by the rule of money, whose sway was readily calculated to corrupt government. Economically, the well-known symptoms of capitalist disequilibria were prevalent, giving rise on a large scale to the "social problem." And Lavrov reacted to this state of affairs with all the more bitterness because of the great promise for political liberty and humane democracy which had been embodied in the Declaration of Independence. He, however, would probably have admitted that the American conditions which he found so objectionable could similarly be traced back to inadequacies in the program of the revolutionary thinkers of those earlier times.

In line with the beliefs held by most of his radical contemporaries—Proudhon was a notable exception— [48] Lavrov, as just observed, was opposed to Negro slavery in America and favored the Northern cause in the Civil War. But certain factors, principally the opportunity to observe a decade of Republican political supremacy after the war and the general perspective of ten years of corresponding development in American life, vitiated his near-complete partisanship for the Union side. In the *Historical Letters*, Lavrov wrote that the Southern states "had no right to assert themselves in opposition to a constitution that was the best . . . that history had as yet offered." He condemned the Southern

[48] J. Salwyn Schapiro, "Pierre Joseph Proudhon, Harbinger of Fascism, *American Historical Review*, L (July, 1945), p. 729.

separatists for setting only an "apologia of slavery" against
an instrument which would fully realize "the equal rights
of races." [49] Lavrov further asserted that the North fought
"against a minority" of the Southern population, which
"strove to maintain its power over the majority." And under
such circumstances, he declared, the struggle was justified
only if the North "genuinely" intended to better the position of "the oppressed majority." [50]

Lavrov's favorable disposition towards the American constitution in this case was unquestionably heightened by his
opposition to slavery and Southern particularism. His attitude to the Civil War and to "the equal rights of races" is
clearly defined; however, a frank discussion of how the
program of racial equality, even as embodied in the Constitution, was to be applied in practice, is lacking—perhaps
discreetly. Furthermore, it is difficult to tell whether in
speaking of equality, he meant a full economic and social
equality, or simply personal liberation, or even something
between the two.

Lavrov wrote, in 1875 in *Vpered,* a penetrating sketch of
the forces and events involved in the struggle over slavery.
Before the Civil War, it stated, the "slaveholders'" Democratic party "oppressed the North American States both in
Congress and in the Senate [*sic*]." Simultaneously, the
"Negrophile" Republicans "suffered a series of political defeats." Nonetheless, the Republican party "bore aloft the
banner of the idea of freedom for the enslaved race." It
"dispatched" John Brown "to arouse the slaves"; "produced"
Abraham Lincoln; "possessed a lofty political program; . . .
served a progressive idea"; and "it appeared to have played
a striking historical role in the development of humanity."
Possessing these virtues, Lavrov declared, "it succeeded in

[49] *Soch.*-Lavrov, I, 336.   [50] *Ibid.,* p. 337.

crushing its enemies and the enemies of the indivisibility of the Union."

But with the fall of the Confederacy, the triumphant Republicans "who had conquered in the name of an idea," revealed themselves as ordinary hypocrites, as "the most common despoilers of the conquered states; as the most ordinary exploiters of the country." In consequence, Lavrov asserted, "venality, plundering, indifference to the common welfare, speculation of the most variegated sort" were more conspicuous attributes of "the model republic" than "even of the decrepit states of Europe." The end product of the victory of "the leading political party in the freest state in the world" was "moral downfall" and political bankruptcy. Lavrov concluded vituperatively that "not one conscientious political idealist" could "now point to the United States as a political ideal. The triumph of the political unity of the American federation caused its historical dethronement." [51]

Lavrov seems to give rather too much credit to the moral level and fervor of the Republican party *ante bellum*. For it must be remembered that even in the election of 1860, the platform of the Republicans demanded only the closing of the territories to any further expansion of slavery. It is also a gross exaggeration to assert that the Republican party "dispatched" John Brown "to arouse the slaves" or even that it "produced" Lincoln. Furthermore, as Chernyshevski himself had pointed out earlier, the platform of the Republicans was by no means confined to the slavery issue, but also embraced enthusiastically such mundane planks as protective tariffs.

Thus as Northern arms triumphed over the Confederacy, it is somewhat less than surprising that the problem of Negro

[51] *Ibid.*, IV, 33–34.

emancipation should to some extent have been shelved.
For at least equally important to the Republican party was
the passage of measures directly favorable to its industrialist
and small farmer wings, measures which had formerly been
thwarted by the slave-holding Democrats in Congress. And
while it is true that corruption and bribery flourished in
Washington, and that speculation and exploitation of the
conquered South were rampant in the decade following Ap-
pomattox, there was also a bright side to this era. These
positive elements were certainly found in the work of many
of the Freedman's Bureaus, and in the personal honesty of
certain Radical Republican leaders, including Sumner and
Stevens. Even the intransigent Bakunin had noted with
favor the existence of positive elements in the Reconstruction period. Therefore one may agree only *generally* with
Lavrov's analysis of the changes and transformations in
American political life in the era of the Civil War.[52]

The Civil War provided a useful example for Lavrov when
he defined the field of sociological theory. What did the
sociologist "learn," he asked, from the "American Civil War"
—this war which "caused" such "fearful loss of men and
money in America, and . . . an economic crisis in Europe"?[53] Lavrov then contrasted the outlook of the sociologist and the historian towards "these events." "Within the
group of phenomena connected with the . . . American
Civil War, the sociologist" would "discover . . . a series of
examples for *general laws* of the different branches of social

[52] For a bitter commentary on attempts by extremist Southerners to sup-
press the newly emancipated Negroes by violence after the Civil War, cf.
Vpered, no. 42 (Oct. 1, 1876), pp. 611–12. At the same time Lavrov was
also conscious of the very real danger to the United States of persisting
separatist feelings after the War. He urged that the "goal of progress" in
this connection lay in stifling these tendencies, *Soch.*-Lavrov, I, 320.

[53] *Soch.*-Lavrov, I, 181.

life." An historian, on the other hand, would regard these "events" as "isolated phenomenon[s] . . . observed once," and ones that in their "very totality and complexity" did "not admit of recurrences." [54]

It is unfortunate that Lavrov offered no specific examples from this war to clarify his definition of sociology as the science of recurrent phenomena in contradistinction to the discipline of history, which dealt with non-recurrent phenomena. [55]

The pattern of Lavrov's attitude towards the state and public life in America revealed certain ambiguities, as in the case of most of the Russian radicals under consideration. On the one hand, he rejected the republican state as an instrument of coercion and exploitation essentially no different from any absolutist type. Grudgingly and infrequently, he admitted, however, that a republican state did have some benefit for the masses, if only political liberty. Though Lavrov of course believed the infant American state offered much promise to humanity, he felt that the contemporary United States in no way accorded with Herzen's sporadic feeling that an American "exceptionalism" existed. In fact Lavrov desired to *combat* such tendencies of thought. The task of the socialist movement in America was, as he saw it, to organize, grow, and finally to smash the exploiting capitalist state. And curiously enough, the *Narodnik* sociologist was far more determined on this subject than the volatile and vociferous enemy of the state, Bakunin.

In 1876, Lavrov wrote that America, together with Switzerland and France, possessed "more democratic constitu-

[54] *Ibid.*, p. 182.
[55] Cf. Masaryk, *op. cit.*, II, 119–20, for an incisive critique of this view of sociology and history.

tions" than did other countries.[56] He also reluctantly conceded the existence, if not the effectiveness, of a public opinion in America. Moreover, this force would be strong enough in the "future society" to deal with such anti-social phenomena as "judge lynch in America." [57]

On the important question of the efficacy of American federalism, that great issue in mid-nineteenth-century socialist thought, Lavrov did acknowledge the real worth of the American experiment. He declared this experiment in federalism to represent "the widest . . . attempt . . . in history" so far "to unite a strong governmental state unit . . . with as full an independence as possible of the provincial centers." The federated "units," however, were "still too large" for the people to participate universally in the "most important functions of the political life of a state [unit]." Hence the American federal union offered "no guarantee that the whole population" of such "a state would consider itself in actual solidarity with . . . the constitution" of the central state. In other words, Lavrov criticized the United States for still possessing too many attributes of the *unitary* state. Indeed, he advocated the devolution of "many elements . . . to local centers." This, he believed, could be accomplished "without loss of the ability of the whole Union to act as a single governmental entity." In contrast to the American system, Lavrov asserted, the Paris Commune had pointed the way to a higher program of political federation "with a more significant share of self-government for local centers." [58]

Lavrov's adverse criticism of the relatively minor role of the population at large in the affairs of the federal govern-

[56] *Vpered, Nep.*, vol. IV, part I, p. 2.
[57] *Ibid.*, p. 62.
[58] *Soch.*-Lavrov, I, 323.

ment and even of the states is one of the most telling criticisms of the American governmental system. In modern democracies an unhealthy gulf exists, which almost invariably separates the elected representatives of the people from their constituents, even granting the dubious premise that universal suffrage is really universal. Yet the venality of American public life against which Lavrov so constantly inveighed was partly a result of that famous system of "rotation in office," originally one of Andrew Jackson's means of minimizing the gap between electorate and government.

At the same time Lavrov neglected the fact that there were many areas in the United States where local self-government persisted with the active participation of the citizenry, despite the rapid growth of the political machine and the rising influence of the immigrant in this period. Yet even the growth of machine politics brought many to participate in government, albeit in a perverted and distorted manner.[59] Aside from the unfortunate separation between voters and deputies, the net effect of the American federal system seems to have impressed Lavrov. And the "program" of the Paris Commune which the *Narodnik* sociologist counterpoised to the American federal union was actually no program at all. He himself admitted that it remained stillborn because of "war conditions" and could not even be dignified by the name of "political experiment." [60]

But this was the high-water mark of Lavrov's regard for the American political order. Complete rejection now came

---

[59] The question of immigrant responsibility for political corruption is, however, another matter. Cf. A. M. Schlesinger, "The Rise of the City: 1878–1898," *A History of American Life,* ed. A. M. Schlesinger and D. R. Fox (New York, 1933), X, 392, "The immigrant was often blamed for the sorry condition of affairs, but outside New York City, the bosses and grafting politicians were usually of native stock."

[60] *Soch.*-Lavrov, I, 323.

to the fore. And his consequent denunciations of "senile" constitutional monarchies and parliamentary bourgeois republics in Europe and America fall in with those by now familiar to the reader.[61] "The contemporary state has become a tool of the bourgeois order and is decaying under the influence of the development of that order." [62] The fundamental thing which all governments have and have had in common, including the American government, has been the element of force and coercion. "One part of the population" has always "imposed its decisions upon another part in a compulsory way." [63]

In 1872, four years before his acknowledgment of the existence of a "more democratic constitution" in America, Lavrov had thundered that "no difference" existed between "monarchies, aristocrats, constitutionalists, republicans, dictators, demagogues." At that same time he asserted sweepingly that "governmental power was . . . the same in all forms," "a beast of prey that devoured the people; a mechanism for their intellectual torpor" and "economic ruin"; an instrument "for the exploitation of millions in favor of the few." [64]

A negative and more penetrating critique of American governmental institutions was contained in Lavrov's ob-

---

[61] *Ibid.*, II, 8.

[62] *Vpered. Nep.*, vol. IV, part I, p. 42. Also cf. *ibid.*, p. 194, for Lavrov's quotation from Tom Paine's *Common Sense*, " 'Society in any form is a good, but government, even the best, is a necessary evil only; the worst is an unbearable evil.' "

[63] *Ibid.*, p. 13.

[64] *Soch.*-Lavrov, III, 99. Cf. also *ibid.*, I, 318 ("Historical Letters") and *ibid.*, IV, 15, for two of many examples of heavy sarcasm at the expense of the political institutions of "free America." These generalized attacks extended to American foreign policy as well. Cf. *ibid.*, I, 329, for condemnation—even more sweeping than Bakunin at his most intransigent—of the "North American democracy" in what Lavrov termed its unrestrained quest for "natural boundaries."

servation that whereas one could "calmly discuss tariffs and loans in the parliaments of Europe and America," it was, however, "impossible" to engage in "a radical discussion of the question of wealth distribution." In elaboration of this argument, Lavrov declared that while "debates on the responsibility of ministers" were "permissible," the "replacement of one dynasty by another or the shift from a monarchical government to a republican" could "occur only by means of revolution." In short, he insisted that whereas internal class relations were "subject to examination, the essence of these relations" could "not be touched upon." [65]

Whatever objections may be raised against specific charges in these passages, Lavrov's basic assertions about the underlying pre-suppositions and restrictions upon debate in any republican or constitutional monarchical parliament may not be questioned—at least up to the most recent times.

One important explanation for Lavrov's bitterness towards American political institutions is undoubtedly the great corruption which existed in the national government during the immediate post-Civil War years. This situation, almost completely overlooked by the fiery Bakunin a little earlier, touched off a series of attacks by Lavrov against the "venality" of American public life. Typical was his denunciation of "the great American republic," where seats in "Congress and the Senate [sic]," as well as "the judges on the bench" all had "their market price." [66] But the United States was not alone in this respect; interestingly enough, Lavrov joined Russia to "the great American republic" when making this charge of corruption in public life. He asserted that "perhaps nowhere else in the world (with the possible excep-

[65] *Ibid.*, I, 209.

[66] *Vpered, Nep.*, vol. IV, part I, p. 32. Cf. also *Soch.*-Lavrov, IV, 79, for a similar arraignment of "venality."

tion of the North American States) . . ." had "fraudulent
stock-jobbing reached the position" it had currently attained "in Russia under the patronage of the higher state
dignitaries and the princes of the imperial house." [67]

Lavrov, however, did not limit himself to generalities when
denouncing American venality, but hurled specific accusations against the Grant Administration. The Russian asserted
that "not one cabinet member" or "high official" existed in
"Grant's government" who "could not have been prosecuted
for forgery, embezzlement . . . and the sale of offices." Indeed, "the president himself was delivered from the sad
necessity of figuring in court" only because of the aid of
"those officials" who retained "some . . . honesty and brav-
ery." And Lavrov was forced to the pessimistic conclusion
that "bribery at the elections" and "misappropriation of
monies" in favor of the reigning political party was "a common and even a very honorable thing" in America.[68]

In like manner, Lavrov wondered cynically if this were
really the end product of that Civil War fought ostensibly
for such high purposes; for which so many thousands of men
had perished on both sides. His attitude truly represented
the nadir of feelings generated by the American Civil War,
a far cry from the inspired enthusiasm of Chernyshevski.

In a final generalization, Lavrov linked the decay of American political institutions after the Civil War with the then
triumphant and expanding system of industrial enterprise in

[67] *Vpered, Nep.*, vol. V, part I, p. 114.

[68] *Vpered*, no. 42 (Oct. 1, 1876), p. 611. For the corruption of the Grant
Administration and municipal corruption, cf. James Ford Rhodes, *History of
the United States*, VI (New York and London, 1899–1906), 247–57, 392–
410; Don C. Seitz, *The Dreadful Decade* (Indianapolis, 1926), pp. 51–137,
158–233, 260–92. For a rather devastating picture of President Grant, cf.
The Education of Henry Adams [original publication date, 1918], pp.
260–67.

America. He declared in 1875 that the single controversial "issue" left between the two bankrupt old parties in the United States was "the question of payment of governmental obligations in gold or in paper." There was no doubt in Lavrov's mind that "as the money kings, the real tsars and legislators of our time," constantly expanded "the domains of speculation, . . . the representatives of the old political and social forces" were revealed "to be ever weaker, ever more insignificant." [69]

Perhaps Lavrov dismissed too readily the importance of the "sound money" issue both in regard to politics and in relation to the new disposition of industrial capitalism in America. In any case, in these strictures one may observe Herzen's attack upon the baneful role of money in American life brought up to date.[70] That Lavrov's accusations were mainly true for that period is not to be denied.[71] And the Russian's attack upon the "money kings" was not to cease at this point; for in discussing the "economic question" in America, he reached even more resounding crescendos.

[69] Soch.-Lavrov, IV, 205.

[70] Also cf. ibid., IV, 195, for another expression of such views.

[71] Cf. Matthew Josephson, The Robber Barons . . . 1861–1901 (New York, 1934); The Politicos, 1865–1896 (New York, 1938), for colorful confirmation of this process.

CHAPTER IX

"The Freest of Free Constitutions"

PETER LAVROV (concluded)

THE American labor movement harmonized with Lavrov's intransigent views on the "economic question"; and appropriately enough, it concerned him particularly during the period that witnessed his closest approach to Marxism. Quantitatively, the labor issue accounted for a high percentage of Lavrov's published references to American problems. In *Vpered*, for example, a *Chronicle of the Labor Movement* and a *Chronicle of Struggle* always appeared. These two features were carried to report constructive achievements in the working-class struggle throughout the world and to contrast them with "the chaos of bourgeois civilization." In these reports, the progress of the American working class occupied a prominent place.

Lavrov was diligent in reporting every American strike and labor disturbance to the readers of *Vpered*, and ample material was available since *Vpered* was published in the midst of the "great depression" of 1873. In the very first number, for example, appeared a closely written and detailed account of dockers' strikes in New York, Brooklyn, Jersey City, and Hoboken.[1] In the next issue there was a detailed, grim but optimistic presentation of the strike of the Pittsburgh iron founders. This account was continued in the following issue of *Vpered*, and there Lavrov's optimism

[1] *Vpered*, no. 1 (June 15, 1875), p. 31.

gave way to sober realization that the strike would probably be defeated. Strikes from such scattered places as Fall
River, San Francisco, and Jersey City were also recorded.[2]
The "long strike" of the anthracite coal miners in the spring
and summer of 1875 was the most dramatic manifestation of
American workers' discontent in that year and it, too, was
faithfully reviewed in *Vpered*.[3]

All of these accounts contained a detailed summary of the
facts, derived usually from one or more radical foreign-
language newspapers published in America and having contact with the First International; for example, *Vorbote*.
Lavrov also relied upon secondary sources of information
like the *Bulletin de la Fédération Jurasienne*. In discussing
America's strikes, he usually was ardent, sometimes sentimental; and frequently coupled with his uncompromising
sympathy towards the strikers was a pronounced optimistic faith in their success—success which possibly would have
revolutionary implications. Such an attitude usually gave
way to sober realism in the face of approaching defeat, for
most if not all of these strikes were unsuccessful. The lesson
then drawn by Lavrov was that the American worker was
as much exploited as any European worker—that his conditions and problems were identical with those of the European labor movement.

The anthracite coal strike of 1875, which Lavrov followed with intense interest, illustrates these reactions. When

[2] *Vpered*, no. 2 (Feb. 1, 1875), pp. 62–63; no. 3 (Feb. 15, 1875),
pp. 93–94. Other American strikes chronicled by Lavrov may be found in
ibid., no. 7 (April 15, 1875), pp. 221–23; no. 9 (May 15, 1875), pp. 280–
82; no. 23 (Dec. 15, 1875), pp. 732–33; no. 29 (March 15, 1876),
pp. 159–60.

[3] Cf. *Vpered*, no. 6 (April 1, 1875), pp. 189–90; no. 8 (May 1, 1875),
pp. 254–55; no. 9 (May 15, 1875), p. 285; no. 12 (July 1, 1875), p. 383;
no. 13 (July 15, 1875), pp. 413–15; no. 14 (Aug. 1, 1875), pp. 443–44.

first discussed within the pages of *Vpered,* the story reported the basic facts of extensive wage reductions and general hardship and suffering among the miners prior to their strike. This was fortified by a quotation from *Vorbote:* "The workers decided that it is better to die fighting than to work starving." Lastly the solidarity of the striking workers was noted.[4] One month later Lavrov emphasized that "the Pennsylvania coal miners' strike, or . . . more accurately, the war of the Pennsylvania workers against the coal tsars, has erupted ever more fiercely."[5] After the governor of Pennsylvania had issued a proclamation warning the miners to cease their "illegal" activity and return to work, Lavrov exclaimed with some emotion that "the republican government . . . openly stood on the side of the exploiters . . . against the hungry workers." As a result of such governmental action, Lavrov freely predicted "the hastening of a general explosion."[6] By mid-July, however, he was summarizing the course of the strike, had practically conceded defeat, and was already drawing lessons from it. It was "not very probable" that the strikers could "force the bosses to retract the twenty per cent wage reduction." On the contrary, it seemed "more probable" to him that the workers would be "driven again into the mines by hunger pangs and bayonets," despite their "daring and energetic six months' struggle." But "whatever the outcome," Lavrov asserted, the "significance" of this strike would not be diminished "by a hair." For this strike furnished a "brilliant," "self-evident" and "characteristic" illustration of "the predatory nature of the capitalist order." Indeed, "the lesson of the Pennsylvania strike" demonstrated fully that "in

[4] *Vpered,* no. 6 (April 1, 1875), p. 189.
[5] *Ibid.,* no. 8 (May 1, 1875), p. 254.
[6] *Ibid.*

the richest country in the world, with the freest of free constitutions . . . the American worker" was "as much a slave
as the German, the Russian and any other." [7] And in the
next issue, Lavrov concluded definitively that "the strike of
the Pennsylvania coal miners has actually been ended by
the defeat of the workers." [8]

Lavrov's prognosis of the course of this particular strike,
optimistic as it was, was more reserved than in the case of
most others with which he dealt because of the really for-
midable combination of coal company, railroad, newspaper,
and state government opposition to the miners. This was,
however, a good example of the pattern of Lavrov's treatment of strikes in the United States, whether they involved
textile workers in Fall River or Chinese tailors in San
Francisco.

Lavrov's factual background of the strikes was generally
accurate except for exaggerations as to the number of people
involved and the possibilities of the workers' winning. But
certain exaggerations were inevitable, perhaps, since all of
Lavrov's sources were radical publications partisan to the
strikers. In any case, Lavrov's alertness to the affairs of the
American working class is clearly demonstrated. Far more
significant, however, was the moral which this uncompromising revolutionary reiterated: America was not a source
of hope for either European workers or socialists and
America was far from unique. Indeed, American exploitation was no better (and possibly was worse) than that found
elsewhere. For this reason "maximalist" socialist tactics were
to be pursued in the North American republic as well as in
Europe. It is striking, too, that the Russian Populist considered the American working class to be the dynamic

[7] *Ibid.*, no. 13 (July 15, 1875), pp. 414–15.
[8] *Ibid.*, no. 14 (Aug. 1, 1875), p. 444.

revolutionary force rather than the American farmer—who, one may note, was contemporaneously organizing into the Greenback Party. For the latter there was hardly a word in all of Lavrov's published writings.

The strength of Lavrov's denial of any American singularity in regard to the exploitation of the working class by capital was constant even in the face of the opinions of his radical friends who sojourned in the United States. Taking issue with some of the opinions expressed by William Frey, who had written a long expository letter to *Vpered* about the American social and economic scene from his settlement in Cedar Vale, Lavrov insisted that "in America conditions of class hatred and class struggle are exactly the same as in the Old World." [9] Lavrov believed, in fact, that the United States had entered upon the "fatal process" of capitalist development and maladjustment under conditions similar to those of the advanced countries of Western Europe as early as the decade of the thirties.[10] Furthermore, he pointedly observed to his "respected colleague" who directed the Russian Utopian colony in Kansas, that in 1873, American workers were in no position to conduct Utopian "experiments." On the contrary, they could only "prepare themselves for battle with their exploiters for a slice of bread . . . and for the future of the working class." [11]

Such attitudes were pursued to even greater extremes. After the failure of the Fall River textile workers' strike in the autumn of 1875, Lavrov mocked bitterly at Lincoln's

[9] *Vpered, Nep.,* vol. III, part I, pp. 124–25.

[10] *Ibid.,* vol. II, part I, p. 179.

[11] *Ibid.,* vol. III, part I, p. 125. Also cf. *Vpered,* no. 1 (Jan. 15, 1875), p. 4: "The working population suffers everywhere from the Danube to the Far West of the American republic." Other expressions of this kind may be found in *ibid.,* no. 5 (March 15, 1875), pp. 153–55; *Vpered, Nep.,* vol. III, part III, p. 129, and *Soch.*-Lavrov, IV, 165.

famous dictum of "government of the people, by the people and for the people." This government, he declared sarcastically, was rather "the submissive servant of the capitalists and the mortal enemy of the workers." He insisted that one factor alone distinguished the American trinity of "capital, the courts and the army" from its European counterparts: In the United States, "the bourgeois" acted "openly." They had "no crowned allies like their brothers in Europe." But this, he asserted, was to the good. For the American worker "has no need to seek out his enemy; he is present and at hand."[12]

Closely related to these convictions were Lavrov's warnings directed to those "tired of Europe" to stay away from the false "promised land." This was in sharp contrast to many earlier Russian radicals' views. America, in Lavrov's opinion, was not to be the source of consolation for the disillusioned European socialist. He even tried to influence the course of migration back upon itself, or at least remarked with triumph the return to Europe of immigrants dissatisfied with conditions in the New World. "Let us take a look . . . at that 'promised land,'" he wrote, "where those who are 'tired of Europe' rush so." Thereupon he quoted several unpleasant facts from *Arbeiter-Zeitung* and *Volksstaat* on the widespread character of unemployment, woman and child labor, and unhealthy conditions of work, prevalent at that time of great depression in the chief cities of the eastern seaboard. After this description Lavrov again reminded his readers: "Evidently the exploiters beyond the seas do not lag even a half-step behind their European kinsmen." He bitterly deplored the fact that "nevertheless, ship after ship" sailed from Europe "bearing . . . people . . . filled to excess with suffering," who "naïvely" expected to

[12] *Vpered*, no. 23 (Dec. 15, 1875), pp. 732–33.

find "a different life in the New World." Finally Lavrov castigated the "clever swindlers" who organized "special gangs" to "scurry around among the European proletariat," taking advantage of their "suffering" and "naïveté," to "sell them into servitude to the American exploiters." [13]

Yet, a reverse trend was growing, he believed, because of the painful realities of "suffering" which so many immigrants had discovered in American life. This was evident in the "movement . . . constantly increasing in strength" of "those . . . 'tired of America,' " who were "returning to Europe." These people, "formerly 'tired of Europe,' " were "returning" now "even more poverty-stricken," if that were possible, than when they "had forsaken her." And Lavrov added grimly, "Let them return . . . we need fighting forces . . . we need merciless avengers." [14]

Lavrov knew well the vulnerable places in the American immigration system of post-Civil War days. The great abuses of this traffic of directed migration under the contract system, caused principally by a desire for cheap labor, for passenger fares and to sell land, combined with the widespread suffering and discontent among the laboring masses of America in the years of the great depression of 1873 and after, to offer a fertile field for his probing eye.

It is undoubtedly true that the hardships of migration to America were then severe, and that many tens of thousands of immigrants did return to Europe, but at least conditions of Atlantic passage had improved with the change from sail to steam power. And despite all suffering and hardship, the bulk of the now vastly increasing stream of immigrants did remain in the United States.[15] Furthermore Lavrov himself

---

[13] *Ibid.*, no. 1 (Jan. 15, 1875), pp. 29–30.

[14] *Ibid.* Also cf. *ibid.*, no. 2 (Feb. 1, 1875), p. 59.

[15] The law of 1864 which permitted the importation of immigrants under a contract to work was not finally repealed until 1885, and even after this

recognized, just as Herzen and Chernyshevski had, the rapid process by which European immigrants were transformed under conditions of American life—conditions that would cause many difficulties in reversing the immigration process. He declared that "the isolation of nationality" was "removed" where the state approached "ideal" standards even remotely. And to support this statement he pointed to the United States, where "immigrants from the whole world become simple Americans in the second and sometimes even in the first generation." [16]

Lavrov took an active interest in the work of the moribund First International, stricken first in 1871 and again in 1872. Despite the tendency to display greater realism in regard to this organization than Bakunin had, Lavrov's revolutionary faith in the International was constant even unto its formal dissolution in 1876. "Many may have been broken and have died," he wrote defiantly in 1874; nevertheless, "the International is alive, . . . whole," and "ready for battle." [17]

Although Lavrov usually sided with the Marxian "centralists," he thought their decision in 1872 to remove the

---

date the new law was badly enforced. Cf. H. P. Fairchild, *Immigration* (New York, 1913), pp. 274–80, for a brief but lucid description of the padrone and contract labor systems in the period following the Civil War. Also cf. *ibid.*, p. 91, for the shift from sailing to steam vessels and its importance for the immigrant. For the main facts of immigration legislation in the second half of the nineteenth century, cf. H. U. Faulkner, *American Economic History* (New York and London, 1924), pp. 612–14. One authority has noted the "balancing" of the immigration movement in the nineteenth century by that of emigration from the United States. This same source tends to discount the belief that immigrants were "imported" in large numbers by capitalists; I. A. Hourwich, *Immigration and Labor* (New York and London, 1912), pp. 3–4.

[16] *Soch.*-Lavrov, I, 336.

[17] *Vpered, Nep.*, vol. III, part III, p. 107.

International's headquarters to New York City was unwise. After the expulsion of the Bakuninist "federalists" this step would, in Lavrov's opinion, weaken the International even more. "The centralists by this move themselves destroyed the influence of their central institution for Europe without attaching strength to it in America." [18] Lavrov considered American industrial development as "advanced" as England's in this period and important to the labor movement, but this did not alter the fact that the United States was far removed from the Western European labor scene in terms of transportation and communication.[19] Hence removal to New York, he believed correctly, cut the International off from the main stream of socialism.[20] Four years later, the International did collapse, yet during its brief existence in America, "the International . . . unquestionably . . . dominated the labor movement in New York City"—so Samuel Gompers has written in his colorful memoirs. [21]

Lavrov devoted much attention to the activities of those small, sectarian groups still dignified by the term "American Section of the International," after the disappearance of the National Labor Union at the outbreak of the economic crisis of 1873. In this case, his somewhat self-contradictory belief that the splits and conflicts which beset the International in America would have no lasting harmful effects upon the proletarian movement of America was illusory.[22] Here Lavrov's revolutionary optimism paralleled Bakunin's

[18] *Ibid.,* p. 53.

[19] *Soch.*-Lavrov, II, 267. Elsewhere Lavrov expressed the opinion that "in no country in the world has the development of industry forged ahead so rapidly as in the United States"; *Vpered, Nep.,* vol. II, part I, p. 179.

[20] *Soch.*-Lavrov, II, 302–3, 317–18.

[21] Gompers, *Seventy Years of Life and Labor* (New York, 1925), I, 60; copyright, 1925, E. P. Dutton & Co.

[22] Cf. *Soch.*-Lavrov, II, pp. 255–56.

exaggerated confidence when the latter was confronted by a similar situation.

The *Narodnik* sociologist, indefatigable to the end, even found enthusiasm for the new Workingmen's Party of the United States.[23] It was painful coincidence that the final issue of *Vpered* to be published under Lavrov's guardianship reprinted "the last word of the Centralist International," which met in Philadelphia in July, 1876. Lavrov responded to this event with outer fortitude but ill-concealed inner despondency.[24]

The catholicity of Lavrov's approach to the American labor movement was indeed noteworthy. In the period when the Negro in the South was frequently beaten back to a state of semi-slavery and when the Chinese on the West Coast were looked upon with great hostility by American labor, Lavrov ardently defended these depressed groups. He asserted that the labor movement recognized no "ethnic and racial" differences. On the one hand it embraced "the Negroes of America," on the other it called "the Southern Slavs to the social struggle." [25]

Shortly thereafter, Lavrov greeted with delight the protest movements of Negro workers in Washington and the

[23] This party was organized in Philadelphia in 1876 by a group of dissident socialists who had left the International in 1874. The Workingmen's Party came into being almost on the very morning after the International expired. The new organization was Lassallean in its approach to socialism. Its platform included such demands as the eight-hour day and the establishment of workers' coöperatives. In 1879, it is estimated that its total membership was ten thousand, of whom ninety percent was foreign born. Cf. *Vpered*, no. 40 (Sept. 1, 1876), pp. 549–51, and Anthony Bimba, *History of the American Working Class* (New York, 1927), pp. 163–65.

[24] *Vpered*, no. 48 (Dec. 31, 1876), pp. 811–12.

[25] *Ibid.*, no. 2 (Feb. 1, 1875), p. 36. On American labor's hostility to the Chinese, cf. Bimba, *op. cit.*, p. 159. Local members of the Workingmen's Party, however, apparently took no part in the widespread anti-Chinese rioting of 1877 in San Francisco.

strike of Chinese tailors in San Francisco. "Even the colored workers little by little are beginning to be stirred," [26] he declared.

In discussing the American labor movement, Lavrov emphasized his belief that a socialist revolution was just as necessary in the New World as in the Old and equally desirable as well; and he pointed out the proletariat as the primary social group to effect this fundamental change. The influence of Marxism upon Lavrov's thought is clearly revealed here.

The most overt expression of these convictions was contained in Lavrov's passionate greeting to "the socialist workers of America." The entire editorial board of *Vpered* and two Slavic revolutionary groups joined him in sponsoring this message at the centenary of the American republic. The first part of this greeting lauded Jefferson and the Declaration of Independence. An attack followed, in a manner already familiar, upon the corrupting role of money in the United States, and such speculators as Jay Gould and "Jim" Fiske. It continued with an exposure of what the writers termed the sham freedom of the American proletariat. Lavrov then declared that just as "the exploiters of all countries" were gathered together in Philadelphia for the "peaceful celebration of wealth and luxury, . . . the workers of all countries" were assembled "to celebrate" the coming "social revolution." He asserted that "Europe and America . . . together" would "prepare this day" of "victory." And he

---

[26] *Vpered*, no. 14 (Aug. 1, 1875), p. 444. Lavrov was especially pleased at the strike of the Chinese tailors because he understood that the Chinese were the lowest-paid workers in that region of America and were "the most dangerous competitors for the local workers." For this reason, their continued docility in the face of a depressed wage scale could only lead to a growing resentment of the American workers—which indeed did occur a few years later.

assured his American "brothers" that whereas "the republic of the past belonged to the rich . . . the republic of the
future" would "belong to the working proletariat." [27]

This flaming optimism for the prospects of socialism in
America was expressed at almost the same time that the First
International was dissolved; and like Bakunin's statement
under analogous circumstances, it was an expression of
revolutionary desperation.[28]

In the same year, Lavrov emphasized in more sober terms
the theory of the primacy of the proletariat in the revolutionary movement. But he confined this role of proletarian
hegemony to Western Europe and the United States in
contradistinction to conditions of struggle in Russia. "The
main element," he declared which unified "the labor movement in the countries of German, Anglo-Saxon, Scandinavian and Romance languages" was "the factory proletariat"; the "agricultural proletariat" in these regions either
was "not touched at all by the movement" or played only
"a secondary role" in it. In "Slavic lands," however, and
"especially in Russia," the peasantry possessed "a significance altogether different"; the "organization of a socially
revolutionary group" had "to conform to this peculiarity."
Therefore, Lavrov continued, just as the task in Russia con-
sisted of creating "solidarity" among the widely dispersed
suffering population, in precisely the same way, "all the
forces of the social revolutionaries in Europe and America"
had to "strive" to turn this "labor movement" into "*one* international struggle of the organized proletariat . . . against
its exploiters." "This goal," he asserted, "was definitely es-

[27] *Vpered*, no. 37 (July 15, 1876), p. 453.
[28] This was by no means an isolated example of Lavrov's glowing faith
in the possibility of American socialism within the measurable future. Cf.
Vpered, Nep., vol. III, part II, p. 224, and *Soch.*-Lavrov, IV, 171.

tablished almost thirty years ago in . . . the *Communist Manifesto* . . . This goal was near to realization in the International Workers' Association of 1864." [29]

The influence of Marxism upon *Narodnik* theories as applied to Europe and America, but not to Russia, is readily apparent in Lavrov's assignment of a primary role to the "factory proletariat" in the class struggle, and relegation of the "agricultural proletariat" to a "secondary" position. Indeed Lavrov freely cited the *Communist Manifesto*. Equally, if not more interesting, is that Lavrov raised no question as to America's part in the achievement of socialism. Unlike Herzen, he made not the slightest attempt to couple America with Russia in the socialist struggle, but maintained that the fate of socialism in America was dependent upon the same forces operative in all the advanced countries of Western Europe.[30]

Within the whole complex of Lavrov's views towards the labor movement and socialism in America, attitudes of this character occur explicitly and abundantly. Only Bakunin before him appears to have dealt at any length with this issue of the proletariat's role in effecting socialism. For Herzen the social question in the United States was really the issue of Negro slavery, and for Chernyshevski the question of slavery certainly overshadowed the problems of American labor.

America for Lavrov appeared as an advanced capitalist

[29] *Vpered, Nep.*, vol. IV, part I, p. 191.

[30] Interestingly enough, energy and individual initiative were traits that Lavrov considered peculiarly American. He believed they would prove highly valuable in removing the pragmatic difficulties encountered by a socialist order "on the morrow of the revolution." At that present moment, however, Lavrov asserted angrily, "this energetic, individualistic activity" is "manifested in abominable forms: judge lynch hangs the thief or the bandit." *Vpered, Nep.*, vol. IV, part I, p. 125.

state with all the economic problems and dislocations common to the states of Western Europe. Significantly too, in contrast to the views of the earlier Russian radicals, Lavrov devoted no attention whatever to the American frontier and the "safety valve" theory. America, in his estimation, was no longer a land of hope, nor unique refuge for the tired European radical or the mass of potential immigrants. Rather, it was a fertile area in its own right for the attainment of a socialist order. And this order, as qualified by Lavrov, was to be neither the Utopian variety of Frey or Chaikovski, nor the agrarian socialism of the Russian *Narodniki*, but one almost Marxian in its stress upon the industrial proletariat. The peculiarly Russian *Narodnik* element was the emphasis laid upon the attainment of "maximalist" goals within a relatively short time.

Lavrov's analysis of the American situation in terms of the labor problem, though largely sound, was unbalanced, since he observed this phase of American life during a time of great depression which inevitably intensified existing contradictions in the nation's society. Then, too, the frontier was still a factor to be reckoned with, as may be illustrated by the fact that modern pragmatic trade unionism with its primary concern for equitable hours, wages, and conditions of work did not enter the picture until 1886 with the formation of the American Federation of Labor. Beyond this, America, notwithstanding all adverse factors, was able to absorb large numbers of immigrants even to the end of the century and later. And their general political conservatism may be taken as an indication that conditions in the New World were significantly better than in the Old World. Finally, Lavrov's cosmopolitan revolutionary impulses blinded him to the fact that socialism in America—no matter

what labor disturbances there were—was not really on the
agenda for that generation. This was especially true after
the disintegration of the First International.

Logically enough, Lavrov was a firm believer in the equality of the sexes. His belief in women's rights was most probably founded on Chernyshevski's well-known convictions;
joined with these were the teachings of Saint Simon, Georges
Sand, and John Stuart Mill, all of whom held advanced
views on the "woman question." The general revolutionary
desire to shatter all social barriers, as in Herzen's case, played
its part here, too. Lavrov observed first that "the movement
that is now called the woman question arose in Europe and
America outside of any relation to workers' socialism. These
two movements were "linked together . . . only . . . in
Russia," but even there "more empirically than in a strictly
scientific way." [31]

Lavrov was quite right in asserting that the "woman
question" in America was not linked to the movement for
"workers' socialism." It was, however, a concern of many reformers who were active before the Civil War. After that
conflict and with the seeming solution of the slavery issue,
a transfer of the reforming impulse took place with such
issues as the "woman question" receiving stronger attention.
But it was still not linked with the issue of "workers' socialism" except, possibly, in the thought of Wendell Phillips.[32]

Then when Alexander II issued a decree directing Russian
women students to return home from the Swiss universities,

[31] Vpered, Nep., vol. III, part I, p. 62, and Soch.-Lavrov, II, 196.

[32] Cf. A. M. Schlesinger, New Viewpoints in American History (New
York, 1922), pp. 126–59. On Wendell Phillips and the labor movement, cf.
V. L. Parrington, Main Currents in American Thought (New York, 1927),
II, 256 and III, 140–47; also Encyclopaedia of the Social Sciences, XII,
117–18.

Lavrov wrote irately that those Russian women were seriously intent on receiving not "the very limited diploma of midwife" but the "fullest . . . rights of medical practice." Similarly "in America," he asserted, "the movement for the emancipation of woman has long been going on . . . women are striving for equality of medical rights." [33]

Lavrov's observations on the "woman question" in the United States were generalities offering none of Chernyshevski's specific detail and incisiveness on this subject. The same can be said of his observations on the American periodical press. In a sense, the press served Lavrov as merely an illustration of what concrete advantages a politically liberal government might possess. He declared that the periodical press in the infant "liberal-bourgeois states," the United States and France, had "an enormous role" assigned to it as a "bar" of public opinion, as a "check to force," and as a "banner" of progress. And "with this significance it went over into the nineteenth century." However, by the "second quarter" of that century, the periodical press "became more and more a weapon in the struggle of the new forces guiding events." The newspapers became predominantly "speculative enterprises in the hands of competing capitalists." [34]

This view of the American press despite over-schematization coincided with Lavrov's general views on the historical transformation of republican government and political liberty in the United States. Elsewhere he did concede, however, that "the organs of the Social Democratic party in America" might, because of "the conditions of free speech

[33] Soch.-Lavrov, II, 10. The first woman in America to receive a diploma in medicine was Elizabeth Blackwell, in 1848; Schlesinger, New Viewpoints . . . , p. 141. It is certainly a social reality that this "equality of medical rights" for women has still not been completely attained in the United States.

[34] Vpered, no. 40 (Sept. 1, 1876), p. 524.

. . . express themselves more directly and frankly than . . . the socialist press of Bismarck's Empire." [35]

This is one of the few instances where contemporary America was not denigrated by Lavrov as a decadent country. With a free press, the republican United States definitely offered favorable opportunities for furthering the socialist end, opportunities not to be found under absolutist or semi-absolutist regimes.

Lavrov's acquaintance with certain outstanding American literary figures of the last century has already been mentioned. It should also be noted that he had alert critical judgments on American authors and writings, as is verified by his *Studies of Western Literature*.[36] Not only did Lavrov reveal a reflective critical sense and literary taste, but he seems also to have been the first actually to have introduced Whittier, Lowell, and Whitman to the Russian reading public.[37]

His main venture into appraisal of American letters appeared in an essay on Longfellow, written in 1882. This essay presented a detailed critique of the man and his achievement.[38] It also contained significant commentary on the work of Whittier, James Russell Lowell, Walt Whitman, and others. Lavrov indicated that this study was prompted in part by Longfellow's recent death, and he characterized the bard as "one of the most famous poets of America [whose] popularity was great." Then, using American newspapers as his source, Lavrov commented on the fact that Longfellow's portrait was hung in memorial in the bookshops of

[35] *Ibid.*, no. 46 (Dec. 1, 1876), p. 718.

[36] These essays were written from about 1860 to 1882, and were collected in 1923 in Leningrad by A. Gizetti and P. Vitiazev as *Etiudy o Zapadnoi Literature*.

[37] *Ibid.*, editors' "Introduction," pp. xxiii, xxiv.

[38] *Ibid.*, pp. 152–81. All quotations on Longfellow are from this essay.

the principal American cities. A biographical sketch followed and an enumeration of Longfellow's poetical productions. Here mention was made of Longfellow's work at Bowdoin College and his professorship at Harvard, where he replaced Ticknor, "the historian of Spanish literature." In turn, Longfellow was succeeded by Lowell, "the present American minister to England."

Lavrov next turned to Longfellow's three journeys to Europe. The critic considered these most important for his development. This poetic growth, characterized by "an almost religious respect" for the Old World, in Lavrov's eyes, rendered Longfellow's work almost completely non-American. He supported this characterization of Longfellow by citing the parallel judgments of Charles Waite in his *Sketch of the History of American Literature*.[39] Thus a picture of deracination emerged.

Longfellow, wrote Lavrov, belonged to the class of "writers . . . so susceptible to the diversified impressions of historical epochs and various nationalities that their own time and homeland" failed to "evoke a strong response in them." There were "people," he continued, "who, resting upon the firm soil of the sympathies, tasks and aspirations of their epoch and nation," broadened such "sympathies, tasks and aspirations, because of their energy, to the point that they" became "common to mankind." Others existed, however, who considered it "possible to satisfy their own personal interests, tasks and aspirations" only by ignoring "all" that was achieved by the "members of a definite nation, by the participants in the vital struggles of a given epoch." Such people, Lavrov insisted, suffered from "cosmopolitan" diffusion of talent because of their weak "ties with epoch and nation." On the one hand, the "world sympathies" of Walt

[39] Careful search has failed thus far to unearth this text.

Whitman, "Longfellow's rival," developed "in the soil of a passionate . . . even a blindly-fanatical American patriotism." The "same" was true of James Russell Lowell. On the other hand, Longfellow "belonged to the second type and this . . . may most clearly explain why his poetry has a 'cosmopolitan' character." [40]

Apart from depreciating Longfellow's poetic stature (perhaps to an unwarranted exaltation of Lowell), Lavrov illustrates in these passages that sociological approach to literature which has been the main trend of Russian literary criticism from Belinski to Lunacharski.[41] In practice, aesthetics is always subordinated to ethics in such presentations although the written or unwritten presupposition calls for equal appraisal of form and content. In addition, Lavrov anticipated, "both in life and literature," the Soviet view of achieving internationalism from the variegated contributions of diverse nationalities.

Lavrov sustained the sociological approach in this essay by asserting that Longfellow's weak "ties" to his epoch were indicated by the large element of romanticism in his work. He pointed to *Outre-Mer* and to *The Poets and Poetry of Europe* as illustrations of this. In Lavrov's estimation, the romantic movement was a complicated phenomenon which differed in various regions, but which, nevertheless, was conditioned in all countries by the struggle of revolutionaries and reactionaries. This struggle, Lavrov believed, was

[40] In this passage, Lavrov specifically cited two Whitman poems: "Salut au Monde," and "To Field Pievolter or Pievoltress." The latter actually refers to a poem entitled, "To a Foiled Revolter or Revoltress." He also mentioned with praise four of Lowell's poems: "The Fatherland," "The Poet," "To the Future," and "Ode to France (1848)."

[41] Anatoli Lunacharski (1876–1933), People's Commissar of Education during the first ten years of the Soviet regime, was an outstanding playwright and literary theorist.

a phase of romanticism that did not concern Longfellow, yet similarities between the romantic movement in America and Russia made his position therein more understandable to Lavrov. The Russian critic amplified his point by declaring: "absence of historical traditions capable of evoking inspiring tones of the past inevitably tore Russian romanticism from Zhukovski's rootless fantasies." As a result of this deficiency, Russian romanticism, after a period of "Byronism," was "reworked into pure realism, leaving the glorification of the past to . . . Zagoskin." Likewise, "in America . . . romanticism was fatally reworked into cosmopolitan sympathy for all peoples and past epochs," from "the ancient Hebrews and Scandinavian Vikings to the patriots of New England." [42]

As examples of this, Lavrov enumerated the mythology of the Indians in the *Song of Hiawatha,* and accounts of the North American Puritans of the seventeenth and eighteenth centuries in the *Tragedies of New England* and the *Courtship of Miles Standish.* It is not appropriate here to embark upon a long digression on the nature of romanticism, but one may comment that it is difficult to see why Lavrov regarded the struggle of reactionaries and revolutionaries as alien to Longfellow. Such a struggle was actually occurring in America at that time, as James Fenimore Cooper,

[42] Basil Zhukovski (1783–1852) was one of the greatest Russian romantic poets of the early nineteenth century, a contemporary of Pushkin. He is particularly noted for translations of pre-romantic and romantic poetry from Western European languages, Gray's *Elegy,* for example. Zhukovski was also the tutor of the future Alexander II.

Michael Zagoskin (1789–1853), a prolific writer of secondary talents, was very popular in the early nineteenth century. He wrote historical novels with a pronounced patriotic "Russian" bias. Zagoskin's best work, *Iuri Miloslavski* or *The Russians in 1612,* was written under the direct inspiration of Scott's works and is the first Russian historical novel. Cf. D. S. Mirsky, *A History of Russian Literature* (New York, 1934), pp. 97–101, 148.

for one, well realized.[43] Even in this synoptic view of the Russian and American romantic movements, Lavrov was more correct than not, within a "Western" frame of reference, in pointing out the common quest for historical traditions undertaken by certain writers of both countries in this period. In Russia, Chaadaev's philosophical letter bitterly critical of his country's history and destiny, and in America, the writings of Hawthorne, Cooper, and Charles Brockden Brown, to mention but three, bear witness to this concern.

But romanticism had more within its scope than interest in antiquities. It had also its revolutionary and religious aspects, as Lavrov did not fail to mention. Then, too, in breaking with certain narrow and outworn traditionalisms of the past, romanticism had attracted such divergent figures as Philip Freneau, Emerson, Bryant, Melville, and Thoreau. Thus to consider Longfellow as the archetypal American romantic writer, as Lavrov seemingly implied, was certainly an ill-proportioned view both of Longfellow and of the American romantic movement.

In connection with the romantic element in Longfellow, Lavrov rightly maintained that any genuine understanding of the historical process was lacking in his subjects of different epochs and peoples. In fact, romanticism was apparently nowhere able to work out such an understanding because it lacked the necessary philosophical framework. Therefore, the Russian believed that Longfellow's lack of what we would call a philosophy of history existed because the Hegelian idealistic theory of evolution remained outside of romanticism and what Lavrov called the Darwinian

---

[43] Cf. *The American Democrat of 1838*, in which Cooper offers some significant "hints on the social and civic relations of the United States." For the evolution and subsequent evaporation of Cooper's "radicalism," cf. Arthur M. Schlesinger, Jr., *The Age of Jackson*, pp. 375–80.

realistic theory of history had not yet appeared. Hence in Lavrov's view, Longfellow was not to blame for this lack.[44]

The Russian critic also called attention to the religious element of romanticism visible in many of Longfellow's works and pointed out William Ellery Channing as a responsible and important influence. Noteworthy in this respect was the dedication of Longfellow's *Poems on Slavery* (1842) to Channing. Longfellow, in company with Channing, declared Lavrov somewhat surprisingly, tried to avoid committing himself to any contemporary Christian sect.

Leaving the issue of religion, Lavrov examined Longfellow's work for specific repercussions of the slavery question and the Civil War. The Russian approved of Longfellow's dedication of his slender volume of *Poems on Slavery* to Channing, but he surely exaggerated when he characterized Channing as one of "the most" energetic preachers against slavery.[45] At the same time, Lavrov was convinced that

[44] It is of some interest to note that Hegel's doctrines were not introduced to America on any large scale before 1866. In that year, Henry Brokmeyer, a German refugee, and his protégé William T. Harris, organized the St. Louis Philosophical Society. "For more than a decade . . . the St. Louis Movement . . . spread the glad tidings of German idealism throughout the Middle West and influenced to no inconsiderable degree the development of its culture"—mainly through the *Journal of Speculative Philosophy*. But Longfellow was sixty years old when this movement got under way. Cf. E. S. Bates, "Henry C. Brokmeyer," *Dictionary of American Biography*, ed. Allen Johnson (New York, 1929), III, 64–65. However, at least two American "romanticists," contemporary with Longfellow, were interested in Hegelianism: Whitman and Emerson. "The North American thinker," Emerson, was criticized severely by Lavrov for what the Russian termed his "heroic" and "picturesque" concept of history; Lavrov, "Thomas Carlyle," *Zap. Lit.*, p. 145.

[45] Cf. S. M. Crothers, "William Ellery Channing," *Dictionary of American Biography*, IV, 4–7. The Unitarian preacher is described (p. 7) as insisting that "slavery . . . is an unspeakable evil. But so also is war and of all wars, the most dreadful to contemplate is a civil war. He could not dismiss as did many abolitionists the possibility of a war between the states." Hence "in

Longfellow's poetic opposition to slavery was decidedly weak compared to that of Whittier and of Whitman and Lowell as well.

In regard to Whittier, Lavrov believed that as a "convinced Quaker, religious motives were . . . a very characteristic trait of his genius," and therefore of his poetic opposition to slavery. It is interesting to notice that Lavrov, the otherwise uncompromising atheist, acknowledged in the cases of Channing and Whittier the positive role which religion in America could play in directing activity for a righteous secular cause. He reported sarcastically that one critic had called Longfellow's *Poems on Slavery* "inoffensive little pictures" which "any Southern baron could read without taking offense at the author." The Russian critic concluded that slavery in that time was "a burning question for America," but for Longfellow it was only one of many questions for which he had sympathy.

In keeping with his theory that literature is not an autonomous art, Lavrov condemned not only Longfellow, but also Whitman, Lowell and Whittier—poets "incomparably more energetic in thought"—for their alleged failure to be moved by the "illnesses" of post-Civil War America. Among the "illnesses" adumbrated here by Lavrov were "terrible stock exchange scandals," corruption of legislative bodies, unblushing exploitation of the country by great capitalists, and finally, the "workers' disorders" of 1877, "which overflowed from ocean to ocean."

Along with Longfellow's rootless cosmopolitanism, historical romanticism, and weakness on the slavery issue and

---

his discussions of slavery he addressed himself to the conscience of the South rather than to the New England conscience." As a result, "he was attacked from both sides, but his addresses did much to prepare people to understand and follow Abraham Lincoln."

"social question," Lavrov also considered his poetic reticence in regard to sex and to "the sensual side of love" as a great failing.[46] This "modesty" was, appropriately enough, one of the sources of Longfellow's great popularity in Victorian England. Beyond this, Lavrov asserted, Longfellow was neither passionate nor energetic in either the tragic or the satirical sense. The passion and sadness which Longfellow himself had insisted a great poet must feel were missing; there was only a quiet yearning. Lavrov wrote bitingly that Longfellow's "whole horizon of 'activity in the living present,' his whole horizon of life," was limited to "family joys and family sorrows." "Even Schiller's *Bell*," the Russian critic declared, "rang out in more challenging tones." And of Longfellow's works, Lavrov repeated approximately what George Ticknor had said of Longfellow's personality in his memoirs: "a very amiable and kind man whom all love very much."

Lavrov finished his probing critique of Longfellow by delving for the sources of the poet's popularity. "The majority could grant popularity," he asserted, "only" to those writers who would "sincerely repeat in artistic form" clichés which served to disguise the plundering activities of the men of affairs of that time. This was a "disguise of piety and patience, of love of freedom and self-denial, of sympathies common to mankind and of philosophic breadth of thought." Longfellow was "a representative of this . . . category . . . in the epoch when art in all spheres ever more" conformed "to the demands of comfort." In Longfellow's work, Lavrov declared cynically, it was therefore fitting to find "patriotic hymns on the ship of state which the speculators" now steered "in quest of the Golden Fleece." And "behind these

[46] Unlike Walt Whitman who, Lavrov observed, was not inhibited thus, as evidenced in *Leaves of Grass*.

argonauts of the new age the world followed with 'all its hopes and prayers.'" Lavrov concluded that "the average reader of a future era" would not experience in Longfellow's poetry "the higher spiritual currents of our time." On the contrary he would discover only "a comprehensively and beautifully expressed feeling of grief, accessible always to the great majority."

With this sweeping consignment of Longfellow to the realm of mediocrity, Lavrov ended his study of the poet. Lavrov's prose in this critique at times becomes almost as lyrical as Herzen's, and although but scantily concerned with aesthetic considerations, it is provocative. But there is at least one question which one may legitimately pose in the face of Lavrov's theoretical assumptions. And that is, in condemning the representative of "the great majority" for being unresponsive to "the battle of contemporary theoretical and practical parties" (i.e., for not really being a "critically thinking individual"), was not Lavrov in a sense throwing "the great majority" to the discard, and revealing as well the individualist-aristocratic aspect of his own teaching? This flaw is probably one of the most revealing clues to Lavrov's weakness not only as literary critic but also as political activist. Within the somewhat circumscribed framework of sociological canons of literary criticism, however, Lavrov's analysis of Longfellow's achievement offers much for the critical reader of today to ponder.

In reviewing Lavrov's attitudes towards these various aspects of American life and culture, one may confidently assert that in company with his contemporary mid-century Russian radicals, he displayed great interest in and extensive factual knowledge of American life. Despite certain errors of dates and geography, his knowledge of the American scene was reasonably extensive, albeit largely derivative, and ranged from American government and politics to American literature. Lavrov viewed America primarily from a long-range historical standpoint. Hence his opinions have a certain self-consistency which belie the usual accusation of eclecticism. He is thus free from those almost cataclysmic variations to be found in Herzen.

The striking difference between Lavrov's opinions and those of his predecessors was his almost completely negative attitude towards the America of the 1870's. This negative quality characterized his views of government, business, and the "social question" in the United States. The mature republic had reneged its youthful promise of being a constant beacon of hope for the future. This significance of America to which Herzen had so frequently quickened, had now vanished from the sight of the European socialist. Indeed the United States was now anything but the near paradise that Chernyshevski dreamed of, once the slave owners and their system were extirpated.

Lavrov believed that the only features which the United States and Russia possessed in common were a widespread venality in public life and an "absence" of inspiring historical traditions in the "Western" sense. Paradoxically enough, the two countries also shared a certain revolutionary tradition, although in the one it was bourgeois and constitutional whereas in the other it was popular and elemental. Perhaps Lavrov's sense of disillusionment with the United States was enhanced because of that very promise shown by both the Declaration of Independence and the armed struggle to destroy the slave power. In this regard, the bloody suppression of the Paris Commune doubtlessly contributed to Lavrov's hostility towards the America he looked upon. For with the Commune gone, it was a bitter thing that America more and more should disappoint Lavrov's "maximalist" hopes. Hence, in his firm rejoinders to the Utopian optimism of William Frey, he emphasized the common character of the economic and political evils which beset America in company with Europe.

It is clear that Lavrov over-estimated the "progressive" character of post-Revolutionary America, failing to note, for example, the essential change in spirit between the Declaration of Independence and the Constitution. Conversely, his condemnation of post-Civil War America was too general. This may be partially explained by the fact that Lavrov overlooked the strong democratic elements which opposed the tidal wave of monopoly swiftly engulfing American industry. Yet the omission is extremely curious since these democratic elements (e.g., the Grange, the Farmers' Alliance) were in great part the very agrarian elements upon which Lavrov presumably based his hopes for socialism in Russia. Finally one should note that Lavrov was able to use the phenomenon of the American Civil War as specific illustration of certain sociological theories peculiar to him.

Positively viewed, Lavrov displayed a critical judgment as interesting if not so shrewd as that of previous Russian radicals in his observations of the United States. Above all, his negative judgments stand out in bold relief, even when compared with those of the intransigent Bakunin.

CHAPTER X

America: The "Sullen Stepmother"

NICHOLAS CHAIKOVSKI

WE have observed how Peter Lavrov fulminated against those European and Russian radicals who were "tired of Europe" and who sought the "promised land" in America. More specifically we have seen how Lavrov admonished William Frey for his facile conclusions in regard to the labor movement and the social struggle in America. That there was sustained interest in America during the early seventies on the part of certain Russian radicals is evident from sources other than Lavrov's own strictures against this tendency.[1] One concrete manifestation of this positive interest was the actual migration of several Russian *Narodniki* across the Atlantic in the decade of the seventies. They left Russia with the hope of finding "a new

---

[1] Cf. for example, the testimony of Vladimir Debagori-Mokrievich, a fairly outstanding Bakuninist-*Narodnik* in the 1870's. "At the end of the sixties," he wrote, "the attraction of America, of American life and of American free institutions was noticed. . . . Certain individuals travelled there, observed the mode of life there and wrote about it in Russian magazines: thus as I recall . . . a book was published by Zimmerman on his travels over North America, which was very much read at that time. . . . Our cousin was one of those attracted to America. He migrated to the United States and after spending about a year there, returned to Russia . . . to organize a company for emigration and for the establishment of an agricultural commune there"; *Ot Buntarstva k Terrorizmu* (Moscow-Leningrad, 1930), I, 91–92. Edward Zimmerman's book was *Soedinennye Shtaty Severnoi Ameriki iz Puteshestvi 1857–1858 i 1869–1870 gg.* (Moscow, 1873). Also cf. V. I. Mezhov, *Russkaia Istoricheskaia Bibliografiia za 1865–1876 Vkliuchitelno* (St. Petersburg, 1885), VI, 427.

earth and a new heaven" in America, and with the aim of establishing Utopian, agricultural communes. The experience of Nicholas Chaikovski is instructive in this connection. For insofar as Chaikovski lived in the United States for several years, his reactions to American life may profitably be compared with those of the radicals who had little or no primary knowledge of America.

Chaikovski was born in 1850 to a family of petty nobles in the provincial capital of Viatka, where Herzen had once sojourned in exile.[2] He attended school in St. Petersburg and received a bachelor's degree from the physico-mathematical faculty of the University in 1872. From an early date Chaikovski attended student meetings, but was opposed to the extremist tactics advocated by Bakunin's wayward disciple Nechaev, then a popular figure among the revolutionary youth.[3] After minor participation in certain radical activities at the University in 1871, Chaikovski became one of the leaders of the circle which took his name. This circle was organized in the northern capital for purposes of self-education so that the members might train themselves as cadres for propaganda work among the people.

In those student years, the influence of Auguste Comte was "too heavy," as Chaikovski himself reported.[4] But within the "circle of the Chaikovtsy"—which soon expanded, as several smaller "circles" in various cities of the Empire were formed—we hear no more of Comte, but rather of

[2] For details of Chaikovski's biography, cf. V. Miakotin, "Chaykovsky," *Encyclopædia of the Social Sciences*, III, 362, and *Deiateli* . . . (Moscow, 1929), vol. II, parts 3–4, pp. 1919–22.

[3] The plot of Dostoevski's *Possessed* is built in large part upon a sensational murder engineered by the amoral Nechaev in 1869. For details of "the *affaire* Nechaev," cf. Carr, *Michael Bakunin*, pp. 375–93.

[4] Cf. *Nikolai Vassilevich Chaikovski* [in Russian], ed. A. A. Titov (Paris, 1929), I, 38.

John Stuart Mill, Chernyshevski, Karl Marx, Dobroliubov, Pisarev, Nekrassov, Kostomarov, and Lassalle. Lavrov's *Historical Letters* and Louis Blanc's *History of Ten Years* [5] also had impact on the circle's thinking. The influence of Bakunin, however, was extremely slight if it existed at all. As one member of the Chaikovtsy, Charushin, expressed it, "There were no followers of the Bakuninist tendency among us except for [Peter] Kropotkin." Indeed, he added, "even Bakunin's very teaching was known to us in only the smallest degree in . . . 1873." [6]

The practical activities of the circle in the three years of its work (1871–74) developed in three phases: book-education and propaganda among the youth; propaganda among the workers; and preparation for propaganda among the peasants. Thus educational rather than "militant" action characterized this group; in fact, to the end, they remained "bookish people." [7]

Many of the Chaikovtsy, however, dropped their sedentary pursuits towards the end of 1873, and joining the "going to the people" movement of that winter they went out with great eagerness to spread socialist propaganda among

[5] *Ibid.*, pp. 41, 48, 61. Chaikovski acutely perceived the trend of the revolutionary youth away from Pisarev's nihilistic "healthy egoism," and towards the "critically thinking realists," ushered in by Lavrov's "notable" *Historical Letters* in 1869. Chaikovski also referred to Herzen and to Chernyshevski as "sovereigns of the thought of the Russian youth of the sixties," *ibid.*, pp. 71–72.

[6] *Ibid.*, p. 74.

[7] *Ibid.*, pp. 69, 86. Cf. Peter Kropotkin and his high esteem of the circle of Chaikovski in *Memoirs of a Revolutionist* (Boston, New York, 1899), Houghton Mifflin Company, pp. 304 ff. "Never did I meet elsewhere such a collection of morally superior men and women as the score of persons whose acquaintance I made at the first meeting of the Circle of Tchaykovtsy. I still feel proud of having been received into that family," p. 306. "It played an important part in the history of the social movement in Russia and . . . will go down in history," p. 304.

the *narod*. But "to the extent that the fighting spirit grew among the Chaikovtsy, the divergences between . . . Chaikovski and his circle became ever more clearly defined."[8] For at that time, Chaikovski's own views were shifting—to the point that he felt need for "*a new religion*." In August, 1874, Chaikovski met for the last time with those members of his group who had survived the pilgrimage to the people. There was no possibility of reconciliation, and so the friends parted. "True to his new aspiration of 'creating the good from yourself alone,'" the former Populist agitator "quickly forsook Europe 'to realize the God-man in his life' upon the American prairie."[9]

Chaikovski has tersely summed up this Petersburg period of his life. It was "fitted into the one decade (1861–72) of the great reforms" and coincided with the flowering of the Russian intelligentsia, the Russian civil state and society." Next followed "the social self-education of the students" who went "to the people bearing the propaganda of Utopian socialist ideas." For this they were persecuted by the government. As a result, "the Populist organization was transformed into a politically revolutionary group with terrorist and conspiratorial activity." Chaikovski declared fervently that he "never had any inclination" for the "latter ends." And he "renounced this activity for another reason—the religious deepening" in himself and "the practical search for social forms" to embody this quickening impulse. Accordingly, he "was forced to travel to the American prairie since the Russian regime lent no aid for that kind of activity."[10]

[8] Titov, *op. cit.*, pp. 89, 90.

[9] *Ibid.*, pp. 92, 94, 96. For an exposition of this belief, which had much in common with Frey's religious views, cf. *ibid.*, pp. 107–11.

[10] *Ibid.*, pp. 12–13. Cf. Stepniak (Sergei Kravchinski), *Underground Russia*, tr. (New York, 1883), preface by Peter Lavrov, pp. 1–42, for a concise and well-written summary of this period by a revolutionary practitioner,

The pattern of events and ideas that impelled Chaikovski to cross the Atlantic stands clear: the seeming failure of the "going to the people" movement, his own temperamental aversion to tactics involving violence and terrorism, a deeply religious sense, and the belief that the United States was the country best suited to work out his new religious and communal ideas. The matter of geographical location was, however, not quite agreed upon as yet by Chaikovski's followers.[11]

Already established on the great plains in Kansas was William Frey's Utopian colony. Frey had migrated in 1868 to America, "the great social laboratory of all ideas and aspirations that agitated the contemporary world," in search of "the good, the true and the just." More specifically he sought to realize "the religion of humanity"—the positive religion of Auguste Comte.

Frey was indeed a "repentant nobleman," born to the name of Vladimir Constantinovich Geinss and destined for

which generally corroborates Chaikovski's views without, however, taking account of the religious strain in the revolutionary movement after 1873–74.

[11] Debagori-Mokrievich reports rather different motives for the momentary "Americanism" of the Kievan circle to which he belonged. His elder brother Ivan proposed to establish a commune in America, where the migrants would divest themselves of the "demoralizing" circumstances of their privileged lives, rid themselves of the "fundamental evil" of private property, and raise their bread "morally," placing the greatest emphasis upon "physical labor." In this way they would harmonize their pattern of life with that of the Russian peasants. The projected colony itself was looked upon as a nucleus from which redeeming forces would eventually spread the propaganda of "moral" and "militant" communism over Europe and America.

In the end there were disagreements among the members of this circle. The plan of migration to America was, therefore, shelved in view of the rising tide of "muzhikophile" sentiment, which failed "absolutely" to "harmonize with the concept of migration." Cf. *Vospominaniia* (Paris, 1894), I, pp. 1–16, 17–38; and *Deiateli* . . . , vol. II, parts 1–2, 335–38.

a military career. But the problem of the "suffering and oppressed masses" overwhelmed him. He sought an answer in the *Zemlia i Volia* secret revolutionary society—to which Chernyshevski probably once belonged. But soon Geinss became "disillusioned" with the group and at that point decided that no answer was possible in Russia. Abandoning social position, career, friends, and family, he migrated to America "to experience for himself all the stages of hard, heavy labor."

After "long, disastrous roaming about with . . . wife and child," Geinss "became an American citizen and assumed the name of William Frey." Then, taking up about three hundred acres of land under the Homestead Act in Cedar Vale, Kansas, Frey settled down with his family and a few others to live the life of Comte's "religion of humanity." This life, Frey believed, would serve as "the ideal of another life" for suffering humanity. Once apprehended by the mass of the people, it would reveal to them the solution of their sufferings and enable them to build their heaven on earth. Unfortunately, Frey's belief in "the wonder-working influence of the 'religion of humanity' on people" had most disappointing results, as Machtet, one of the five colonists, concluded after eight months of this mode of life.[12] The

[12] All citations from Titov, *op. cit.*, pp. 100–8. Cf. also Machtet's vivid description of the sufferings and hardships endured in Frey's commune. Even when Machtet first arrived at the colony, he felt a keen sense of homesickness: "Upon meeting here, under this unfamiliar heaven, on this broad plain, our first word was—Russia . . . The wonderful broad prairie faded away from our eyes, the clear sun set, the transparent azure distance was slowly covered with shadows . . . and we suddenly felt the desire—passionately and strongly—to be under our own poor gray sky, surrounded by naked and cold plains and forests! . . . and in our smoky huts."

Frey himself is depicted in very unflattering terms as a weak but despotic character: G. A. Machtet, *Polnoe Sobranie Sochineni*, ed. D. P. Silchevski (St. Petersburg, 1911), I, 184–214. Citations from pp. 197, 201.

colony lingered on for a time, however, and was finally absorbed by the Chaikovski community.[13]

By autumn 1874, having determined upon his course of emigration, Chaikovski made his way abroad illegally, first to Switzerland, and thence to Paris and London. At about this time a letter by Frey which expounded the principles of the communistic theory upon which he founded his colony appeared in *Vpered*. In all probability, Chaikovski saw this letter. In it, Frey appealed to all intellectuals seeking the truth to join his American commune.[14] Simultaneously, Chaikovski was in contact with other *émigré* Russians who had settled in New York, Kansas, and California. Thus by the summer of 1875, the location of the new colony was definitely settled in favor of the United States.[15]

Chaikovski crossed the ocean in the summer of that same year and landed in New York. Here he awaited the fifteen-odd comrades who shared his religious beliefs and who were to be the future colonists. They arrived in the autumn, when Chaikovski was already in correspondence with William Frey, who persistently urged the new migrants to unite with his Progressive Colony. The Chaikovski group decided to send three deputies, of whom Chaikovski himself was one, to investigate the situation at Cedar Vale. The first disillusionment occurred with this investigation.

The autumn of 1875 in Kansas was extremely cold and

[13] For the prospectus and top-heavy constitution of the Progressive Colony, cf. Charles Nordhoff, *Communistic Societies in the United States* (New York, 1875), pp. 353–56.

[14] Cf. pp. 173–74 *supra* for discussion of the letter's contents, also for Lavrov's objections to Frey's optimistic concept of the position and tasks of the American working class.

[15] Titov, *op. cit.*, I, 119–21. One of the reasons for the time lag lay in the fact that in these months Chaikovski was working on a study of a history of religion in English, *ibid.*, p. 120.

windy. The delegation from New York, arriving at this "savage locality," was greeted by the dismal sight of Frey's "badly built house with cracks that allowed draughts to enter." Then "Frey came out to meet them, racked by fever . . . his wife followed with a suffering expression upon her tortured face." Both he and his wife "were dressed in blue military greatcoats . . . bought by Frey at a rummage sale after the Civil War." Clearly, "the setting spoke for itself: in the 'progressive' community, poverty and want peeped from every corner." [16]

It is not surprising that the Chaikovski group categorically refused to join with Frey. But when establishing their own community, they bought land in the very same Cedar Vale, near the city of Wichita. Eventually they were joined by Frey, his wife and little daughter, when the Progressive Community finally collapsed.

The believers in "God-manhood," like Frey's followers, knew very little of this pioneer mode of life. None of them had more than the slightest acquaintance with the hard work demanded on the frontier, and all suffered the usual privations of the inexperienced, civilized immigrant who takes up life in a savage country. They were not farmers, although they sincerely and ardently set out to work as such, and, as might have been expected, they tilled their soil inefficiently. Their buildings were as bad as the ones in Frey's colony. They suffered cold and hunger and many other hardships. Inevitably, rumblings of discontent began to be heard. But here Frey's "deep faith in the commune, his enthusiasm, steadfastness and self-sacrifice undoubtedly produced a strong impression." These qualities indeed "held the believers in God-manhood together even . . . after they had otherwise long been prepared to disperse." [17]

[16] *Ibid.*, I, 121–22.   [17] *Ibid.*, I, 125.

Nevertheless even Frey could not stem the tide of misery and homesickness, and the Chaikovski commune broke up in the summer of 1877 after two years of precarious life.[18]

The majority of the colonists returned to Russia. Chaikovski himself deemed it inadvisable, however, to follow this course of action. Many of his adherents and disciples were then languishing in tsarist prisons, awaiting trial for their part in the propaganda among the peasantry. Moreover, in that year of 1877, tsarist fury against the radicals was reaching a peak with the famous "trial of the 193." [19] Therefore, leaving wife and daughter with William Frey (who "preserved the keys" to the colony and heroically awaited the "inevitable return" of the dispersed colonists), Chaikovski set off in the direction of Philadelphia. There he hoped to find work and earn money.[20] Thus the first half of his stay in American ended.

Here one may logically ask, what impressions did the United States make on the leader of this lonely band of idealistic Russian migrants in the first two years of his sojourn in this country? The answer seems to be: surprisingly few. In regard to the growing feeling of loneliness in the colony at Cedar Vale, we are told, for example, of "tears" of homesickness and of "unexpected yearning for fatherland." Temperamentally, "the souls of the believers in God-man-hood were attuned to a cosmopolitan harmony." America, however, "greeted them coldly." The farmers of the vicinity "regarded the commune warily at first, as though the Rus-

[18] *Ibid.,* I, 126–27.

[19] For details of the open trial of these one hundred and ninety-three *Narodniki,* cf. M. Kovalenski, *Russkaia Revoliutsia v Sudebnykh Protsessakh i Memuarakh* (Moscow, 1923), I, 163–223, especially pp. 169–75, which discuss the government's extreme alarm over the "circle of Chaikovtsy" as distributors of revolutionary propaganda.

[20] Titov, *op. cit.,* I, 127.

sians might have decided to preach and then practice both atheism and free love." But after convincing themselves that "these fears were unfounded, the Americans left the 'freaks' in peace." However, "the members of the commune clearly had no points of contact with the life that surrounded them." The truth of the matter was that "America was a cold and sullen stepmother." [21]

Such an unhappy reaction to America on the part of the Chaikovski colonists was typical of immigrant experience on the remote American frontier in the second half of the nineteenth century. And feelings of incredible loneliness in the face of both overwhelming natural forces and the latent hostility of the "different" farmer-neighbors combined to have decidedly deleterious effects even upon this most extraordinary group of migrants.

The material conditions of wresting a livelihood from the soil, joined with a doctrinal interest in their new theology, surely tended to isolate the Chaikovtsy from the main currents of American life. Accordingly, their lack of detailed interest in the life around them might well have been true if they had settled on the Argentine pampas.

Thus only the most generalized psychological reactions to America are recorded for this group, and none of them refers to specific American institutions.[22] These generalized impressions, however, were to be of some value later on in Chaikovski's own evolution. More important was their partial confirmation of Lavrov's warnings to those "tired of Europe" against the tendency of flight to America.[23]

Despite the fact that Chaikovski himself described his

---

[21] *Ibid.*, I, 126.

[22] Except, as remarked earlier, in the case of William Frey.

[23] For Stepniak's opposition to Chaikovski's "temporary flight from Russian affairs," cf. Titov, *op. cit.*, I, 178.

experiences on the American prairie in gloomy tones and complained bitterly of the "dull suffering and hopelessness of Kansas life," he clung to his belief that the fundamental reason for the failure of the community lay in the fact that "the members . . . were not equally united by a religious feeling." [24] Completely glossed over in this idealistic explanation were the physical and psychological difficulties encountered by the colonists.[25]

Indeed, Chaikovski maintained to the end of his life that the failure of his commune did not signify the failure of the commune idea, that is, of Utopianism in general. And he believed this firmly although in later times when he returned to Europe, he became successively a member of the *Narodnaia Volia*, an anarchist, a Socialist-Revolutionary, and a People's Socialist.[26] Future men, he believed, would be prepared for a communal mode of life such as had been practiced in Kansas. However, "at present, people" were "not yet ready for it, not . . . capable of constantly sensing the presence of divinity in themselves." Chaikovski asserted that without this sense, "communistic life" was "unrealizable." [27]

To what extent the Russian's tenacity of belief can be ascribed to the American environment would be most difficult to determine.

Now at the midpoint of his stay in the United States and with the ruins of the Kansas experiment behind him, Chaikovski gathered his resources and prepared for the long and difficult journey to Philadelphia. He planned to ask a friend who lived in that city to aid him in seeking work. And so,

[24] *Ibid.*, I, 127.

[25] William Frey seems to have concurred with Chaikovski's view of the colony's failure. However, he naturally thought more in terms of his own Comte-like "religion of humanity," *ibid.*, p. 128.

[26] *Ibid.*, I, 167.

[27] *Ibid.*, I, 129.

with "poor command of . . . English . . . a dilettante knowledge of carpentry, with a specialist's diploma in chemistry from a Russian university . . . and with ten dollars," Chaikovski was forced to make his way east as a "tramp." [28] To aggravate his difficulties, the great railroad strikes and riots of 1877, which had so attracted Lavrov's attention, broke out during his journey. The trip lasted twenty-three days and cost Chaikovski—to use his own words—"ten years of life, without exaggeration." He was literally "face to face with the problem of a piece of bread." [29]

The weary pilgrim finally arrived in the Quaker metropolis and with his friend's help secured a job as ship's carpenter on the Chester wharves. This first taste of life as a worker in American industrial society was, however, anything but pleasant. The greatest difference existed between the former voluntary labor on the Kansas farm and the job in Chester whose every aspect was constantly under the oppressive eye of the overseer. Chaikovski did his job no worse than any of his fellow-workers, but his main thought lay always in anticipating the end of his twelve-hour shift so that he might enjoy the next twelve hours in "complete freedom."

He recorded very few impressions at all analytical of American institutions which might have been gleaned from his journey east and from his experiences in Chester and Philadelphia. Describing his twenty-three-day trek across the continent, he declared somberly that "sometimes I fell into such despair that I began to cry." [30] On the Chester wharves he observed that the workers were very distrustful and noted the bad impression an Irishman made upon him. And he told of a German friend who worked in a sugar

[28] *Ibid.*, I, 131. "Tramp" appears in English in the original.
[29] *Ibid.*, I, 135.
[30] *Ibid.*, I, 132.

refinery, "very nice, but horribly stupid." [31] These comments are all highly personal and contain little that is valuable for an understanding of American life. At the utmost, they reinforce the observations already recorded about America, "the sullen stepmother." [32]

After various hardships in Chester and Philadelphia, when seemingly there were no opportunities of any kind for the miserable immigrant, one of Chaikovski's compatriots advised him to leave Philadelphia, and look for work in the Groveland Community of the Shakers, a colony located in "Son Yea," New York, some forty miles from Rochester. [33] Taking this advice, Chaikovski traveled north.

The trip to the Shaker colony was made early in 1878, and upon arrival there Chaikovski was welcomed by the

[31] *Ibid.*, I, 133.

[32] It is amazing that the widespread railroad strikes should have left so slight an impression upon Chaikovski since he was involved, although involuntarily, in them. The attention that Lavrov devoted to these events is noted *supra*. Lavrov's interest was shared by the editors of *Obshchina*, an anarchist journal published in Geneva in 1878; cf. M. Nettlau, *Bibliographie de l'Anarchie* (Brussels, 1897), pp. 195–96. Men such as Stepniak, Dragomanov, Axelrod, and indeed certain former Chaikovtsy contributed to this magazine. In the February issue, a long analysis of the railroad strikes appeared, written by Elisée Reclus, a French anarchist and Communard who lived in exile for many years in Geneva; cf. Kropotkin's warm and respectful remembrances of him in his *Memoirs*, p. 392. The lesson that Reclus derived from the social ferment in America closely approximated Lavrov's conclusions: "The American [railroad] strike serves as new and obvious confirmation of the fact that, in general, no strike, no matter how insignificant, can be crowned with . . . success for the workers" unless it "grows into a revolution." The French anarchist went on to reject decisively any idea of American "exceptionalism." He asserted in this connection that "Americans . . . stop at nothing to reach their goal . . . In accordance with his European confrère, the American boss exploits his worker to the very extreme, but he does it without hypocrisy," *Obshchina*, pp. 27, 28.

For a vivid and factual account of the railroad labor disturbances of 1877, cf. Louis Adamic, *Dynamite!* (New York, 1931), pp. 22–37.

[33] Titov, *op. cit.*, I, 134.

members of the sect. He spent a year in the Groveland Community, during which time he recovered slowly from his previous adversities. His days were filled with a good deal of work. And in time Chaikovski "experienced a spiritual restoration that vindicated, deepened and altered somewhat his feelings and theories about God-manhood." [34] Indeed, Chaikovski asserted that among the Shakers, "I returned to a religious soil upon which I had not yet stood in Kansas." [35]

Chaikovski's first impressions of the Shakers were troubled. The Russian "God-seeker" found these "submissive disciples of Christ" quite alien to him. He was prepared to leave at any moment if the Shaker elders raised the question of his actually becoming an integral member of the settlement. And at one point Chaikovski asked himself in desperation why he was "here" and lending his "sanction" to "what has grown senile from head to foot." He pondered what course he should take: "a hired laborer—a lie; an independent farmer—a lie; privileged work—a lie." Where then, he demanded, was "peace for the moral feeling"? Was it "among the people who avow destruction"? This he denied emphatically, for "religion" was "rising." And so, he concluded passionately, "I shall seek it no matter where, even in the most outworn and dying Christianity." [36]

---

[34] Titov, *op. cit.*, I, 134. On the Shakers, cf. Margaret F. Melcher, *The Shaker Adventure* (Princeton, 1941), and Daryl Chase, *The Early Shakers: An Experiment in Religious Communism* (Chicago, 1938). The elevation of woman to the level of equality with men in the divine pantheon of the Shakers, besides the more familiar aspects of a religious-Utopian colony, would have great appeal for a man like Chaikovski. For the Groveland Community itself, cf. Charles Nordhoff, *op. cit.*, pp. 198–200.

[35] Titov, *op. cit.*, I, 137.

[36] *Ibid.* Chaikovski confided to his diary, in this time of growing underground terrorist activity in Russia, not only of the "uselessness, but even of the harm of the revolutionary struggle, from the point of view of the ideals of the 'God-seekers.'" But if he were forced to choose between the

Fortunately Chaikovski's inner doubts came to be stilled for a time. The Shaker elders did not persist in seeking his formal allegiance to the colony; he himself worked physically and energetically, thought and wrote a good deal about the religious subjects close to his heart, and achieved some rapport with the men about him. His second conversion to God-manhood occurred in this period. But despite the persistence of elevated religious feelings which Chaikovski considered important, the surrounding environment could not completely calm his agitated soul. His disquietude was due in great measure to the insoluble dualism which in his estimation rent the Shaker community: the discord between the founders' ideals and the current degeneration of those ideals.

The Shakers had withdrawn from the world in protest against the vanity fair of civilization, which deified the dollar and personal happiness only. To the establishment of what they considered a truly Christian life, they enforced celibacy, a rigorous program of work, and the renunciation of private property. By Chaikovski's time, however, "business" had made inroads upon the sect. The striving for comfort and wealth, the appearance of hired labor, and the penetration of ideas of "progress" had tended greatly to transform the inner content of Shaker life. The residue was only such stranded forms as similar garb and manifestations of respect for the elders. Almost inevitably, the persisting "narrowness" and "dualism" of the Shakers compelled Chaikovski's decision to depart.

At the end of 1878, Chaikovski left the Son Yea colony and by February, 1879, he was again with his family in New

---

persecutions of the tsarist government and the terrorist acts of the revolutionaries, his place, he asserted, would be with the revolutionaries, *ibid.*, I, 140.

York. There he awaited the money collected by his friends in Russia for his return passage to Europe. In May, 1879, Chaikovski landed in Liverpool, "a prodigal son of the Old World," . . . "having learned much but also having become disillusioned in much." [37] He quickly crossed to Paris and not long afterwards plunged into the work of the European émigré-revolutionaries. Although he became successively an anarchist, a Socialist-Revolutionary, and a People's Socialist, it is significant that late in life he recorded that his "heart was not in it." [38]

Almost thirty years later Chaikovski again visited the United States. This time he came under the auspices of the Russian Socialist-Revolutionary party, to lecture on the state of Russia's internal affairs following the suppression of the 1905 revolution. This second visit and the later phases of Chaikovski's long and stormy career lie, however, beyond the bounds of our study. [39]

Chaikovski's stay in the Groveland Community, in fact his whole experience in America after he left Philadelphia, provoked a disappointingly small output of recorded observations on American life beyond the immediate province of Shakerism. On the eve of leaving the Shakers he evaluated

[37] *Ibid.*, I, 171; 13.

[38] *Ibid.*, I, 141, 265. At the end of his life, Chaikovski, surveying his American religious commune in retrospect, emphatically announced: "I see that I was right when I said to myself: it is impossible to live . . . in the Kingdom of Caesar, when you do not have the Kingdom of God with His absolute Good, absolute Truth and absolute Love in your very self; for in the struggle with wickedness, the victory lies not in the annihilation of the enemy, neither in vengeance nor in wickedness towards him, but *in the creation of a new blessedness from your very self*, that is, from your own absolute self"; *ibid.*, I, 284.

[39] *Ibid.*, I, 216. Notable in Chaikovski's subsequent political career was his leading role in the intervention at Archangel in 1918; cf. W. H. Chamberlin, *The Russian Revolution* (New York, 1935), II, 285, 400–1, and Leonid I. Strakhovsky, *Intervention at Archangel* (Princeton, 1944).

their position and his own relation to it. The Russian declared that "notwithstanding the . . . terrible gulf" that
separated them from us, "notwithstanding the fact that we
[Russians] are historically . . . farther advanced than they
are and despite even the fact that we cannot live with
them," they could "nevertheless, help us in our spiritual
troubles." [40]

And, of course, the Shakers did help Chaikovski in his
spiritual, and, for that matter, material troubles as well.
Even though this restless man could find no lasting satisfaction in the Groveland Community, he did find it served
as a kind of sanitarium where he might recuperate from the
physical hardships which he had lately undergone. Concurrent with this, the Shaker experience enabled the Russian
"God-seeker" to reorient and recast his theoretical ideas of
"God-manhood." And so this sect, and therefore America,
played some part in Chaikovski's future development.[41]

Of greater importance than the subtle differences in humanistic theology experienced by Chaikovski, which after
all did not come to very much upon his return to practical
revolutionary activity in Europe, was the insight gained
into the dynamics of this Shaker type of Utopianism. Such
insight is evident in his analysis of the decline of the Shaker
colony—which, one may note in passing, finally died out
in 1892. Chaikovski's realization of Shaker decadence may
have been one of the reasons for his rapid plunge into more
orthodox revolutionary activities upon returning to Europe.

Based upon the Shaker experience were a very few shrewd
observations that he later made concerning the nature of

[40] Titov, *op. cit.*, I, 139.

[41] For a discussion of this phase of Chaikovski's thinking, cf. *ibid.*, I,
142–56. When Chaikovski returned to Europe, he surely communicated his
experiences with the Shakers to his radical colleagues, thereby familiarizing
them with at least one American religious institution.

American life. Chaikovski saw in America an unpleasant example of the effects of the dissolution of old religious ties.
The former bond in Christ, in Chaikovski's view, had come,
contemporaneously, to be supplanted by the impersonal
and cold nexus of hard cash. Every institution and idea was
subordinate "to the golden calf and individual interest." And
he exclaimed passionately that "hidden in the very kernel
of the Christian idea, in-humanity becomes ever more manifest, until finally it overflows into purchase and exchange,"
whose standard is "the *dollar*" only. Moreover, this "in-
humanity" now joined men together "in exactly the same
way as by God's spirit they were once linked in Christ." The
difference, Chaikovski asserted, now lay "only in the fact
that people have degenerated and squandered their elevated and poetic feeling to small purpose." [42]

Chaikovski's condemnation of the devastating effects of
money and of the liberal society upon "humanity" was explicit. His was an attack against the spirit of capitalist accumulation, of that energetic and ceaseless pursuit of the
"dollar" in "business" often at the expense of great personal
hardships, and with little purpose beyond that of mere accumulation.[43] Chaikovski's analysis, which relates elements
of Christianity to certain aspects of American capitalism, is
close to Chernyshevski's presentation of the "saving,"
"miserly" quality of Americans.[44] This anti-, or precisely,
"pre-capitalist" attitude towards accumulation in the *laissez-
faire* society was the result, no doubt, of Chaikovski's ad-
mixture of socialist and religious modes of thought, each of
which, in this case, reinforced the collectivism of the other.

The American experience also clarified for Chaikovski
some problems in the struggle for socialism. Before leaving
America in 1879, he received persistent invitations from

[42] *Ibid.*, I, 147.   [43] *Ibid.*, I, 147 n.   [44] Cf. *supra*, pp. 97–98.

William Frey to remain in the New World and establish
a new commune. Chaikovski's reply to Frey was significant.
He declared that he and all others who deeply felt the "need
for a full renovation of people" had to return to Europe. For
in Europe, the work of renovation was "organically tied up
with the very course of civil life." There the socialist movement possessed "definite forms, a position . . . in society."
And in Russia, he insisted, "the people . . . understand
us." On the contrary, in America the work was of "individuals, of chance circumstances"; for the Americans did
not "understand" the Russian migrants. There was no rapport and the Russians lacked those peculiar ties with American life which they possessed in common with "significant"
elements of Russian society. Chaikovski concluded wearily,
that in the United States, "the soil is lacking and even if it
were present, it is beyond the strength of our brothers and
of me in particular" to persist in our activities.[45]

This attitude, closely linked to the viewpoint expressed
earlier about the lack of contacts between the Kansas Commune and its neighbors, is a more advanced formulation of
the problem; for Chaikovski here viewed the socialist movement, by which term we may understand everything from
Utopianism to Marxism, not as a cosmopolitan abstraction
to which every historical entity might somehow be pressed to
service, but as a more supple process, one that had to be
flexible enough to accommodate the varying peculiarities
and special characteristics of different nations. In addition,
Chaikovski clearly inferred that socialism could best flourish
where oppressive historical developments had conditioned
the masses so as to make them objectively receptive to socialist teaching.

Such a view may be interpreted as corroboration of Lav-

[45] Titov, *op. cit.*, I, 141.

rov's negative attitude towards America as refuge and beacon for those tired of Europe. But it also represents a certain advance over the "cosmopolitanism" often expressed by Bakunin. One may say, too, that it agrees to some extent with Herzen's views of the differentiation of national development.

Finally, these passages heighten our realization of the curious contradictions in Chaikovski's outlook. He was convinced of the immediate futility of William Frey's brand of Utopianism in America at the same time as he realized the need for a more practical revolutionary activity to win the masses to socialism. Contrariwise, the Russian "God-seeker's" long-conditioned aversion to terrorist tactics and his deeply humanistic religious sense compelled him to cling to the tatters of the idea of community settlement withdrawn from "the world." [46] This insoluble dichotomy unquestionably palsied Chaikovski's future radical activities.

In estimating the impact of the American experience upon Chaikovski, one must note the relatively slight number of observations recorded during his four years' residence. The most generalized impression was one of disillusionment with the "sullen stepmother." Allied to this was the attack upon the *laissez-faire* system in the United States.

On the basis of his stay in America, the Russian "God-seeker" was able to become acquainted with Shakerism and was also in a better position to formulate and elaborate his own religious beliefs. Finally the failure—with certain reservations—of the Utopian idea was brought home to Chaikovski, along with a better understanding of the nature of the struggle for socialism.

[46] Frey himself finally returned to England in 1884 and promptly proceeded to establish a "religious commune of positivists" near London, *ibid.*, I, 159.

Catherine Breshkovski, "the little grandmother of the Russian Revolution," has probably best summed up Chaikovski's four years in America. She here perhaps defers overmuch to Chaikovski's acumen, and erroneously compresses all of Chaikovski's later political experiences into the equivocal term "anarchism":

With Frey and some other Russian intellectuals besides, Chaikovski succeeded in getting to North America so that he might there realize in practice the possibility of joint, laboring, brotherly love, without outsiders' interference. And this group of sincere people really invested all of their strength in getting such an enterprise going. Time passed, and the too unbearable labor told ever more sharply upon all. The small resources brought over were exhausted and the young families, despite all suffering, were forced to disperse in different directions. Want reached its limits. Chaikovski threw himself into the search for work and with a few dollars in his pocket, went off into the heart of the rich country. Here he really ran up against cruel disillusionment. The free democratic republic turned its seamy side to him. He met a soulless . . . attitude each time he turned to the official staff of one or another institution. They drove the homeless foreigner away. This experience did not pass over him without a trace.

Nikolai Vassilevich, defeated by such customs in this free country pondered over the justice of her political regime and by this road came to the acknowledgment of anarchism. But it was anarchism from the point of view of his old comrade, Peter Kropotkin.[47]

Despite the few impressions left as record by Chaikovski, the experiences of this Russian religious-*Narodnik* in the United States, considered objectively, seemed to confirm Lavrov's warnings against flight to the New World. Thus America was not destined to be a unique area for the experimentation with and the resolution of the problems of socialism. The bright hopes of "exceptionalism" found in Herzen had dissolved at least for a time in the mists of the disillusionment of the *Narodnik* radicals.

[47] *Ibid.*, 1, 8–9.

CHAPTER XI

Conclusion

WE have now seen how several representatives of various strands of mid-nineteenth-century Russian radical thought considered the United States in relation to their own world outlooks. It emerges clearly, both from their lives and their theoretical analyses, that American influence and example were of much more than passing importance to them. Russian intellectual life, long since familiar with the culture of Western Europe, now expanded across the oceans to explore the hitherto almost unknown institutions of the first republic of the New World.

Only two of the thinkers we have considered ever actually touched American shores; and paradoxically enough, Bakunin's impressions formed during a few weeks' time in 1861 seem more significant than those garnered by Chaikovski over a period of four years in the seventies. Thus the main sources of information of these radical intellectuals were restricted to writings on America, and contacts with travelers and visitors to this country. In this connection the importance of Alexis de Tocqueville's *Democracy in America* was very great. Western European intermediaries were still indispensable for bridging the informational gap between Russia and the United States.

The attention which these Russian radicals devoted to America is immediately manifest in their display of a large amount of factual information, much of it surprisingly accurate, on almost every important issue in American life. The questions relating to the United States which reappear time and again in their works, often treated at great length and always from a radical point of view, are among the central issues of the nineteenth century: the nature of the state, government, and federalism; slavery in its ramifications and the Civil War; the question of women's rights; the "social" question, i.e., the labor problem; and socialism. To this extent they communicated, to their Russian disciples at least, a certain understanding of the basic forces at work in American society during those times. The undoubted influence of the mid-century Russian radicals upon subsequent generations of revolutionaries unquestionably included American example—which previously had played so large a part in the early radicals' formulations.

The sure grasp with which these men handled the large issues involved in American life was vitiated by some mistakes; yet these stemmed naturally enough from untrustworthy information, occasional bias, and the clinging to previously formulated ideology.

In terms of an "over-all" view of America, the evolutionary pattern of their thought emerges as follows: For Ogarev and especially for Herzen the United States was both the example of high democratic development and the beacon of hope and consolation to those "tired of Europe." Sometimes America was even the "exception" to the normal pattern of economic and social developments in Western Europe. With Chernyshevski, the view of America as the present ideal of radical democracy—except for the institution of Negro slavery, which had to be destroyed—almost reached the level of adulation of every institution in "the free North," from the "ploughmen" to the protective tariff. Bakunin reveals only fitful glimmerings of the belief in America either as a "consolation" or as an "exception." It is certainly true, however, that Bakunin's otherwise intransigent statements of doctrine were mitigated by American actuality. It is with Lavrov—and Chaikovski to some extent despite the fact that the "God-seeker" represents far less of a trend than does Lavrov—that a qualitative transformation of attitude occurred. This metamorphosis represented a great and partly justified disillusionment with the United States, either as a refuge for those "tired of Europe" or as a model to be utilized by radical and socialist Europe. Lavrov especially launched a veritable tirade against the land of promise now so sadly fallen from grace. The era of the Civil War, with the rise to dominance of industrial capitalism and the ruthless captain of business enterprise, seems to mark the watershed for this change of opinion.

Closely allied to these developments, was the early joining by Herzen and Ogarev of the destinies of the United States and Russia in terms of their respective "exceptionalisms" in relation to Western Europe. By Lavrov's time, a common bond still exists between Russia and America, but a different one. It consists now of a parallel incidence of public corruption and venality, the lack of a "historical past" in both countries, and, lastly, a common revolutionary heritage (albeit of different orders). Lavrov and surely Chaikovski, too, had ceased to believe in American "insularity" and uniqueness. The tendency after the American Civil War to rank the United States more and more with the advanced states of Western Europe may be taken as a sign that the Russian revolutionary movement was fast reaching maturity. America of the late nineteenth century could teach Russian radicals less and less as they became ever more aware of the growth in the United States of the dislocations of capitalist development already familiar to them. The limits of even the American democracy became ever more visible. The conclusion was fast crystallizing that there could be no simple transfer of American example and institutions into the Russian radical concept of the future socialist state. From the decade of the nineties onward, the Russian revolutionary movement turned more and more to Marxism, and concomitantly tended to lose its lingering illusions in regard to the United States.

Selected Bibliography

CHAPTER I

Figner, V., *Memoirs of a Revolutionist,* tr. New York, 1927.

Iakovlev, V. [Bogucharski], *Aktivnoe Narodnichestvo Semidesiatykh Godov.* Moscow, 1912.

Valuable study of Populist movement and the various trends within it during decade of seventies.

Sakulin, Pavel, *Russkaia Literatura i Sotsialism.* Moscow, 1924.

Important early Soviet treatise on relation of nineteenth-century Russian literature to socialist trends.

Semevski, V. I., *Politicheskiia i Obshchestvennyia Idei Dekabristov.* St. Petersburg, 1909.

Penetrating analysis of the Decembrists' political thought.

CHAPTER II

Herzen, Alexander, *Polnoe Sobranie Sochineni i Pisem,* ed. M. K. Lemke. 21 vols. Petrograd, 1919–23.

———, *Kolokol.* London, 1857–65.

Herzen's uncensored newspaper, to which Ogarev also occasionally contributed.

Separate Works of Herzen in Western European Languages

ENGLISH

The Memoirs of Alexander Herzen, tr. J. D. Duff. Parts I and II. New Haven, 1923.

The Memoirs: My Past and Thoughts, tr. C. Garnett. 6 vols. New York, 1924–27.

Memoirs of the Empress Catherine II . . . , with preface by A. Herzen, tr. from the French. London, 1859.

My Exile in Siberia. London, 1855.

FRENCH

Camicia Rossa (Garibaldi à Londres). Brussels, 1865, and Lausanne, 1882.

La Conspiration de 1825. . . . London, 1858.

De l'autre rive, tr. Geneva, 1870.

Du Développement des idées révolutionnaires en Russie. Paris, 1851.

La France ou l'Angleterre? London, 1858.

Le Monde russe et la révolution; mémoires de A. Hertzen, 1812–1835, tr. Paris, 1860.

Le Peuple russe et le socialisme; lettre à Michelet. Paris, 1852.

Lettres de France et d'Italie, 1847–1852, tr. Geneva, 1871.

Oeuvres; récits et nouvelles. Paris, 187–?

GERMAN

Aus den Memoiren eines Russen. Hamburg, 1859.

Die russische Verschwörung und der Aufstand vom 14. Dezember 1825. . . . Hamburg, 1858.

Erinnerungen, tr. 2 vols. Berlin, 1907.

Konstantin Kawelins und Ivan Turgenjews sozialpolitischer Briefwechsel mit Alexander Herzen, ed. M. Dragomanow; tr. Stuttgart, 1894.

Russlands Soziale Zustände, tr. Hamburg, 1854.

Wer ist Schuld?; novel by Alexander Herzen, tr. Leipzig, 1888.

ITALIAN

La Camicia rossa di Alessandro Hertzen, tr. Milan, 1885.

CHAPTER III

Deiateli Revoliutsionnogo Dvizheniia v Rossii. Moscow, 1927. Vol. I, part I, p. 134.

Kolokol. London, 1857–65.

Ogarev, N. P., *Izbrannye Stikhotvoreniia,* ed. I. Z. Cherniak. Moscow, 1938. Includes mediocre biographical sketch of Ogarev.

——, "Zapiski Russkogo Pomeshchika," *Byloe,* XXVII–XXVIII (Leningrad, 1924), 14–17.

Some biographical notes left by Ogarev, which in tsarist Russia appeared only in mutilated form.

Separate Works of Ogarev in Western European Languages

FRENCH

Essai sur la Situation Russe; lettres à un anglais. London, 1862.

SELECTED BIBLIOGRAPHY 223

CHAPTER IV

Bakunin, M. A., *Sobranie Sochineni i Pisem,* ed. I. M. Steklov. 4 vols. Moscow, 1934.

Incomplete Russian edition of Bakunin's works; no definitive edition has yet appeared.

Separate Works of Bakunin in Western European Languages

ENGLISH

God and the State, preface by C. Cafiero and Elisée Reclus; tr. Boston, 1883.

——, tr. Columbus Junction, Iowa, 1896.

——, tr. London, 1893.

FRENCH

Correspondance de Michel Bakounine, lettres à Herzen et à Ogareff, ed. M. Dragomanov. Paris, 1896.

Oeuvres de Michel Bakounine, ed. James Guillaume. 6 vols. Paris, 1907–13.

GERMAN

Beichte aus der Peter-Pauls-Festung an zar Nikolaus I. . . . Berlin, 1926.

Die bekämpfung des zarismus . . . rede . . . in Bern . . . 1868. Berlin, 1925.

Gesammelte Werke, ed. Erwin Rholfs and M. Nettlau. 3 vols. Berlin, 1921–24.

Gott und der Staat, tr. Leipzig, 1922.

Sozial-politischer briefwechsel mit A. I. Herzen und Ogarjow, ed. M. Dragomanow. Stuttgart, 1895.

Zwei Schriften aus den 40er Jahren des XIX Jahrhunderts von Michael Bakunin. Prague, 1936.

ITALIAN

Dio e lo stato; preface by F. Turati and L. Bissolati. Milan, 1914.

Il socialismo e Mazzini; lettera agli amici d'Italia. Rome, 1905.

Risposta d'un internazionale a Giusseppe Mazzini. Milan, 1871.

CHAPTERS V, VI, AND VII

Chernyshevski, N. G., *Dnevnik, 1848–1849.* Moscow, 1931.

Diary containing some hitherto unpublished materials.

——, *Polnoe Sobranie Sochineni,* ed. M. N. Chernyshevski. 10 vols. St. Petersburg, 1906.

——, *Polnoe Sobranie Sochineni,* ed. B. P. Kozmin. 16 vols. Moscow, 1939.

Only Volumes I and XI have yet appeared in the United States.

Popov, V., *Ukazatel Statei, 1830–1884.* St. Petersburg, 1885.

Detailed index of articles in leading Russian magazines of the period. One or two foreign periodicals which had wide circulation in Russia are also covered.

Separate Works of Chernyshevski in Western European Languages

ENGLISH

A Vital Question; or What Is to Be Done?, tr. New York, 1886.

What's to Be Done?, tr. Boston, 1886.

FRENCH

L'Economie politique jugée par la science; critique des principes d'économie politique de John-Stuart Mill, tr. Brussels, 1874.

Lettres sans addresse sur l'abolition du servage en Russie, tr. Liège, 1874.

La Possession communale du sol, tr. Paris, 1911.

Que faire?, tr. Milan, Paris, 1875.

CHAPTERS VIII AND IX

Deiateli. . . . Moscow, 1930, Vol. II, parts I–II, pp. 729–30.

Lavrov, P. L., *Izbrannye Sochineniia,* ed. I. A. Teodorovich. 4 vols. Moscow, 1934.

——, *Etiudy o Zapadnoi Literature,* ed. A. A. Gizetti and P. Vitiazev. Petrograd, 1920.

——, *Vpered!* London, 1875–77.

——, *Vpered! Neperiodicheskoe Obozrenie.* London, 1874–77.

Separate Works of Lavrov in Western European Languages

FRENCH

Lettres historiques, tr. Paris, 1903.

La Propagande socialiste; son rôle et ses formes . . . *Conférence* . . . *à Paris, 1887.* Paris, 1898.

GERMAN

Historische briefe, tr. Berlin, 1901.

CHAPTER X

Breshko-Breshkovskaia, E. K., *Hidden Springs of the Russian Revolution; personal memoirs* . . . , ed. Lincoln Hutchinson. London, 1931.

Debagori-Mokrievich, Vladimir, *Ot Buntarstva k Terrorizmu*. Moscow, Leningrad, 1930.

——, *Vospominaniia*. Paris, 1894.

Deiateli. . . . Moscow, 1929. Vol. II, parts I–II, pp. 335–38, and parts III–IV, pp. 1919–22.

Kropotkin, Peter, *Memoirs of a Revolutionist*. Boston, New York, 1899; Houghton Mifflin Company.

Machtet, G. A. *Polnoe Sobranie Sochineni*, ed. D. P. Silchevski. Volume I. St. Petersburg, 1911.

Mezhov, V. I. *Russkaia Istoricheskaia Bibliografiia za 1865–1876 Vkliuchitelno*. Volume VI. St. Petersburg, 1885.

Nettlau, M., *Bibliographie de l'Anarchie*. Brussels, 1897.

Nikolai Vassilevich Chaikovski, ed. A. A. Titov. 2 vols. Paris, 1929. [In Russian.]

Obshchina. Geneva, 1878.

Stepniak (Sergei Kravchinski), *Underground Russia;* preface by Peter Lavroff, tr. New York, 1883.

——, tr. New York, 1892.

INDEX

Abbott, John, writer, 87

Abolition, American, 97–120; sentiment, in Unitarian church, 68, in Canada, 110; extremist point of view, 114–115

Absolutism, dangers to independent judiciary, 43; paternalistic, 80–81, 121; in republic, 162; conditions under, 185; mentioned, 39, 40, 50

Acculturation, American, 129, 131, 176

Aestheticism, 6, 193

Aesthetic Relations of Art and Reality, 82

Agassiz, Louis, naturalist, 57

Agriculture, political influence, 161; for revolution, 173, 181; socialistic elements, 195; Southern, 100, 113, 114; Northern, 102. *See also* Land

Alabama, Confederate privateer, 35

Alaska, sale of, 40

Alexander I, 17

Alexander II, reforms of, 8, 46; disillusionment in, 47; refusal to pardon Bakunin, 52; mentioned, 4, 13, 22, 143, 183

Alexander III, 13

Alfieri Cesare, Italian patriot, 140

Allgemeine Zeitung, 86

America, "exceptionalism" of, *see* "Exceptionalism"; influence on Western Europe, 27, 33, 87, 89, 90; in relation to Russia, *see* Russia and America

American Federation of Labor, 182

American Revolution, 18, 45, 153; in South, 105

Anarchism, 48, 53, 206, 216

Andrew, John Albion, governor of Massachusetts, 57

Annals of the Fatherland, 82

Annuaire de l'Economie Politique, L', 87

Arakcheev regime, 17

Arbeiter Zeitung, 151, 174

Artel, artisans' guild, 148

Assassinations, 8, 13, 143

Atheism, 205

"Atheism, collectivism, anarchism," Bakunin aims, 53

Athenaeum (London), 87

Atlantic cable, 29

Atlantic Monthly, 70

Attorney-general, American, 45

Autocracy, limitation of, 44, 47; mentioned, 83, 84, 85. *See also* Monarchy

Bakunin, Michael, 48–76; early life, 48–50; exile, 50–53, 55; influence, 54; journey to America, 55–57; on America, 58–77; on American socialism, 3; influence of Belinski on, 49; meeting with Ogarev, 49; association with Herzen, 49, 52, 53; acquaintance with Turgenev, 50; residence in Switzerland, 51; refusal of Alexander II to pardon,

Women: emancipation of, in Russia, 6; failure in America, 45; Herzen's concern with, 35; position in society, 132; rights of, 174; emancipation mentioned, 129, 131, 183, 184, 218

Wonder Book for Boys and Girls, 138

Workers, American, character of, 58; exploitation of, 171, 172, 173, 174; British, pressure on Palmerston, 118; mentioned, 74, 169. *See also* Labor movement

Workingmen's Party of the United States, 178

World Power, U. S. as, 61, 91. *See also* Imperialism

Writers, American, *see* Cooper; Clemens; Emerson; Hawthorne; Prescott; Ticknor; Whitman; Whittier; Longfellow; *also* Literary criticism

Yancey, William Lowndes, Southern extremist, 114

Zagoskin, Michael, Russian author, 188

Zemlia i Volia (Land and Freedom), Russian society, 12, 41, 143, 201

Zemski Sobor (Estates General), 46

Zemstvo institutions, 46

Zhelcheviki, term applied to *Contemporary* group, 83

Zheliabov, Andrei, revolutionist, 12

Zhukovski, Basil, Russian Romantic poet, 188